The Biblical Basis
of Christian Counseling
for People Helpers

THE
BIBLICAL BASIS
of CHRISTIAN
COUNSELING *for*
PEOPLE HELPERS

Gary R. Collins, Ph.D.

NAVPRESS

BRINGING TRUTH TO LIFE

NavPress Publishing Group

P.O. Box 35001, Colorado Springs, Colorado 80935

OUR GUARANTEE TO YOU

We believe so strongly in the message of our books that we are making this quality guarantee to you. If for any reason you are disappointed with the content of this book, return the title page to us with your name and address and we will refund to you the list price of the book. To help us serve you better, please briefly describe why you were disappointed. Mail your refund request to: NavPress, P.O. Box 35002, Colorado Springs, CO 80935.

The Navigators is an international Christian organization. Our mission is to reach, disciple, and equip people to know Christ and to make Him known through successive generations. We envision multitudes of diverse people in the United States and every other nation who have a passionate love for Christ, live a lifestyle of sharing Christ's love, and multiply spiritual laborers among those without Christ.

NavPress is the publishing ministry of The Navigators. NavPress publications help believers learn biblical truth and apply what they learn to their lives and ministries. Our mission is to stimulate spiritual formation among our readers.

ISBN 1-57683-081-0
Cover Illustration: © SuperStock/Diana Ong

Unless otherwise identified, all Scripture quotations in this publication are taken from the Holy Bible: New International Version® (NIV®). Copyright © 1973, 1978, 1984 by International Bible Society. Used by permission of Zondervan Publishing House. All rights reserved. Another version used is the *King James Version* (KJV).

Collins, Gary R.
   The biblical basis of Christian counseling for people helpers /
Gary R. Collins.
     p. cm.
   Includes bibliographical references.
   ISBN 1-57683-081-0
   1. Counseling—Religious aspects—Christianity. I. Title
BR115.C69C65   1993
253.5—dc20   93-6435
                                        CIP

Printed in the United States of America

4 5 6 7 8 9 10 11 12 13 14 15 16 17 / 07 06 05 04 03 02

Contents

Preface

Shortly after completing the manuscript of one of my earliest books I was having lunch with the publisher when our conversation drifted to the topic of book prefaces. He listened to the summary of what was included in the preface of my book, then he smiled and said, "It's too bad that nobody reads the preface."

I protested and explained that I always read the preface, but my friend argued that probably I was in the minority. If that is so, you are in the minority too because you are reading this introduction to the pages that follow. But whether or not they are read, these paragraphs give my reasons for writing and indicate what you can expect as you read.

The idea for this book came when I was asked to teach a course in theology for Christian counselors. Previous classes of students had been required to study theology, and the professor was well acquainted with his subject. But the lectures never mentioned counseling, they were filled with theological jargon, and the class periods were spent in discussion of the technicalities of eschatology, historical theology, ecclesiology, and other issues that seemed far removed from the counselor's work. Stated more concisely, the lectures were dull and the students were bored. I was challenged to do something different.

You can guess what happened next. I agreed to teach the course, looked at a stack of potential textbooks, and despaired. None had any relationship to the challenges of people-helping, and apart from a handful of notable exceptions, they all seemed dry and irrelevant. When I was a seminary student enrolled in theological courses, we were told that theology is alive and relevant to Christian living and problem solving. I have always believed this, but my survey of contemporary textbooks showed the need for an introduction to basic Christian beliefs that would be clear, jargon free, interesting, and of consistent value to counselors. The result is this book.

This is not intended to be a systematic theology. It is not a survey of all the doctrines of the Christian faith, an evaluation of diverse theological positions, an introduction to theology for ministerial students, or an argument in favor of one approach to theology. Of course, my theological perspectives will shine through the pages, and I have tried to write from a clearly evangelical perspective. I respect the various evangelical traditions and hope that readers who represent a variety of perspectives will find the following pages to be of interest and practical value. I hope, too, that counselors at all levels—psychologists, psychiatrists, social workers, pastoral counselors, lay counselors, and others—will find that this book gives clear and helpful information about what we believe and a fresh perspective on how these beliefs have a bearing on everything we do in the counseling room.

Several special people have encouraged me along the way and have given their help during the months that this book has been in the making. To each I am very grateful. My wife, Julie, has stuck with me cheerfully and faithfully, showing her consistent love and support through yet another book. Tim Clinton and Joy Olson each made significant contributions—not the least of which was Joy's protecting me from interruptions when I was trying to write. I appreciate the people at NavPress, especially Steve Webb, who believed in this book from the beginning, even when I wondered if it should be written. And thanks to Brett Helvie for preparing the index.

But the major responsibility for what follows has been shouldered by my friend and colleague Bill Smith. For six months he worked as my researcher, consultant, evaluator of every phrase I wrote, and challenger of ideas. Innumerable times I called his office to get an opinion about how I had phrased something, to ask a theological question, to inquire about a reference. Bill made library calls, found obscure references, combed bookstores to find newer books that I wanted to buy, showered me with ideas that needed to be considered, made occasional suggestions about illustrations, and prayed with me and for me as I made my way, sentence by sentence, through the manuscript. At times we had debates and even a few friendly theological disagreements, but Bill was a constant source of encouragement and guidance. Although I wrote every word of the book, Bill's influence is on every page. When the manuscript was completed he commented about the experience of going with me through the writing of a book. "It's like the army," he said. "It's fun to look back on but terrible when you're going through it." I am grateful for Bill Smith's input throughout the whole project.

Most of all, I am grateful to God for giving me the opportunities and the abilities to write in ways that I hope will bring honor to Jesus Christ.

Some time ago I read that many Christian counselors have graduate training in psychology but their biblical knowledge and theological training is often very limited. I send this book forth with the prayer that it will increase your knowledge of what we believe as followers of Jesus Christ, that it will improve your helping skills, that you will be encouraged in your own relationship with Christ, and that you will have an increased awareness of the need to build Christian counseling where it has to be built, on a strong biblical foundation.

CHAPTER ONE

What Makes Counseling Christian?

THE WEIGHT OF DEPRESSION almost never left. He prayed about it, argued with God about it, fought the Devil over it, talked with his physician about it—but its relentless torment persisted. At times the despair was so intense that he longed to end his life. He was reluctant even to pick up a carving knife for fear that he might destroy himself.

Over the years he developed an assortment of gimmicks to cope with the gloom. There were times when he felt better, even elated. His wife often brought comfort and so did the friends who would distract him with talk about irrelevant topics. It helped to sing, and dance, and joke, and eat—even when he wasn't hungry—and often he would try to ignore the emotional pain by plunging into his work. He tried to avoid being alone, looked to the aid of wise counselors, sought help in the church, and turned often to seek solace in Scripture. Once he concluded that there were three rules for dispelling despondency: the first is faith in Christ, the second is to get really angry, the third is the love of a woman. He tried them all.[1]

Critics argued that a believer, especially a Christian leader, should never be depressed. He himself wondered why he struggled so often with questions about the goodness, presence, and justice of God. The troubled theologian was writing books with ideas that were shaking the church to its core, but so often he sat alone, wondering if God even exists, and swayed by moods that fluctuated like the weather in April.

For decades, theologians, historians, and psychiatrists have analyzed the depression that plagued the life of Martin Luther. Some have concluded that his emotional agonies were caused by the many physical problems that he endured: constipation, insomnia, gout, hemorrhoids, ringing in the ears—to mention the best known. Others have linked the depression to outward, sometimes traumatic, events that marked his life. Some have wondered about the influence of his personality, which allowed him to be traumatized by a bolt of lightning (the experience led him to become a monk), shaking with fear when he said his first mass, deeply distraught when his followers were being martyred, but bold enough to take a highly unpopular and life-threatening stand for what he believed. Luther's own analysis attributed the depression to attacks from the Devil, and there were times when he wondered if intense emotional upheavals were necessary for anyone, like him, who sought to find hope and the answers to difficult religious questions.

How would you have diagnosed Martin Luther? How would you have treated his depression? How would you have responded to his shifting moods?

Your answer could say something about Luther; it might say a lot more about you.

IT ALL DEPENDS ON YOUR POINT OF VIEW

I have a friend who is a diehard football fan. He attends all the home-town games, reads the sports pages religiously, and delights in telling everybody when his team is victorious. (He is very silent when the team loses.) I don't always share his enthusiasm because I live in a different city and root for a different team. When "his" Oilers play "my" Bears, we see everything from different points of view.

Most of life is like that. We differ from one another in the ways that we view sports, politics, education, marriage, standards of right and wrong, news events, mental illness, and a host of other issues, including religion. Each of us has a set of lenses through which we view the world. Instead of talking about lenses, philosophers say that we each have a *worldview*.

A worldview, according to one definition, is "a set of presuppositions (or assumptions) which we hold (consciously or subconsciously) about the basic makeup of the world."[2] This is what we really believe, whether we have thought much about it or not. These are views of life and the world that we rarely question, almost never mention to friends, and usually ignore unless somebody disrupts what we believe by showing a different perspective.

A person's worldview helps him or her make sense of life, choose values, decide what is right or wrong, make decisions, settle on a lifestyle, and plan for the future.

In counseling, our worldviews determine how we think about human nature, evaluate the causes of emotional problems, decide on treatment strategies, and evaluate counseling progress. If we have a worldview that is limited or inaccurate, we can make a lot of mistakes in counseling and bring harm instead of healing. Most counselors realize this, but many appear to be like the masses of people who rarely think about their own worldviews and how these are affecting themselves, their work, and the lives of others.

Consider, for example, how our worldviews influence counseling. In attempting to help the despondent Martin Luther, some counselors would start immediately with his physiology. They would order a complete physical examination and put "the patient" on antidepressive medication. Others might focus on Luther's stress, helping him understand how pressures can lead to depression and teaching him stress-management techniques. Some counselors might be more inclined to look inside the man, to see how his past experiences and unconscious conflicts were leading to overt despair. Had the counselor been a systems theorist, he or she would have emphasized the role of Luther's system of family, friends, and colleagues in both creating and helping to bring recovery from his problems.

Among his Christian friends, some might have encouraged Luther to "just pray about it and trust God" to take the depression away. Others might have held a healing service for Luther or met together for a "power encounter" with the demonic forces that appeared to be pulling him down spiritually as well as psychologically.

Most of us may have tried a combination of approaches: approaches that reflected the worldviews that each of us developed and accepted while we were growing up and going through our training.

It is popular to assume that using a variety of approaches is healthy. Since no two counselors, counselees, or problem situations are identical, shouldn't we develop an assortment of techniques that can be pulled out and adapted to each unique counseling situation? Counselors are not very effective when they always use the same rigid methods, applied without much variation to every person who comes for help. Most of us agree that some blend of responsible eclecticism is good for everybody.

But worldviews operate here as well. A counselor's worldview influences what he or she assumes to be helpful in reducing conflicts and what is worth bringing into the blender of methods that will be used in our people-helping. Most counselors look for methods that are effective and practical for bringing changes in people's lives.[3] We may realize that some of these therapeutic techniques are built on philosophical presuppositions that are not consistent with what the Bible teaches, but we feel confident in our ability to use each method without accepting its underlying philosophy. Often we are successful in making this distinction—buying the method without the philosophical underpinning—but when we have no awareness of the secular, humanistic, and new-age foundations that undergird many therapies, we are in great danger of being swept innocently into error.

C. S. Lewis once made this thought-provoking observation:

> Our faith is not very likely to be shaken by a book on
> Hinduism. But if whenever we read an elementary book on
> Biology, Botany, Politics, or Astronomy, we found that its
> implications were Hindu, that would shake us. It is not the
> books written in direct defense of Materialism that make the
> modern man a materialist; it is the materialistic assumptions
> in all other books.[4]

As Christian counselors, our beliefs might not be shaken by a book in defense of humanism or new-age philosophy. But if we read books on therapy and personality theory that are steeped in nonChristian philosophy, we might be shaken. Too often, however, we don't even recognize the philosophical assumptions that underlie many contemporary psychological writings. We fail to realize that nonbiblical and even anti-Christian assumptions in psychology can mold our values, influence our counseling, and lead us to promote ideas that are in opposition to Scripture.

Christian counselors are much more able to spot errors in modern psychological worldviews when they have a clear perspective on the Christian worldview. We must be able to state what we believe and how this influences our counseling. When we are aware of our worldview perspectives, we are far less likely to naively pull together a combination of assumptions, values, goals, and techniques that are in conflict with one another and in opposition to the basics of the Christian faith.

WHAT GOES INTO A WORLDVIEW?

I enjoyed teaching personality theory. It was stimulating to lead my students as we dug into the theories of Freud and those who followed, looking at what each theorist wrote and pondering how these conclusions might relate to counseling. Sometimes, at the end of the course, I would ask the students to choose the theory or theorists that they preferred. Most students had clear theoretical preferences, but few had any idea why they made the choices they did. I suspect that something similar is true with worldviews. Many people have some idea what they think, but they aren't sure why they believe as they do or whether some other worldview would be better.

A well-rounded and useful worldview deals with at least five major topics: what we believe about God, the universe, knowledge, right and wrong, and the nature of human beings.[5]

- ❖ What we believe about *God* is our theology. This includes whether or not we believe God exists, what this divine being is like, and the extent to which God influences our lives. There are vast differences, for example, between the views of Christians, atheists, Hindus, Muslims, and new-age pantheists, who believe that God is in everything and that each human being is a god.
- ❖ What we believe about *the universe* (philosophers refer to this as "metaphysics") includes our answers to questions like these: How did the universe come into existence? Is there a purpose in the universe? Does the universe operate in accordance with natural laws? Is everything orderly or chaotic? Do supernatural interventions ever occur?
- ❖ How do we know anything with certainty? This is the philosophical issue of epistemology, our views about *how we get knowledge*. Can we trust our senses? Will logic get us to the truth? What is the role of divine revelation? Is the Bible trustworthy? What about the Koran? How do we

know if we are getting accurate information from CNN,
the daily newspaper, or the "facts" that come from a political news conference?

❖ Debates over abortion, homosexual rights, business practices, euthanasia, or the behavior of some televangelists,
all point to moral issues and the determination of what
is *right and wrong*. Morality issues surface frequently
in counseling. How we respond shows, in part, what we
believe about whether there are absolute standards of right
and wrong, or whether some or all morality depends on
the situation (situation ethics). Do you think it is okay for
each person to do what is right in his or her eyes, or are
there standards that are greater than individuals? If you
believe the latter, then who sets the standards, where do
they come from, why should they be followed, and who
determines what to do when moral standards are violated?
Do the standards ever change? How do standards apply
to business people, politicians, preachers, or counselors?
How does a counselor respond if his or her moral values
differ from those of a counselee?

❖ What we believe about *the nature of human beings* concerns us even more personally. Here we consider whether
we are free to make choices or whether we are pawns of
deterministic forces. We have beliefs about life after death,
human limitations and potential, and whether or not people
have souls. Are we really any different from animals, and
if so, what sets us apart?

"Whether we know it or not—whether we like it or not—each of
us has a world-view," wrote Ronald Nash.[6] These worldviews influence
how we see the world, think, act, and do counseling. When we have
conflicts and other differences of opinion, often the differences reflect
the underlying worldviews of the people involved. A prominent example is the national conflict over abortion. Pro-choice and pro-life advocates have different worldviews that lead to conclusions that clash.

TESTING AND CHOOSING A WORLDVIEW

Like my personality theory students, it seems that most people drift
into a worldview, picking up ideas from their past experiences and

subconsciously piecing together a way of viewing the world that might be fuzzy and even filled with inconsistencies.

Does this describe the worldviews of many counselors? If a counselor overlooks worldview issues and comes to the counseling room with no coherent life perspectives, there is a much greater potential for confusion, fumbling, and misunderstanding. As we have seen, our worldviews influence how we think about people, evaluate their problems, and make interventions to help them change. If we have a limited or unclear worldview, our work in counseling can be much more difficult than it might be otherwise.

Like a well-founded counseling theory, a clear worldview helps us make sense of life. The best worldviews are plausible, coherent, able to answer most questions, and useful in helping us to make decisions. Inadequate worldviews, like faulty eyeglasses, can cloud our vision and hinder our efforts to see things clearly. A good worldview clarifies a lot of things and gives us a clearer basis on which to operate. But how do we choose a good worldview or test the one we have?[7]

1. *Use reason.* Do our views of the world hold together logically? One test of this is whether or not there are inconsistencies. B. F. Skinner built his theories on the idea of determinism. But if all behavior is determined, that has to include Skinner's behavior in speaking about determinism. And if everything is determined, we have no reason to counsel because our clients have no freedom to change their thinking, actions, or perceptions. Skinner's worldview is contradictory, and for this reason it is not useful. It doesn't make sense.

2. *Think about past experiences.* Every counselor knows that experiences often are tied into emotions that are changeable and subjective. Even so, there are things that we know subjectively to be so. It is hard for me to believe, for example, that pain is an illusion, that we can go through life without ever being discouraged, or that human beings, as a whole, are innately good. These conclusions are at the basis of some worldviews, but they simply do not fit with most human experience. We should be suspicious of a worldview that fails to explain something we experience or that seems to be opposite to our experiences.

3. *Check with others.* Several years ago, psychologists in Minnesota introduced the term "*groupthink*" into our language. This is the tendency for likeminded people to support each other's beliefs, even though the beliefs may be wrong. Errors are exposed and faulty

thinking can be eliminated when we challenge one another. "As iron sharpens iron, so one man [or woman] sharpens another" (Proverbs 27:17). Since our own experiences can be distorted, we can avoid error, including groupthink, when we test our worldviews against those of others. Be careful, however, not to become like those who conclude that "if most people believe it, it must be right." That isn't always true.

4. *Look at the data.* Psychologist Albert Ellis once wrote that religion is "at its core, some kind of faith unfounded on fact." In reading the Ellis writings, however, I get the impression that he has never taken the time to look closely and honestly at the factual evidence in support of religion, especially Christianity. Empirical evidence doesn't tell us everything (according to my worldview), but a worldview is suspect if it goes against strong evidence.

5. *Test it out.* Does the worldview work consistently? Can we live, counsel, and build a lifestyle or a career on the worldviews that we hold? If a worldview does not work in the realities of life, it is not very useful, not very clear, and probably not right.

You will notice that these five suggestions all focus on how to evaluate worldviews that exist. Since all of us have a worldview, these questions can be useful for looking at what we have come to believe.

But suppose you already know that your worldview is unclear or inadequate. Suppose you have discovered that your worldview is not serving you well in your counseling work. How, then, do you come up with something better? That is the message of this book. The following chapters look at the basics for building a worldview that is effective for all people, but especially for counselors.

THE CHRISTIAN WORLDVIEW

If we are to be faithful followers of Jesus Christ and effective Christian counselors, how can we filter out the theological and philosophical error that pervades so much of modern counseling? How do we profit from counseling courses, books, seminars, journals, and workshops, without embracing faulty methods that arise from anti-biblical worldviews?

To answer, we must look at the field of theology. In a powerful indictment, a recent writer noted that Christian counselors often are limited in their grasp of the basics of the Christian faith. In many cases,

Those who practice psychology know their respective psychological schools and theories better than they do their systematic theology, with the result that they end up "integrating" a Sunday school training in theology with a graduate school training in psychology. No wonder such popular works tilt in favor of psychological concepts and phrases, notwithstanding the abundance of proof texts and Bible words.[8]

Christian counselors (like all other believers) need a basic understanding of what they believe and why they believe as they do. Literally thousands of books exist to help with this understanding, but very few seek to apply this understanding to the process of helping others. Many of the massive theological books that line the shelves of my office are filled with complex jargon and writing that is just plain dull. Of course, theology is not unique in having a professional literature that is technical, written for specialists, and not intended to be easy or fun to read. This is true of psychology and every other field of knowledge. But theology—the study of God and His creation—has practical relevance to all of us, and it needs to be presented in language that non-theologians can understand and apply to their lives.

This is my goal in the following pages. I have tried to write a basic summary of the biblical-theological worldview that forms the core of Christianity and that must be at the basis of any Christian approach to counseling. The following pages are intended to be interesting, relevant, practical, and as free of jargon as possible. This will not be a systematic theology that seeks to summarize and analyze all Christian doctrines. Although it is likely to reflect my personal theological position, it will not be an argument for one theological point of view. Instead, it will be a broadly evangelical volume that presents the basics of the Christian faith and points out the practical implications of these basics for the counselor and for the art of counseling.

WHAT IS CHRISTIAN COUNSELING?

I wish I had known Jim Stringham better. As a young boy he sensed God's call to be a medical missionary in China. Although he resisted for a while, he and his new wife sailed for China in 1933, shortly after his graduation from Yale Medical School. Life abroad was difficult, and the young doctor was surprised to see so much bitterness, resentment, and many broken relationships among the committed missionaries who were his fellow servants. In time, Jim returned to the United States, became a psychiatrist, opened a private practice, and discovered quickly that many of his patients struggled with problems that were basically spiritual.

One of his first patients was a single woman whose recurrent attacks of acute gastrointestinal upsets were making it difficult for her to continue in nurses' training. Extensive tests showed no organic basis for her condition, but the psychiatrist discovered that she harbored intense guilt over her past sexual experiences. When this issue came into the open, the patient was able to face her shame and find forgiveness from Christ. Shortly thereafter her physical symptoms disappeared and never came back.

Cases like this seem obvious when they appear in a book, but Dr. Stringham was learning about the spiritual side of emotional illness at a time when this was not widely accepted. He began lecturing about his discoveries and one day received a letter from E. Stanley Jones, the renowned missionary, who invited Jim Stringham to speak in India. A short time later he accepted a position as clinical director of NurManzil Psychiatric Center in Lucknow, India, where he and his wife stayed for ten years. In all of this time their worldview was being refined. Jim Stringham became increasingly convinced that spiritual issues are at the root of most problems, and he sought to develop a "Christian spiritually oriented therapy."

Several years ago, Jim wrote to me and began to call periodically, urging that I develop a clear definition of what we mean by Christian counseling. I confess that sometimes I resisted (and even resented) his frequent contacts. I was busy and not always inclined to talk to this stranger who gently and persistently pushed me to reevaluate my own counseling perspective. Nevertheless, I admired his commitment to Christ and his determination to build psychiatry on a clear Christian foundation.

A few months before his death we met for lunch. He never mentioned the cancer that was eating away at his body, but he talked enthusiastically about his work and the need for all counselors to give periodic spiritual checkups to themselves and to their clients.

More than anybody else, Jim Stringham prompted me to think through a practical definition of Christian counseling, a definition that seeks to be built on a biblical worldview. I presented this in an earlier book, but it needs to be repeated here because it gives a picture of what is meant by counseling in the pages that follow.

> Attempts to define or describe Christian counseling tend to emphasize the *person* who does the helping, the *techniques* or skills that are used, and the *goals* that counseling seeks to reach. From this perspective the Christian counselor is:
> ❖ a deeply committed, Spirit-guided (and Spirit-filled) servant of Jesus Christ
> ❖ who applies his or her God-given abilities, skills, training, knowledge, and insights
> ❖ to the task of helping others move to personal wholeness, interpersonal competence, mental stability, and spiritual maturity.
> Christian counselors are committed believers, doing their best to help others, with the help of God. Such a definition includes believers who come from different theological perspectives, use different approaches to counseling, and have different levels of training and experience.[9]

Like everybody else, Christian counselors are unique. We don't all proceed in the same way, use the same methods, or agree on the same explanations of why people behave as they do. But as followers of Jesus Christ, we all accept some basic Christian beliefs. These beliefs form the core of the Christian worldview and undergird Christian counseling and other forms of people-helping.

THEOLOGY AND CHRISTIAN COUNSELING

After completing my formal training in psychology, I enrolled in a theological seminary. I had no plans to earn a degree; I wanted instead to learn more about theology and the Bible, without having to worry about all of the term papers and tests that make student lives so miserable. Unlike today, when almost every theological school has courses in counseling and psychology, I went to seminary at a time when such courses were rare and psychology was mistrusted by many Christians.[10] Probably I was the first psychologist-seminary student the faculty of that little school had ever encountered.

But I learned a lot. I continued to read psychology books, of course, but I also found myself reading heavy theology books and taking courses that discussed bibliology, pneumatology, hamartiology, and other issues that are foreign to psychologists.

Most of us know that writers of introductory psychology books divide their subject into categories that include learning, perception, abnormality, motivation, and how the scientific method is used in psychology. Theologians divide their field in a similar way. Table 1.1 lists the major parts of Christian theology and shows how we deal with these issues in the following pages.

Table 1.1
BASIC CHRISTIAN THEOLOGY

Bibliology:	the doctrine of Scripture	(chapters 2–3)
Theology Proper:	the doctrine of God	(chapter 4)
Paterology:	the doctrine of God the Father	(chapter 4)
Christology:	the doctrine of God the Son	(chapters 4,7)
Pneumatology:	the doctrine of God the Holy Spirit	(chapters 4,9)
Anthropology:	the doctrine of human beings	(chapter 5)
Hamartiology:	the doctrine of sin	(chapters 6–7)
Soteriology:	the doctrine of salvation	(chapters 7–9)
Ecclesiology:	the doctrine of the church	(chapter 11)
Angelology:	the doctrine of angels	(chapter 10)
Eschatology:	the doctrine of the future	(chapter 12)

As promised, the following pages avoid technical terms, and I hope you will find that they are helpful and interesting even if you have never had a course in psychology or counseling. We will cover the basic Christian doctrines as they apply to all of us, but especially as they relate to the Christian counselor's work.

To begin our journey, the next two chapters (2 and 3) will describe how Christians can know about God, about the ways in which He has revealed Himself, and about the methods that we can use to interpret the Bible accurately—without too much distortion by our own biases and perceptions.

With this foundation, in chapter 4 we will focus on the nature of God. What is He like? How does His power and place in the universe make a difference in the lives of counselors and their counselees?

Every theory of counseling, and every counselor, has a perspective on the nature of human beings. What are people like—at the core? Why do we exist? How do the answers to questions like these have relevance to helping people change? Our discussion of human nature (chapter 5) will move us into the topic of sin (chapter 6).

Christians realize that we cannot deal with sin on our own. The core of the gospel concerns the coming of Jesus Christ to redeem sinners and help us find forgiveness. Chapter 7 summarizes the work of Christ and the following chapter deals with the issue of guilt and forgiveness (chapter 8).

Then we will look at the work of the Holy Spirit (chapter 9), and after considering the sometimes controversial issue of miraculous intervention, we will move on to discuss supernatural agents and their influence in both our lives and our counseling (chapter 10).

There is good reason to believe that the Church, the Body of Christ, is crucial in Christian caregiving—even though much modern Christian counseling takes place in professional offices far away from any religious setting. Our discussion of the Church will consider how Christian counseling relates to the local congregations of believers (chapter 11).

Then we will look at the future (chapter 12). Eventually, all of us will die, but the Christian worldview has a perspective on death and on life after death that differs from many of the perspectives appearing in counseling books. The bottom line is that Christians have hope and Christian counselors can offer hope to their counselees. That in itself is encouraging.

After considering these basic theological issues, we will look again at ourselves—those of us who are Christians and Christian counselors. What are we like? How should we be growing? How does all of this relate to the current emphasis in counseling on spirituality? We deal with these issues in chapter 13 and then pull together our conclusions in a brief concluding chapter.

Martin Luther never knew about Christian counseling as we understand it today. Perhaps he would have been helped out of his depression if modern psychotherapeutic methods had been available in sixteenth century Europe. We now have these methods. Some are new; many are based on centuries-old forms of Christian caregiving. In drawing on these methods to help others, we must be sure that our techniques and counseling goals are consistent with the Christian worldview that we begin to consider in the next chapter.

SO WHAT?

Over the years I have come to the conclusion that there is one question we should ask after every sermon or lecture we hear and after every article or book chapter we read. It is a question that I ask myself whenever I give a talk or write. It's the question, *So what?*

We will ask it in every chapter in this book. You have a right to ask, "I have read the chapter, but *so what* does this have to do with me or with my counseling?" The study questions in the back of the book (see pages 253-260) will help you find answers and so, I hope, will the summary-conclusions with which I end each chapter.

So what can we conclude from chapter 1?

Every counselor (and counselee) brings assumptions, values, beliefs, and viewpoints into the counseling session. These perspectives—some of which may be poorly developed and rarely thought about—make up our worldviews and mold a lot of our thinking and behavior. A worldview helps us make sense of life, including what is right or wrong, what causes personal problems, and what treatment strategies we should use.

In our efforts to be effective counselors, we sometimes use techniques and ways of analyzing behavior that reflect worldview assumptions that are anti-Christian. When we give no thought to worldviews—our own or those of others—we risk building our counseling on presuppositions, values, goals, and techniques that are in conflict with one another and even in opposition to the Christian faith. Good worldviews, in contrast, are plausible, coherent, able to answer most questions, and useful in helping us to make clearer decisions in counseling.

To evaluate a worldview, or to build a better worldview, use your reason, think about your experiences, check with others, look at the evidence, and then try it out to see how it works. Counseling cannot be considered Christian unless it is built on a clearly stated Christian worldview. That worldview must be understood clearly by counselors if they are to be of maximum effectiveness. To understand the worldview that undergirds Christian counseling, we must take a careful look at theology.

That is what this book is all about. To begin looking at our Christian worldview, we must consider the question of epistemology (where and how we get accurate knowledge), but we want to do this without using too many long words like *epistemology*. That, fellow people-helpers, is what we will do in the next chapter.

CHAPTER TWO

The Bible and Counseling: Revelation

NATHAN WAS A HARD-WORKING student who quickly grasped the basics of counseling, wrote good term papers, and did well on exams. It was easy to see that he would become an effective counselor, in spite of his first formal counseling session.

"I was scared to death," he told me after his client had left. "She came in to talk about her anxiety, and I knew she was uncomfortable seeing a counselor. But *she* wasn't the most anxious person in the room. The most anxious person was me."

Perhaps all counselors have had similar experiences. Like Nathan, we have felt anxious, especially near the beginning of our counseling careers, but eventually we have learned to relax. Some of this sense of relaxation comes when we accept the fact that a counselor's first responsibility is not to give advice and answers to complex problems. The counseling process must begin with listening.

In the counseling room, listening involves much more than passively hearing the words that come from another person's lips. Effective listening is an active process that involves using both your ears and your eyes. The counselor listens to words but also is aware of what the counselee reveals through tone of voice, gestures, posture, facial expressions, and other nonverbal clues. We get to know our counselees and to understand them better as we hear what they say and see what they do or have done.

This learning is not limited to counseling; it applies to all human relationships. We learn about others by listening to their words and observing their behavior. When a couple is in love, for example, they express their feelings verbally and through loving actions. God has chosen to reveal Himself in the same two ways.

KNOWING ABOUT GOD

Does God know how we feel when we get depressed? Does He care about our anxieties? Does He understand our suffering? Why doesn't He stop family abuse? Does He know how much we struggle in our recovery groups? Can He really help us, and does He care enough to help? If so, where is God when it hurts? Does He give direction when we face difficult problems or important decisions?

Counselors often hear questions like these, and sometimes we ask them ourselves. To find answers we must look at how God communicates and reveals Himself. What theologians call *revelation* is a divine activity in which God tells us about Himself and creation, communicates His purposes, and shows what He is like.

This revelation is of two types. In one of these, *general revelation*, God communicates through what we observe in the world and the universe. In the second type of communication, *special revelation*, God conveys through the words and deeds recorded in the Bible all that we need to know about His character and purposes. For the counselor to understand and help others know God and His purposes, we need to be familiar with both types of revelation.

GENERAL REVELATION

Introductory psychology was the first course I ever taught. While living in Germany, I was invited to give an evening class to U.S. Army personnel who were working on their bachelor's degrees. As I recall, the courses went well, but in those days I didn't know what I know now: that teaching a beginning psychology course is very difficult. Students who expect to learn about themselves and how to "psych out their friends" don't have much enthusiasm when the textbook and lectures focus instead on rats in mazes, perceptual theory, or the need to memorize endless (seemingly useless) facts and terms to be spit back to the professor on multiple-choice tests. Often there is even less interest when the course deals with psychological methods.

But these methods are important. Learning about them enables us to better understand human beings and to know how the basic procedures of psychology are used in counseling. The scientific methods of psychology are designed to give us facts about the universe and about individual people, and they help us discern how the facts fit together.

Psychological journals focus on scientific methods of collecting data—methods that include the use of surveys, carefully controlled experiments, and even animal studies that may uncover basic behavioral principles. In counseling we are more inclined to use the method of carefully observing one or more persons as they talk and interact with each other and with the counselor. These observations, scientific and clinical, are then combined with our reasoning abilities, past experiences, store of knowledge, and intuition. The best counselors, like the best researchers, are able to summarize and analyze the facts (and to help others do the same), so that they better comprehend what might be causing a problem and how it might be resolved.

In all of this activity we are observing and seeking to understand the world and people in the world. The Christian would conclude that this really is observing and understanding God's creation, including ourselves and the other human beings that He has created. To get facts and reach conclusions, we use our God-given minds, intuitive abilities, training, past insights, prior experiences, and personal worldviews.

Of course, there is potential for error, so we seek to prevent bias, to be as objective as possible, and to reach conclusions that are minimally distorted by subjectivity. But all facts must be interpreted, influenced by the observer's perspectives and worldview. Whenever we observe facts in the world and in people, we are learning about what God has created and what sin has destroyed. We are learning through general revelation.

Three Types of General Revelation
Most theologians agree that general revelation is available to all intelligent human beings and comes in three areas. First, we get general

revelation by looking at nature. "The heavens declare the glory of God; the skies proclaim the work of his hands," wrote the psalmist (Psalm 19:1). The Apostle Paul noted that "since the creation of the world God's invisible qualities—his eternal power and divine nature—have been clearly seen, being understood from what has been made, so that men are without excuse" (Romans 1:20).

Many people today assume that nature is self-created and self-sufficient, but many others (Christians included) look to the beauties and complexities of creation and conclude that God is showing Himself through His universe. Ponder the complexities of the people who come for counseling, or watch the physical and psychological development of a young child, and surely it is harder to maintain the self-sufficiency view of the world than to conclude that a superhuman being, God, is holding everything together (Colossians 1:16-17) and revealing Himself to human beings.

The second area of general revelation is history. Several years ago, one of my teaching colleagues published a book titled *Where Is History Going?*[1] The author outlined some of the ways in which we interpret historical events, and he argued that there is a purpose in all of history. We are not going in endless cycles or drifting without direction. God is at work in the world, the book claimed. He created the world, He sent His Son to redeem the world, He has a purpose for this world (and its inhabitants), and ultimately He is in control of history.

There is biblical basis for this claim: "No one from the east or the west or from the desert can exalt a man. But it is God who judges: He brings one down, he exalts another" (Psalm 75:6-7). Paul noted that governmental authorities have been established by God, who allows them to exist (Romans 13:1). He has made every nation, "that they should inhabit the whole earth; and he determined the times set for them and the exact places where they should live" (Acts 17:26). The Bible speaks of God's dealings with ancient nations, especially with the nation of Israel (see, for example, Joshua 23:1-14). We are told that although He sometimes allows a wicked empire to triumph, for purposes that we don't understand, He brings fairness and justice in the end (Habakkuk 1:1–2:20).

Historical documents are not always available, of course. Sometimes historians dig up information that isn't reliable, and like the rest of us, historians bring their own worldviews and biases when they analyze events of the past. Despite these difficulties, when we look at history it is possible to see God's work, purposes, goals, and nature as He intervenes in the affairs of this world.

A third area of general revelation focuses on human nature. C. S. Lewis once wrote that "human beings, all over the earth, have this curious idea that they ought to behave in a certain way," but the universal realization is that none of us, in fact, behaves as we should. Lewis calls this the "Law of Nature."[2] It is the standard of right and wrong that the Bible says is written on our hearts (Romans 2:14-15)—a moral part of us that many people resist but that nevertheless reveals something about God's standards, nature, and existence. Some theologians would add that this innate presence of right and wrong is supplemented by an inborn religious nature. "In all cultures, at all times and places, humans have believed in the existence of a higher reality than themselves, and even of something higher than the human race collectively," wrote Millard Erickson. While religions differ significantly, "many see in this universal tendency toward worship of the holy the manifestation of a past knowledge of God, an internal sense of deity, which, although it may be marred and distorted, is nonetheless still present and operating in human existence."[3]

Before we leave the topic of general revelation, we need to add two observations. First, we must note that none of us can see God perfectly in creation. Our viewing is marred by sin, for even the world that God created has been spoiled (Romans 8:20-21). Second, as every counselor knows, there are great individual differences in how we perceive and interpret the world where we live. (These differences often lead to the conflicts and disagreements that people have with each other.) Because of the differences, there is a danger that we will impose our own interpretations on the world and on events and sometimes make faulty conclusions about whether or how God might be revealing Himself through general revelation. God has declared Himself, but we don't always clearly see what He has revealed (1 Corinthians 13:12). Each of us needs to maintain a sense of humility when we set forth our conclusions.

Psychology and General Revelation
Psychology has always had critics, both outside the Church and within. Dave Hunt has called psychology "the most dangerous and at the same time the most powerful form of modernism ever to have invaded the church."[4] William Kirk Kilpatrick wrote that within the

psychological community there is "an abundance of speculation, wishful thinking, contradictory ideas, prejudice, doubletalk, and ideology disguised as science."[5]

Criticisms like these, extreme and often flawed,[6] point neverthe- less to the limitations of psychology. Even when they are thorough and extensive, the findings of psychology can give us only observa- tions and information about issues—such as how people think, act, feel, learn, cope, mature, and relate to one another. Like every other science, psychology is limited in that it cannot make authoritative statements about the meaning of life or death, about values and mor- als, or about the place of humans in the universe. Of course, many psychologists give their opinions about these ultimate issues, but in doing so, they are expressing their own philosophical ideas and are not citing the findings of psychology.

General revelation, psychology included, speaks to us about God, about the world, and about human beings. But if we want more specific knowledge, especially knowledge about salvation, we must look to special revelation.

SPECIAL REVELATION

When I was taking my psychological internship, I worked for sev- eral months in a center for severely handicapped children. Many of these kids had twisted arms or legs, but their minds were sharp and they could communicate clearly with words. Others were less able to talk. Their words were almost incomprehensible, or their language skills were so poorly developed that I had to do my psychological evaluations completely by making observations of their nonverbal behavior. It is not easy to learn precise and accurate details from and about another person when we don't have access to words.

Perhaps this is why God gave us the Bible—His special, verbal revelation. God did not dictate the Bible. He used human authors, writing in their own styles, to record the words and acts of God. These writers were carefully guided by the Holy Spirit so that their words were true, accurate, inspired ("God breathed"), and of practi- cal relevance (2 Timothy 3:16-17, 2 Peter 1:20-21). They recorded those times when God did speak directly—often these Bible passages begin with phrases like "The word of the Lord came to me saying" —but the writers also recorded what God revealed through the per- son and work of Jesus Christ, through miracles, through prophecy, and through the personal and spiritual experiences of people like David or Paul. The end result of these writings is more than a collection of works by spiritually sensitive writers; it is a book that accurately records the words and events that God wants us to know. The Bible, therefore, claims to be the revealed Word of God.

If this is true, then the Bible must be regarded as an authority when it speaks about the issues of life, including those issues that people bring to us in counseling. The Bible tells us what God is really like. It shows us that while God is perfect and without sin, He is also personal and is able to understand our emotions, struggles, and ways of thinking (Hebrews 4:15). The Bible tells us what God thinks of sin, guilt, forgiveness, lust, greed, anger, anxiety, suffering, relationships, and a host of other counseling-related issues. God's Word tells us about supernatural beings and about life and death. It helps us see how God interprets history, and it gives us a glimpse of the future.

Specific Answers and Biblical Principles

When I was in graduate school, a well-known psychologist published an article titled "Wanted: A Good Counseling Cookbook!" The writer knew, of course, that complex counseling problems can't be solved by recipes and "how-to" formulas, even though most of us might like to have such a manual.

Is the Bible a manual of counseling?

The pages of Scripture give clear guidance on many issues. If we look only in the book of Proverbs, for example, we see specific biblical instructions about counseling-related topics—such as avoiding sex apart from marriage (6:32), maintaining self-control when sexually enticed (7:6-27), not expressing anger verbally and with harsh words (15:1), and avoiding the tendency to get even with somebody who has caused harm (25:28). When the specific instructions are not there, often we can learn from the examples of God-honoring people in the Bible (people like Joseph or Daniel) who faced difficult decisions and responded in ways that were approved by God.

In addition to the specific directions, the Bible gives broad behavioral principles that can guide the counselor. Once again we can look to Proverbs for examples. Is a counselee facing a major decision? Proverbs 15:22 says that it is best to seek the input and observations of several others before we make an important decision.

Has a counselee been successful and inclined to be proud? We must alert that person to the dangers of pride (16:18). What about the workaholic whose life seems dedicated to the pursuit of money? "Do not wear yourself out to get rich," says Proverbs 23:4—a verse that reinforces the New Testament warning that the love of money can create a lot of problems (1 Timothy 6:10). When a counselee has done something wrong, encourage confession in place of efforts to hide the failures (Proverbs 28:13). And when we see people who are powerless to deal with injustice in their lives, we need to take a stand and speak up for the rights of people who cannot speak for themselves (31:8).

Often the biblical principles are more general. We know, for example, that the Bible consistently teaches honesty, treating others fairly, controlling our lusts and emotions, avoiding sexual immorality, remaining faithful to our marriage partner, not filling our minds with harmful influences, and seeking to do what pleases God.

The Bible is not a counseling cookbook. It does not make that claim. Most of the problems we encounter in counseling are far too diverse and complex to be solved by quoting a Bible verse or by applying some pat biblical formula. Certainly the Bible, God's revelation, gives a number of specific directions and many clear principles that can give us a framework for counseling and can form the basis of our Christian worldview. But what does the counselor do if he or she is presented with a problem that isn't mentioned or even alluded to in the Bible?

Finding Answers When the Bible Is Silent
When the answers to our questions are not clearly stated in the Bible, there is nothing wrong with looking for answers someplace else. But where do we look and how can we be sure that the answers we find are right?

For many people, counselors included, the answers are based in the philosophy of *pragmatism.* This is the idea that "if something works, it must be right." British writer Martin Robinson has written that in our society, it is assumed "that since all faith and morality are firmly in the area of opinion and that all opinions are equally valid, the only thing that really matters is whether or not they work: 'Does it work?' is the question that arises again and again. Never mind if the suggested formula is derived from Hinduism, Buddhism, the occult, or Christianity—the main question asked is, 'Does it work?'"[7]

Sometimes pragmatism can be a useful guide. If a counseling technique works to bring change, perhaps it *is* right—but that isn't always necessarily so. Alcohol or illicit drugs can push away the pain of anxiety or depression for a while, but this is neither a wise nor an effective long-term solution. A woman who is beaten repeatedly by her husband can flee to a shelter for battered women and this works to give her safety, but it doesn't solve the problem of the violent husband's lack of control. Christian counselors cannot be dependent on the prevailing philosophy of pragmatism.

So where do we turn for answers? Psychologist Larry Crabb has made the interesting suggestion that if God is interested in all of our struggles, maybe we could assume that the questions He has answered in the Bible are the questions we would ask if we had the sense to ask the right questions. It becomes important, therefore, to see what questions God has answered in the Bible. Then we can develop a framework for thinking through the questions that we ask ourselves or that people ask us in counseling.[8]

The Bible answers questions like these:

- What is God really like?
- Can God be trusted?
- Where did I come from?
- How does God guide?
- What are human beings really like?
- Is God in control of situations?
- What causes us to sin?
- What makes sin attractive?

The Bible's answers to these and similar questions bring us back to the importance of building a Christian worldview. When we look at the issues that the Bible discusses, we can form a worldview that gives us a grid through which we can sift the questions of life that are not specifically addressed in Scripture. And we can find answers that are consistent with biblical teaching even if they are never addressed by the biblical writers.

PERSONAL EXPERIENCE AND THE BIBLE'S AUTHORITY

To this point, we have assumed that the Bible is the Word of God—a trustworthy and authoritative book on which we can build our lives and our counseling practices. I agree with Larry Crabb that "biblical revelation must function as the controlling guide for all our thinking about counseling." As counselors, Crabb wrote, we must come to the Bible with a spirit of expectancy and submission. This does not mean that we disregard the insights of psychology or the ideas of other thinkers. They are stimulating, informative, and sometimes provocative, but we cannot regard them as being authoritative.[9]

But why should the Bible be set up as an authority? Would it be more logical to build our worldviews and our counseling on the latest scientific facts? Would it be wiser to draw on the ideas of great intellectual thinkers or spiritual giants whose ideas might be recorded in religious and philosophical books other than the Bible? In this information age, we have vast quantities of data available at the beck and call of a computer command. Surely, there is wisdom in drawing on this data bank rather than building our counseling and our worldview on an ancient book that was written centuries ago.

It is unlikely that a few paragraphs will convince a skeptic that the Bible is a source of authority, greater than all others, the only true Word of God, and to be trusted even more than our own personal experiences. Others have written persuasively in defense of the Bible's divine authority, and we need not repeat the arguments here.[10]

But two questions do need our attention. The first deals with the question of why we need an authority at all, apart from our own subjective experiences, and the second question concerns the Bible's credibility and why any thinking person should trust it.

Can We Trust Our Experiences?
Near the beginning of World War II, Hitler's forces forged their way across France, demanding the surrender of all Allied forces in Europe and pushing thousands of French and British troops to the shores of the English channel. Weary and footsore, trapped with little hope on the beaches of Dunkirk, the dejected soldiers suspected that they soon would be pushed into the water or wiped out by the Nazis.

In those days there were no CNN reporters to give live coverage of the battle conditions, but there was radio. Three words were sent through the airways to the people in England: *But if not?*

This was no code, according to Charles Colson, who tells the story in one of his books.[11] It referred to the Old Testament experience of Shadrach, Meshach, and Abednego, who were about to be cast into a very hot furnace. The three men stated with confidence, "Our God whom we serve is able to deliver us . . . and he will deliver us. . . . *But if not* . . . we will not serve thy gods" (Daniel 3:17-18, KJV; emphasis added).

The British people understood, and in the days that followed, all manner of boats—pleasure cruisers, yachts, fishing boats, even rowboats—manned by ordinary citizens made their way back and forth across the channel to rescue 338,000 Allied troops.

A similar message today would have no meaning. The prevailing worldview denies the existence of absolute truth. In 1963, about two-thirds of surveyed Americans believed in the absolute truth of all words in the Bible; the numbers today are less than one-third of those polled.[12] Few people read the Bible regularly, and there is little inclination to accept biblical propositions or standards of right and wrong. More common is the view that says, "I am glad Christianity works for you. It is nice that you have found a fulfilling religion and that you have decided to live your life on what the Bible teaches. As long as you don't impose your views on me or try to make me think like you do, I have no objection to what you believe or do or think. I'm tolerant."

People who think this way—and they probably are in the majority today—are rarely swayed by factual data, by logical argument, or by stories of someone's personal experience. Most people realize that we can find a story to "prove" virtually anything, so the personal testimonies convince almost nobody.

Where, then, do modern men and women turn for stability and a foundation on which to build their lives? Many look inside of themselves, assuming that truth and enlightenment come from deep within. This is a modern form of *subjectivism*, a way of thinking that builds one's beliefs, values, and lifestyle on individual reflection and personal experience.

In their sobering book *The Day America Told the Truth*, researchers James Patterson and Peter Kim wrote that in "the 1950s and 1960s, there was something much closer to moral consensus in America. . . . There is absolutely no moral consensus at all in the 1990s. Everybody is making up their own personal moral codes—their own Ten Commandments."[13] According to one report, 69 percent of Americans adhere to the attitude that there is no absolute standard and that ethics should fluctuate according to the situation.[14]

When our lives and our counseling are built only on personal experiences, there can be:

❖ No stability to our beliefs, because what we think will change with our changing emotions.

❖ No enduring ethical standards, because what is right and wrong will change, depending on the situation, on how we feel, and on prevailing attitudes in the society.

❖ No way to validate one's conclusions, because experiences are not subject to testing and there are no standards other than oneself.

❖ No basis for concluding that another person is right or wrong, since one person's experiences and views are assumed to be as valid as those of any other.

❖ No real hope for the future, because my only hope is built on the passing conclusions in my own mind.

Feelings and subjective beliefs are important to all of us. They give life a richness that we would never find otherwise. But the fact that an idea has formed in one's brain is no guarantee that the idea is right or true. If beliefs, worldviews, lifestyles, and counseling practices are built on and validated by subjective experience alone, our lives and our beliefs are likely to be drifting, unstable, and ultimately inadequate.

Can We Trust the Bible?

Assuming that we can't build our lives, worldviews, and counseling on subjective experience, why should anyone choose the Bible as the foundation? When most of us have computers that can tap into data banks containing massive amounts of information, why should we assume that the Bible is a unique book? To answer, we can look to three types of evidence.

The manuscript evidence. When I took an undergraduate philosophy course, nobody questioned whether or not we had a reliable copy of Plato's writings. We all assumed that what we had was accurate. Plato wrote around 380 BC, but seven authentic copies of his writings exist. The oldest is a copy dated about AD 900, 1400 years after Plato wrote.

Compare that with other ancient writings and with the New Testament (see table 2.1). Among the 14,000 existing New Testament manuscripts, most are dated within 200 years of the time when they were written and some writings are within 100 years. In addition, the writings of early church leaders give us tens of thousands of citations from the New Testament. Put this all together and we have a very accurate New Testament text.

Table 2.1
A COMPARISON OF NEW TESTAMENT AND OTHER ANCIENT TEXTS

Author	Date of the Text	Earliest Copy	Number of Copies	Degree of Accuracy
Homer	9th century BC		643	95 percent
Plato	AD 380	AD 900	7	
Caesar	1st century BC	AD 900	10	
Tacitus	AD 100	AD 1100	20	
New Testament	1st century AD (AD 50–100)	AD 130	5,000+	95 percent

There are fewer Old Testament manuscripts, but there is consistency in content among the manuscripts that do exist, including the Dead Sea Scrolls, which were discovered in 1947. Because the Hebrew scribes held the scriptures in such great reverence, the manuscripts were carefully preserved, and scholars consider these documents to be of better quality than any other ancient manuscripts.[15]

The fact that the biblical manuscripts are accurate is not reason enough to build a worldview on these documents, but we would be foolish to continue our discussion unless we could be sure that the ancient biblical text had come to us largely intact.

The internal evidence. The Bible was written over a time span of about 1,500 to 1,800 years by forty very diversified authors who used a variety of literary forms (prose, poetry, biography, letters, parables, prophecies, recorded sermons, and others), but who nevertheless produced a harmonious message with a major theme: the person and work of the Messiah, Jesus Christ. More than one-fourth of the Bible was predictive prophecy at the time of writing, and an amazing number of these prophecies have come true.[16]

Lee Strobel was a hardened and highly skeptical journalist for the *Chicago Tribune* when he decided to investigate the claims of the Bible after his wife became a follower of Jesus Christ. As part of his investigation, Lee discovered that about five dozen Old Testament prophecies concerned the Messiah and that these were fulfilled with amazing accuracy in the life of Jesus. Playing with a calculator one day, the skeptical reporter tried to figure the likelihood of only eight of these prophecies occurring by chance in the life of one person.

> I imagined the entire world being covered with white tile that was one-and-a-half inches square—every piece of dry land on the planet—and having the bottom of just one tile painted red.
>   Then I pictured a person being allowed to wander for a lifetime around all seven continents. He would be permitted to bend down only one time and pick up a single piece of tile. What are the odds it would be the one tile whose reverse side was painted red? The odds would be the same as just eight of the Old Testament prophecies coming true in any one person throughout history![17]

The Bible itself claims to be an accurate account of the events that it records. Most of the New Testament was written between AD 47 and 70, for example, and many of those who wrote were eyewitnesses of the life, teachings, death, and resurrection of Christ (John 19:35; 1 Peter 5:1; 2 Peter 1:16; 1 John 1:1,3). The text appeared before there was time for myths and distortions to be created and spread.

But isn't this circular reasoning, using the Bible's claims as proof that the Bible is true? If you have worked in a hospital for severely disturbed patients, you may have encountered people who call themselves God or who cite life events that they claim to be true. Of course we don't believe these people. Why, then, should we believe the biblical writers? There is no evidence that they were psychotic, but they made some incredible claims. Do we believe these, just because the writers said they were telling the truth?

It is true that we cannot accept circular reasoning, but we are more inclined to take their claims seriously when these reports are backed with impressive evidence that comes from external sources.

The external evidence. Entire books have been written about the geographical, historical, and archaeological data that confirm the Bible's accuracy.[18] Consider, for example, the work of Nelson Glueck, a nonChristian archaeologist who spent much of his life studying biblical archaeology. He reached the conclusion that no archaeological discovery contradicts or disputes the statements of the

Bible and that an impressive body of literature supports the accuracy of biblical statements.[19]

In 1800, the French Institute in Paris issued a list of eighty-two errors in the Bible that they believed could destroy Christianity. Today, largely because of archaeological finds and new manuscript discoveries, not one of these "errors" remains.[20] Even though a few apparent minor contradictions and errors may remain, because they have not yet been resolved, this in itself is no reason to throw out the Bible. To do so would leave us faced with the need to replace Scripture with some other foundation that would be considerably *less* coherent, internally consistent, comprehensive, supported by external data, and able to explain human behavior.

In the pages that follow, we will assume that the Bible is a book of such accuracy and authority that we can build our worldview and develop approaches to counseling that are based on biblical teaching. If you are still unconvinced of the Bible's trustworthiness, I invite you to take an honest and skeptical look at the evidence. In time, you are likely to become convinced. Look to Lee Strobel or Nelson Glueck—among thousands of others.

SO WHAT?

To work with people effectively, counselors need to be knowledge able. In our training, we seek to understand the basic insights and methods of psychology and the other social sciences, and we acquire counseling skills that enable us to learn about our counselees. Effective counselors are always learning—within the counseling room and without.

If we are Christians and/or if our counselees are believers, part of our learning must focus on what God is like and what He has revealed and is revealing to us. Christians assume that God's existence and revelation both have an important bearing on our counseling, our counselees, and ourselves. What God has revealed also has relevance to our building the worldview from which we make observations and do counseling. For these reasons it is important for us to understand divine revelation.

In this chapter we have considered both general and special revelation, have argued that God's revelation is inspired and accurate, and have discussed briefly how this relates to counseling.

Even if we accept the truth of divine revelation, however, doesn't everybody know that different people give different interpretations, especially when they read the Bible? For God's revelation, especially His special (biblical) revelation to be of help to counselors and to our counselees, we must consider how to interpret the revelation accurately. That is the topic of the next chapter.

CHAPTER THREE

❖

Interpreting the Bible

SEVERAL YEARS AGO, a group of denominational leaders decided to develop a biblically based statement on the role of women in the Church. These church fathers (there were no "church mothers" or other women in the group) appointed two biblical scholars to independently develop the basics for the new policy. Imagine the surprise, and frustration, when the two scholars reached completely opposite interpretations of the same passages and made contradictory recommendations concerning the new policy.

Why do people, even biblical scholars, come up with so many different and sometimes contradictory conclusions when reading the Bible? The Bible is not a useful guide for counselors if we can't figure out what it means. How, then, can we be sure that our interpretations of biblical passages are correct?

This question gets us to the topic of *hermeneutics*, the science and art of biblical interpretation. The word is thought to have come from the name Hermes, the Greek god who served as a messenger for the other gods, bringing and interpreting their messages to human beings.[1] Biblical hermeneutics gives us rules for interpreting the text of the Bible accurately and applying it to our lives.

It is easy for any of us to misinterpret the Bible. Most Christians would agree that we are sinful creatures whose minds and perceptions are distorted so that we don't always see things clearly. In addition, the Bible reader must deal with four "gaps." *The historical gap* points to the fact that the Bible was written many years ago and we sometimes fail to appreciate the historical settings in which the biblical books were written. *The cultural gap* emphasizes the vast differences in customs, standards, social expectations, and other cultural traits between biblical times and our own. *The linguistic gap* recognizes that we use a different language and different figures of speech than the biblical writers used, so most Bible readers have to work with translated texts. Then we have *the worldview gap.* The biblical writers often saw the world with perceptions and values that were far different from the mechanistic, materialistic, new-age, individualistic, democratic, naturalistic, cause-effect thinking that characterizes modern worldviews.

When I was teaching graduate students in counseling, I often encouraged them to take a course in hermeneutics—even though this seems far removed from counseling. I had several reasons for this suggestion. On a personal level, I once took a hermeneutics course and found it helpful in my own Bible study. But over the years I have read many books written by Christian counselors who, without apparent awareness of what they are doing, quote Bible verses that are pulled out of context and used in ways that the biblical writers never intended.

The same thing can happen in counseling. If the Bible is to guide us in forming a worldview and in helping our counselees, we must be as sure as we can that we don't misquote or misinterpret Scripture.

Before we look at some guidelines for interpreting the Bible, we must pause to recognize the role of God's Spirit in this process. The Holy Spirit, who guided the biblical writers as they wrote (2 Peter 1:21), today guides us as we seek to receive, properly understand, and apply God's truth (John 16:13). He is at the core of accurate biblical interpretation. Asking for His guidance whenever we approach the Bible is an important first step in keeping us from error and in helping us to interpret and apply the Word of God correctly.

THE GOAL OF BIBLICAL INTERPRETATION

To understand the Bible accurately, we must deal with two issues. First, we start with what the text means, and then we seek to determine its significance.

Meaning

Seminary students take courses in what they call *exegesis*. This involves getting from the text what the writers really meant when they wrote. Some of the confusion in Bible interpretation comes when readers assume that each text can have a variety of meanings. Assume this, and one person's interpretation is as good as any other. This leaves all kinds of room for what the seminarians call *eisogesis*, the tendency to read into the text a meaning that isn't there.

Consider an Old Testament example. Infertility is a common problem today, and apparently it was common in past centuries as well. In the Old Testament, Abraham and Sarah wanted children, but the years passed and she couldn't get pregnant. One day, Abraham had a vision in which he expressed his concern about not having children, but then the word of the Lord came to him and said "a son coming from your own body will be your heir" (Genesis 15:4). This was amazing, because Abraham and Sarah were both old. If you read Genesis 15, it is clear that God is speaking to Abraham at a certain time in history about one man's future parenthood.

Suppose, however, that some counselor reads this passage and concludes that God is indicating that anxiety often prevents infertile couples from getting pregnant. Abraham appears to have been anxious about not having a heir other than his servant (Genesis 15:2-3), but when God gives His reassurance that a son will be born, Abraham seems to relax. Is this God's teaching that infertile couples should learn to relax so that pregnancy is more likely?

While it is true that tension may contribute to infertility in some cases, we can't reach that conclusion from Genesis 15. To assume that God's talk to Abraham means something other than what it says is to impose our meaning on the text. If we want to interpret Scripture correctly, we must seek to determine, as best we can, what the biblical authors meant to say when they wrote. We can't have clarity if we assume that the Bible is a book of riddles; instead, we assume that the biblical writers meant what they said. When we approach the Bible, therefore, our first goal is to determine what it means.

Significance

Once we determine what the text means, we can seek to determine the significance of that text for us, for the world in which we live, or for our counselees.

Let us return to the example of Abraham and Sarah's infertility.

Suppose, now, that an infertile couple reads this passage, correctly recognizes that God was talking to Abraham about a specific situation, but then they conclude, "What this text really means *to us* is that we are going to have a son, from our own bodies." If a pregnancy doesn't follow, they are confused and perhaps angry at God. Their disappointment has come because they assumed that the text was written to give us insight into overcoming infertility. But Genesis 15 was written to show how God supernaturally fulfilled a promise to Abraham and gave him an heir.

Psychologists, counselors, pastors, denominational leaders, and many others too often start with their questions and rush to the Bible to find answers. But often their conclusions are not correct because they have not been careful to first determine what the text means and then to look at its significance to us.

Recently I heard a speaker claim that Moses was rejected as a child (because he was hidden in the reeds) and that his behavior as an adult was a reflection of his childhood rejection and dysfunctional family background. Perhaps! But as I listened to the sermon—preached, incidentally, by a committed biblical teacher whom I greatly respect—I wondered if the speaker started with his views about childhood rejection, imposed meaning on the text that the biblical writer never intended, then reached conclusions that are of dubious validity and significance to us.

Of course, we can't limit God. On occasion He does use a verse that is taken out of context and made to say something that the biblical writer really did not say. Haven't you had the experience of opening the Bible to some passage that seems to speak directly to your situation, even though it is taken out of context, and you have not sought to determine its real meaning first? This *does* happen at times, but when we interpret the Bible in this way, we have slipped into the assumption that this is a magical book that can give teaching or direction without regard for the meaning or context of the words.

Bernard Ramm wrote about this many years ago:

> If a blessing is derived from an improper interpretation of
> Scripture, the blessing has come not because of improper
> interpretation, but in spite of the misinterpretation. . . .
>
> When we force the Bible to say something on specific
> items of our life, we . . . leave the sensible, intelligent use

of the Bible for that which borders on primitive divination. Most notorious is the custom of opening the Bible and putting the finger on a verse and taking that verse as divine guidance. This method dishonors the intelligence of God, the sobriety of the Bible, puts the Christian faith in a ridiculous light, and places the method of determining the will of God on a superstitious, magical basis. It ought to be added: *no promise of the Bible is to be used that is not in keeping with sane, exegetical principles.*[2]

THE METHODS OF BIBLICAL INTERPRETATION

How, then, do we interpret the Bible accurately, using "sane, exegetical principles"? There are three steps, which can be put in the form of questions. Whenever you approach the Bible, ask: What does it really say? What does it really mean? How does it apply? Stated more formally, the interpreter of the Bible is involved in observation, interpretation, and application. Table 3.1 summarizes what the interpreter does at each stage.

Table 3.1
PRINCIPLES OF BIBLE INTERPRETATION

1. *Observation*: Start by asking what the text says.
   a. What does it say?
   b. Who was speaking, writing, being spoken to, or being spoken about?
   c. Where and when does this take place? (i.e., What are the circumstances?)
   d. Does the text tell us why this is reported?
   e. What form of speech is being used? (Is this part of a sermon, history, poetry, a parable, a letter, prophecy, a prayer, or some other format?)
2. *Interpretation*: Continue by asking what the text means
   a. What type of literature is this text?
      ❖ Remember that passages that give direct teaching (didactic passages) take precedence over non-didactic passages when we are developing doctrine or life principles.
   b. What is the context of the passage?
      ❖ The literary context: How does this text fit into the sentences, verses, and chapters that surround it?
      ❖ The historical context: What was going on in history when this was written, and how does this influence was written?
      ❖ The cultural context: What do we know about the culture and customs at the time when this passage was written?
      ❖ The geographical context: Do we know where this passage was written or where the events described took place?
      ❖ The theological context: Assuming that God revealed Himself slowly

over the years, where does this passage fit in to the overall flow of
Scripture?

   c. How is this text made clearer by other, parallel biblical texts?

   d. What do Bible commentaries and other resources say that will help
clarify the meaning?

3. *Application*: Conclude by asking how the text can be applied.

   a. Is there an example here for me to follow?

   b. Is there a sin to avoid?

   c. Is there a promise that can apply to me?

   d. Is there a prayer to repeat?

   e. Is there a command to obey?

   f. Is there a condition to meet?

   g. Is there an error to avoid?

   h. Is there a challenge to face?

   i. Is there something here that I should memorize?

Observation

In one sense, reading the Bible is like "reading" a counselee. In both
cases we look for information. We want to know what was said, but
we also notice what was emphasized, repeated, or told in the form
of a story or figure of speech.

Just as we don't make snap judgments about people, based on
casual observation, so the careful interpreter reads the Bible carefully,
thoughtfully, patiently, inquisitively, humbly, prayerfully, and with the
goal of knowing what it means. I agree with the writers who suggest
that the more time we spend in careful observation, the less time we
will have to devote to interpretation, and the more accurate will be our
conclusions. In contrast, if we hurry past the observation stage, we end
up spending a lot more time interpreting and our conclusions are likely
to be less valid.[3] That is true both in Bible study and in counseling.

Interpretation

How do we respond when two equally committed believers reach conflicting conclusions as the result of their Bible study? Those denominational leaders who wanted to build a policy on the role of women in
the Church responded with frustration—at least in the beginning.

When this kind of disagreement exists, we do not throw up
our hands in resignation and conclude that "it doesn't really matter
what the text says, because one person's interpretation is as good as
any other." Instead, we stick with the assumption that there is really
only one accurate interpretation of each part of Scripture. With our
finite minds, limitations in understanding, and personal biases, we
sometimes disagree with one another.

Even the Apostle Peter had this problem in the early church. He wrote that Paul's "letters contain some things that are hard to understand," and we are warned lest we be carried away by error (2 Peter 3:16-17).

Differences of interpretation persist and probably always will— that is one reason why we have different theologies and different denominations. These differences might not get resolved as long as we are in this world where we don't always see clearly (1 Corinthians 13:12). But many of our differences disappear if we study further and really are willing to seek and to know the truth. We are more likely to know the truth if we follow some basic principles of interpretation.

Principle 1: Notice the type of literature. You don't have to be an English professor to know that people express themselves in different ways, depending in part on the type of language that they are using. Professional journals tend to be boring and difficult to read because the writers want to express themselves concisely, using precise technical terms. In contrast, poetry uses picturesque language that creates impressions and gives us word-images like: "The moon on the crest of the new-fallen snow gave a luster of mid-day to objects below." Much different are articles that include quotations. If I quote somebody who doesn't believe in God, I would hope that the reader would be careful to note that the quotation was not an expression of what I believe. And if I tell my wife, "It's raining cats and dogs," she knows that I am using a figure of speech and not implying that puppies and kittens are falling from the heavens.

Sometimes we misinterpret the Bible because we fail to notice the literary form of the passage. Table 3.2 summarizes the major types of literature in the Bible. An awareness of these differences helps us to understand more clearly.

Most biblical interpreters would agree that we must be cautious about building theological principles and guidelines that are based solely on historical passages. In general, we seek to build theology on the passages that teach—passages like the Sermon on the Mount or the letters of Paul. Much error can come if we turn to the book of Acts, for example, read about some event that occurred, and conclude that because something happened once, we should expect it to happen again. It is a basic principle of hermeneutics that, because they are clearer and more informative, the teaching (didactic) passages take precedence over the historical passages when we are developing doctrine and life principles.

Table 3.2
MAJOR TYPES OF LITERATURE IN THE BIBLE[4]

Types	Characteristics	Biblical Books and Examples
Apocalyptic	Dramatic, highly symbolic material; vivid imagery, stark contrasts; portrays a cosmic struggle between good and evil	Revelation
Biography	Close-up view of an individual's life; selected events reveal positive or negative character development	Abraham, Isaac, Jacob, Joseph, Moses, Saul, David, Elijah, Jesus Christ
Encomium	Description of a subject in glowing terms; exhorts the reader to imitate these qualities	Psalm 119, Proverbs 31:10-31, Song of Songs, John 1:1-18, 1 Corinthians 13, Colossians 1:15-20, Hebrews 1–3
Exposition	Carefully reasoned argument or explanation; terms are crucial; the aim is agreement and action	Paul's letters; Hebrews; James; 1 and 2 Peter; 1, 2, and 3 John; Jude
Narrative	A broad category in which story is prominent; usually historical accounts; events are selected to convey meaning	Genesis–Ezra; the Gospels; Acts
Oratory	Stylized oral presentation of an argument; usually intended to exhort and persuade	John 13–17; Acts 7, 17:22-31, 22:1-21, 24:10-21, 26:1-23
Parable	Brief oral story illustrating a moral; understood as an extended simile with a focal point of comparison	2 Samuel 12:1-6, Ecclesiastes 9:14-16, Matthew 13:1-53, Mark 4:1-34, Luke 15:1–16:31
Pastoral	Deals with rural, rustic themes; heavy on description, lean on action; often meditative	Psalm 23, Isaiah 40:11, John 10:1-18
Poetry	Verse intended to be spoken or sung rather than read; appeals to the emotions	Job, Psalms, Proverbs, Ecclesiastes, Song of Songs
Prophecy	Strident, authoritative presentation of God's will and words; frequently intended to be corrective or motivate change through warnings and foretelling God's plans in response to human choices	Isaiah–Malachi
Proverb	Short, pithy statement of a moral truth; usually has a single point of comparison or principle of truth to convey	Proverbs
Satire	Exposes and ridicules human vice and foolishness; warns readers through a negative example	Proverbs 24:30-34, Ezekiel 34, Luke 18:1-8, 2 Corinthians 11:1–12:1

Types	Characteristics	Biblical Books and Examples
Tragedy	Relates the downfall of a person; problems usually revolve around a critical flaw in the person's character and moral choices; warns by negative example	Lot, Samson, Saul; Acts 5:1-11
Wisdom Literature	A broad category in which an older, seasoned person relates wisdom to a younger person	Job; Psalms 37, 90; Proverbs; Ecclesiastes

Principle 2: Look at the context. It must be difficult to be a celebrity who is pursued by the press. Reporters need quotations to enliven their stories, but often the quotes are pulled out of context and sometimes they completely distort what the speaker said or intended. I have experienced this on occasion in reviews of my books. Once a reviewer cited half a sentence from a book and concluded, *wrongly*, that I believe Jesus was a homosexual. Think of how unfair it would be to me if a reviewer pulled the last six words from the previous sentence and cited this in a review of this book.

To understand what the biblical text means, carefully look at the words and sentences that come both before and after the text that you are reading. Look, too, at the context of the entire book. Letters, like those of Paul, differ from books like Genesis or the gospels, which are historical accounts. It is helpful, too, to be aware of other writings by the same author and of the message of the entire Bible.

Consider, for example, Psalm 73. Here we read that the wicked "have no struggles; their bodies are healthy and strong. They are free from the burdens common to man; they are not plagued by human ills. . . . This is what the wicked are like—always carefree, they increase in wealth" (vv. 4-5,12). This is in the Bible!

But read the context. The writer is describing what was passing through his mind when he looked at the wicked people around him. Then he went into the sanctuary of God and quickly learned that his earlier impressions were wrong, that ultimately the wicked will come to ruin and justice will prevail in the end.

Bible passages should always be read in context.

Principle 3: Be aware of parallel passages. Donald Grey Barnhouse was a Bible scholar who was widely read and highly regarded as an interpreter and preacher of Scripture. He is reported to have said, "You very rarely have to go outside of the Bible to explain anything in the Bible."

This refers to the importance of making comparisons. Often several Bible passages will discuss the same topic, and we get a better overall understanding if we put these passages together. This is of special importance when you encounter something that is unclear. Any unclear passages should be interpreted in light of passages that are clear.

Principle 4: Consult other Bible helps. At some time in the course of their educations, most professional counselors take a course in personality theory. They learn about Freud, Jung, Rogers, Ellis, and lesser-known writers; the class compares and contrasts the theorists' counseling methods. Often the professor uses a textbook that summarizes the theories so that the students never have to read anything else. It is possible, therefore, to learn about Freud in detail without reading even one paragraph of what he wrote. We all know why we do this. It is often easier to read a summary than it is to go to the original writings and read for ourselves.

I suspect some people do this with the Bible. They read books about the Bible, but they never read the Bible itself. Obviously, we need to look at the biblical text if we are to grasp its meaning fully. Each of us is responsible to read for ourselves and to interpret the Bible as clearly as we can.

But that does not mean we ignore what others have written. For centuries, commentators, expositors, linguists, historians, theologians, and many others have studied the Bible and reached insightful conclusions that can help in our interpretations. We can benefit greatly from looking at the interpretations, writings, and conclusions of others.

Go into any Christian bookstore and you will discover that there are many Bible aids available. These include concordances, dictionaries, commentaries, Bible handbooks, and atlases. The appendix lists some of the recommended Bible study aids that were available when this book was published. A bookstore manager or pastor might be able to suggest others.

Application

Someone has suggested that each text in the Bible has one meaning but many applications. Once we are able to conclude what a text says and what it means, we are in a good position to ask how it applies in our lives or in the lives of our counselees.

In a highly practical book dealing with Bible study, Howard and William Hendricks suggest a four-step approach to application.

These steps are concise, easy to remember, and can be helpful for those of us who seek to apply the Scriptures to the problems of our counselees.[5]

Step 1: Knowing. To apply what the Bible says, we have to know what the Bible says. I hesitate to start with something so obvious, but sometimes obvious things get overlooked. The more we know the Bible and the better we understand the text, the more effectively we will make applications. Obviously it is difficult to apply principles from a book that you don't know very well.

After graduate school, I studied for a year in seminary, worked for a while in a university counseling center, and then went to teach psychology at a Christian college in Minnesota. Shortly after my arrival, I got a call from a seminary president who asked if I would be interested in teaching in a school of theology. My answer was immediate and firm: "No!" I didn't want to move so soon after arriving at the college where I was teaching, and I didn't have much interest in teaching seminary students. Maybe you know what happened. Four years later I was working in a seminary and that is where I spent most of my teaching career.

During those years, I hope my students learned from me; I know I learned from them. I discovered that thorough Bible knowledge is not just for young ministers. Counselors need that too. Many of my students were working on graduate degrees in psychology, but they were learning from their Bible courses, acquiring knowledge that would be invaluable in the counseling room—providing they were willing to apply it. If you want to be an effective Christian counselor, be constantly growing in your Bible knowledge.

Keep growing, as well, in knowledge about yourself. Every counseling student soon learns the importance of knowing our own strengths, weaknesses, and tendencies to let our own personalities and struggles influence our counseling. For this reason, many doctoral training programs require students to spend time in therapy, dealing with their own hang-ups, getting to know themselves better, and learning how to keep their own struggles out of the lives of their counselees.

"Watch your life and doctrine closely. Persevere in them," Paul wrote to Timothy (1 Timothy 4:16). This was good advice for a young preacher, because careful self-knowledge and theological knowledge would protect both the preacher and the hearers. The same is true for counselors. Know yourself and your biblically based doctrine well.

In this way you will benefit both yourself and your counselees.

Step 2: Relating. In a later letter to Timothy, Paul wrote, "All Scripture is God-breathed and is useful for teaching, rebuking, correcting and training in righteousness, so that the man of God may be thoroughly equipped for every good work" (2 Timothy 3:16).

This gets us to the core of application: using Scripture to teach, rebuke, correct, and train others and ourselves. Hendricks and Hendricks suggest that we ask several questions whenever we want to relate the Bible to our lives:[6]

   ❖ Is there an example here for me to follow?
   ❖ Is there a sin to avoid?
   ❖ Is there a promise that can apply to me?
   ❖ Is there a prayer to repeat?
   ❖ Is there a command to obey?
   ❖ Is there a condition to meet?
   ❖ Is there an error to avoid?
   ❖ Is there a challenge to face?
   ❖ Is there something here that I should memorize?

These questions enable us to relate the Bible to life. As we look for answers, we will find guidelines for relating to God and to others, for dealing with the Devil, for bringing change within ourselves, and for refining the worldview on which we build our lives. The same questions could guide us as we work with our counselees to deal with the problems in their lives.

Step 3: Meditate. I tend to be an action-oriented person. I like to be involved in many projects, trying new things, keeping on the cutting edge of what is going on. Probably I get caught up in too many activities and this puts me under stress. But am I a workaholic? Of course not! Unfortunately, I can't find anybody to agree with this conclusion.

One thing is certain, however: We all need to stop regularly, to pull away from the activity of our busy lives, to think, to read, and to meditate on the Word of God. If I don't make time for this for more than three or four days, I can feel myself drying up intellectually and spiritually. Then my efficiency begins to slide. I need to read, broadly, but even more, I need to reflect on the Bible. Psalm 1:1-2 stresses the importance of meditating on God's Word "day and night," and Psalm 119 indicates why. When we meditate on the Bible, the Scriptures help to protect us from sin (Psalm 119:11), enlighten us (v. 18), counsel us (v. 24), give us strength (vv. 27-28), clarify our values (vv. 35-37), free us (vv. 45-46), bring comfort (v. 52), give hope (vv. 74,81,147), give us wisdom (vv. 98-100) and understanding (vv. 104,169), guide us (vv. 105,133), and give us an inner peace (v. 165). People who meditate on the Bible are guaranteed to change in ways that will make them more Christlike. This, in turn, makes us more compassionate and able to meet the needs of our counselees.

Step 4: Practice. Whenever I have faced some new decision or challenge, I often have reread the story of Joshua's promotion to become the leader of Israel. Moses had died, and the new leader must have felt at least a little overwhelmed by the awesome responsibility that had fallen on his shoulders. So God gave a formula for success:

> "Be strong and very courageous. Be careful to obey all the law my servant Moses gave you; do not turn from it to the right or to the left, that you may be successful wherever you go. Do not let this Book of the Law depart from your mouth; meditate on it day and night, so that you may be careful to do everything written in it. Then you will be prosperous and successful." (Joshua 1:7-8)

Notice the emphasis on both meditating and taking action. It does little good to read the Bible if we don't obey and put what we read into practice. The New Testament describes this as self-deception. "Do not merely listen to the word," we read in the book of James (1:22-25), "do what it says." It is then that the Bible really permeates our lives, including our counseling.

DOES THE BIBLE ANSWER OUR COUNSELING QUESTIONS?

At this point, we have considered basic guidelines for studying the Bible and applying it to our lives. Often, however, we are faced with specific questions, some of which may be raised by our counselees. "How can I deal with my rebellious teenager?" "Should I accept a new job offer?" "What can I do about my depression?" "Can you help me with my addiction to pornography?" "What can I do to stop my husband from beating me?"

Some Christian counselors say that specific answers to all of our questions are found in the Bible. Since God has given us all we need to know "for life and godliness" (2 Peter 1:3-4) we can go to Scripture to find solutions to all of our problems.

Sometimes, of course, the Bible gives precise direction and answers our questions. Often, however, the Bible does not specifically address the problems that we encounter in our lives and that people bring to us in counseling. When we go to the Bible with specific questions, trying to find biblical answers on issues that are never addressed, there is the danger that we will pull phrases out of context or arrive at interpretations that twist the Scriptures to make them say what they never intended to say. What, then, is a better and more accurate way to help people biblically?

To answer, let's use the illustration of mate-beating. In the United States, and doubtless in many other countries, there is significant evidence of the physical and verbal abuse of women by their husbands. (Husband-abuse by wives also appears to be prevalent, but it gets reported less frequently and is brought to counselors less often.) According to one report, more American women are injured by the men in their lives than by car accidents, muggings, and rape combined.[7] The National League of Cities estimates that perhaps half of all women will experience violence from their husbands at some time in their marriages. Between 22 to 35 percent of all visits by females to emergency rooms are for treatment of injuries that came from domestic assaults.

Let's suppose that one of these women comes to you for counseling. She has chosen you because you are a Christian and she wants counseling that will help her deal with the problem in a biblical way. In addition to listening, showing empathy, and expressing compassion, how do we counsel biblically? There are at least four answers. These are not listed as steps; they all are ongoing as you counsel.

1. Approach counseling as we approach the Bible—with humility and a sincere desire to understand and to respond correctly. We must acknowledge that none of us has perfect understanding. We need to rely on the Holy Spirit to guide our thinking and how we respond.

2. Ask if there are any passages in the Bible that give specific instructions for dealing with the problem. If the battered wife is involved sexually with a man who is not her husband, we know

that for her own good she must stop the adulterous relationship. The Bible is clear: You shall not commit adultery (Exodus 20:14, Matthew 5:27).

But the Bible gives no specific instructions to women who are being beaten by their husbands. This isn't surprising because the Scriptures didn't give answers to every specific problem that might arise. So we move on to our next guideline.

3. If the Bible says nothing directly about the problem, ask if there are related issues to which the Bible does speak. We know, for example, that the wife should respect her husband (Ephesians 5:33) and should determine to stick with him and to be an example to him (1 Corinthians 7:10,13-14). She should be careful not to provoke conflict and should do what she can to live in peace with her husband (Romans 12:18). The counselee can bring her anxieties to God in prayer, be reminded that He is near to her, and expect that she will experience genuine inner peace, even in the midst of her dangerous situation (Philippians 4:5-6).

The counselee can admit her anger without squelching it, but with God's help (she will need it), she can control her natural tendency to respond with bitterness, malice, and revenge. Instead, the Bible tells her to be forgiving and even to show kindness (Ephesians 4:26,29,31-32). She can be reminded that when bitterness gets hold of a life it can cause many additional problems (Hebrews 12:15).

Is seeking to do all of this unnatural? Of course it is. The client is hurting, and she certainly does not need a Bible-quoting judge who sends her on her way burdened with a long, seemingly unrealistic "to-do" list that is likely to leave her feeling guilty when she doesn't put all of the instructions into practice. The counselor needs to be understanding and inclined to show all the characteristics of the fruit of the Spirit (Galatians 5:22-23). He or she encourages the counselee to talk and the counselor listens, like Jesus heard the two confused men who walked the road to Emmaus (Luke 24:1-35). As they talk, the counselor introduces the biblical principles. Both the counselor and counselee recognize that although the Bible does not deal directly with a problem that the counselee presents, there are many relevant biblical texts that can apply, nevertheless.

Larry Crabb reached this conclusion when he wrote,

Yes, the Bible is sufficient to answer every question about life, but not because it directly responds to every legitimate question. The idea of biblical sufficiency for counseling rests on the assumption that biblical data support doctrinal categories which have implications that comprehensively deal with every relational issue of life.[8]

4. Make intervention or action decisions based on your Christian worldview. Should a wife stay in a home where a husband is beating her and threatening the children? The Bible does not say. As we prayerfully think through what we know about doctrine and the issues that Scripture does address, we use our God-given brains to make interventions that, to the best of our ability, are consistent with biblical teaching.

In the book of James, for example, we are told, "Religion that God our Father accepts as pure and faultless is this: to look after orphans and widows in their distress and to keep oneself from being polluted by the world" (1:27). The battered wife may be neither a widow nor an orphan, but the overall strategy seems clear. The Christian helper needs to assist the woman in her distress, undoubtedly protecting her from the rage of the husband, probably by finding another place for her to live temporarily. I would want to talk to the husband if possible and would hope to work with him in dealing both with his anger control and with the issues that are causing his anger explosions.

Since God expects me to obey the laws of society (Romans 13:1, Titus 3:1, 2 Peter 3:13-14), if I live in a place where the reporting of mate-abuse is required by law, I would report the abuse, in ideal circumstances with the cooperation of my counselee. After all, psychological studies show that if the first assault by husbands or former husbands was not reported to the police 41 percent of the women were assaulted again during the following six months. In contrast, only 15 percent of the women who did notify the police were attacked a second time. There is evidence that arrest for abuse often opens abusers to counseling that enables them to prevent future outbreaks of violence.[9]

I once heard about a well-known Christian writer who tried to evaluate everything he heard, read, or saw through a grid that asked, "How would this relate to the Bible and to my Christian perspective?" That is worldview thinking. It is the kind of thinking that we need to develop and apply to our lives and our minds if we are to counsel in ways that are sincerely Christian.

DO WE TEACH CONTENT OR SKILLS?

For several years a local counselor taught an introductory counseling course for seminary students. Every time the course was taught, the teacher and students would get into a debate over the goals of counseling. The students argued that Christian counseling should be like teaching, with the goal of sharing insights and biblical content and instructing counselees on applying these principles to their lives. The classroom teacher argued that counseling goes further. To be effective it must be more than an intellectual exercise.

Many problems, he suggested, have nothing to do with what people know or with what their hermeneutically correct Bible study has revealed. Many Christians know *what* the Bible says about marriage or about relationships, for example, but they don't know *how* to put these principles into operation. These counselees need us to focus less on content and more on the process of acquiring skills. By listening to instruction, observing mentors (including the counselor), and practicing what they have learned, counselees are able to develop communication skills, relationship skills, study skills, parenting skills, job-hunting skills, and other ways of behaving. Often the counselor helps them see where and how they have made errors in their relationships, like failing to be sensitive or failing to listen, and the counselor shows a better, more skillful way to act.

Much of Jesus' teaching was like this. He taught doctrine and biblical truth to the disciples, but in addition to the instruction, He gave them warnings, demonstrations—including many from His own life—practice, and opportunities to discuss what they were learning (Luke 9:1-11).

Most Christian counseling will involve both the teaching of biblical content and guidance in the acquisition of skills. When the Bible does not speak to these skills issues, we counsel from the biblically based worldview that we have developed. That worldview will be built, in part, on our views about God and about the nature of human beings. If we view people as being like tadpoles, with all head and not much else, we will limit our counseling to the sharing of information. In contrast, if we see people as feeling, relating, thinking, perceiving, planning, complex beings, created in the image of God, then we will be more likely to deal with skill acquisition in addition to giving them knowledge.

A lot of what we do depends on our views of God and on our views of human nature. That is the topic of the next two chapters.

SO WHAT?

One day, when I was working on the first draft of this book, I took a break to have lunch with a local pastor. He is a young, sensitive, dynamic, baby-boomer type whom God is using to touch many lives. During the course of our lunch, I mentioned this chapter on hermeneutics and my friend made an interesting observation. "I think everybody in our church should have a brief course on Bible interpretation," he said. "That isn't only for theologians and Bible scholars; we all need to know about hermeneutics."

Knowing how to interpret the Bible accurately certainly is crucial for Christian counselors. The Bible has great relevance in speaking to the problems that people bring to their counselors. But our task is to be sure that we don't pull verses out of context, ignore the real meaning of what the Bible says, or read our own interpretations into the text. We are not being responsible counselors or followers of Jesus Christ if we treat God's Word either like a cookbook of recipes for counseling or a magical volume that we open at random, expecting direction to jump from the page like a genie from some Aladdin's lantern.

Instead, whenever we approach the Bible we must ask: What does the text really say? What does it really mean? How does it apply? Table 3.1 can be a helpful guide for counselors in our personal lives and in our counseling.

When counselees come with questions, remember the principles of good hermeneutics, but try as well to apply the four previously mentioned guidelines. Approach the Bible humbly and with a genuine desire to understand and to respond accurately. Ask if there are passages that give specific instructions for dealing with the problem. If the Bible says nothing directly about the problem, ask if there are related issues to which the Bible does speak. And always seek to make intervention decisions based on your Christian worldview.

Not long ago I was struggling with some career decisions when I read Isaiah 48:17—"I am the LORD your God, who teaches you what is best for you, who directs you in the way you should go." Near the chair where I was reading, the words of another Bible verse hang on the wall in a blue and gold frame. "'For I know the plans I have for you,' declares the LORD, 'plans to prosper you and not to harm you, plans to give you hope and a future'" (Jeremiah 29:11). These are wonderfully comforting words for counselors making career decisions and for anybody else who is pondering the future.

Unfortunately the words were not written specifically for me or for my counselees. The quotation from Isaiah was a message from God to the nation of Israel, which was going through a time of stubbornness. The second quote was directed to the Jewish exiles in Babylon who were being assured that God was making a gracious promise to free them from the bondage of Babylon. To be true to the Scriptures, I have to keep the context of the verses and the intended recipients in mind when I read.

Don't assume, however, that I dismissed these verses as records of history that have no relevance to me. Throughout the pages of the Bible, God promises to care for and to guide His people—individuals as well as whole nations. These two comforting verses tell me something about God and His promises. I can accept them for my own life because they are consistent with the whole of biblical teaching and promises given to specific groups that can apply to all of God's people. When correctly interpreted, the Bible has great relevance, not only to our counselees but to any of us who struggle with decisions, life pressures, and problems.

As you look into its pages, remember that counseling involves both what people need to know and what skills they need to develop. To better understand how human beings can change in their knowledge and skills, we need to know what human beings are really like. But first we need to know about the God who created us and continues to work in our lives. That is what we consider next.

CHAPTER FOUR

God and Counseling

GOD IS ALIVE and very well in America!

That is the conclusion of two respected researchers who did a carefully controlled survey of adults in the United States. Ninety percent of the people questioned said they believe in God.[1] The percentage dropped only a little when people were asked if they could agree that "there is only one true God, who is holy and perfect, and who created the world and rules it today." Seventy-four percent said yes.[2]

That's the good news.

The bad news is that God doesn't make much difference in most of our lives. When they are making decisions, especially decisions about right and wrong, very few of the surveyed people turn to God for guidance. Instead, people look to themselves as authorities on morality. They choose which commandments to believe (if any), and they think of God as "a general principle of life" or as a "distant and pale reflection of the God of our forefathers."[3]

If most of your counseling is with committed Christians, you probably see counselees who hold a view of God that is more traditional. But even among believers, Christian counselors included, there can be misconceptions about what God really is like and how He relates to human beings. When stress builds and God seems far away, some may wonder if He even exists.

DOES GOD EXIST?

Several years ago, a best-selling book advised readers how to start every day. Immediately after turning off the alarm and before putting their feet on the cold bedroom floor, they were to say "I believe!" three times. I had a friend who tried this with enthusiasm. Since he lived in a warm climate, he would throw open his window every morning and repeat his statements of "I believe" in the fresh air.

One morning my friend asked himself an arresting question: "I believe, but in what?"

Social critic Os Guinness has written about the "characteristically American" heresy of having faith in religion in general, rather than having faith in God.[4] Counselors often encourage people to believe—in themselves, in the future, in the possibility of change, in the power of positive thinking—but rarely are there references to God in the counseling room. When God is mentioned, His name tends to be used as an exclamation (as in "Oh, God!") or viewed as a figment from the imagination of unenlightened minds. In most counseling rooms, God does not exist—at least in the words and thoughts of the therapists and their clients. I wonder if God also is left out of counseling by many who call themselves Christian.

Proving God's Existence

Throughout the centuries, theologians, philosophers, and other scholars have sought to prove the existence of God. Their arguments have been carefully reasoned, detailed, thorough, and not always easy to read.[5] The case for God's existence has been built on logical reasoning, subjective experience, and empirical data, but when all of the evidence is accumulated, can we be 100 percent certain that God exists?

The answer is no, but this should not be surprising. We human beings really can't be 100 percent certain of anything. We can compile evidence, however, and reach conclusions that are highly probable. If a person is willing to take the time and make an honest effort to sift through the evidence for God's existence, the seeker is almost certain to conclude that the evidence for the existence of God is stronger by far than the evidence to support His nonexistence. This is what happened to Lee Strobel and Nelson Glueck who were mentioned earlier. It has been the experience of countless others.

Either God exists or He does not. Of the two alternatives, only the assumption of God's existence gives a reason for order in the universe and an explanation for the purpose, dignity, and destiny of human beings, including those we counsel. In contrast, if God does not exist, we are left alone in an impersonal universe, spinning on a planet that is controlled by chance, without any reason to hope, and with no life purpose or ultimate destiny. The existence of God, therefore, has immense importance for mental health and for counseling.

Perhaps it seems strange that the Bible makes no effort to prove God's existence. The biblical writers simply assume that He exists. Look at the first four words in the Bible: "In the beginning, God." There is no further discussion of His existence. For the rest of the Bible we read about His Word, His nature, and His works. The psalmist wrote that the universe gives evidence of God (Psalm 19:1-6). Paul noted that God has made Himself plain, even to those who don't believe (Romans 1:18-21). But detailed arguments for God's existence are not found in the pages of Scripture.

As we begin to understand what God is like, we begin to comprehend why there can be no absolute proof of His existence. God is supreme and far greater than any methods that we might use in an attempt to demonstrate His existence. There are no authorities greater than God to which we can appeal, and He is not confined to any of our methods. We look at the probabilities, therefore, and conclude there is an extremely high likelihood that He does exist. Then, like the biblical writers, we move ahead to see what He is really like.

WHAT IS GOD LIKE?

A London newspaper recorded the views of children who had been asked what God is like. "He has a long white beard and wears glasses," one of the children wrote. According to another, God "eats loaves and fishes for breakfast and when he takes a shower, it rains all over the place."

Similar sentiments were expressed in a book of letters that children had written to God. "Dear God," wrote somebody named

Donna. "We read that Thos. Edison made light. They said in Sunday School you did it. So I bet he stoled your idea."

Here are others:

Dear God,

You don't have to worry about me. I always look both ways.

—Dean

Please send Dennis Clark to a different camp this year.

—Peter

I keep waiting for spring but it never come yet. Don't forget.

—Mark

I bet it is very hard for you to love all of everybody in the whole world. There are only 4 people in our family and I can never do it.

—Nan

Maybe Cain and Abel would not kill each other so much if they had their own rooms. It works with my brother.

—Larry

I went to this wedding and they kissed right in church. Is that OK?

—Neil

Probably a girl named Nora had the best theology. She wrote, "Dear God, I don't ever feel alone since I found out about you."[6]

If you were to write a letter to God, what would you say? If you were to think about the One who would receive your letter, what would He be like? Your answer to that question may say a lot about you. Somebody has said that we tend to move toward our mental image of God. If you think of God as being distant and disinterested, you will act and think differently than the person who thinks that God is compassionate, forgiving, and a helper in times of need.

Every counselor knows that images of God often come from our experiences growing up at home. When one's earthly parent frequently is absent, exceptionally busy, unrealistically harsh, or apparently disinterested in the concerns of his kids, it can be difficult for these kids (even when they have grown up) to accept the idea of a loving heavenly Father who is ever-present and who really cares about His children. Sometimes the parents may be compassionate and good models, but if there is harshness or hypocrisy in a pastor or other spiritual leader, a child may wonder about the God this leader claims to serve and represent.

In reality, all of our images of God are flawed. Our minds are too small to comprehend God accurately, and our experiences are too likely to distort our thinking. But knowing God and knowing about Him are crucially important for our growth as believers and our effectiveness as Christian counselors. Theologian James I. Packer has even argued that knowing God is at the core of why we exist: "What were we made for? To know God. What aim should we set ourselves in life? To know God"[7] (John 17:3). Think of the implications of this for your life and career goals.

Why Should We Know God?

The writer of a recent devotional book caught my attention with these words: "Worship changes the worshiper into the image of the One worshiped."[8] When our kids were growing up, we often warned them to avoid the company of people who might influence them adversely. Sometimes we looked at their heroes and saw how even a distant teenage idol could have an influence. As they matured, our daughters learned what all of us learn sooner or later: We become like our heros and like the people with whom we spend time. "He who walks with the wise grows wise," wrote King Solomon, "but a companion of fools suffers harm" (Proverbs 13:20). In the New Testament we read, "Bad company corrupts good character" (1 Corinthians 15:33).

This gets us back to the words in that devotional book. When we spend time with God and bring Him our worship, we get to know Him better and slowly we become more like Him. Ponder the influence of that on your counselees and on your life. In contrast, when we don't know God very well, we are more easily led into error and more inclined to slide into modern versions of the idolatry that Scripture so strongly warns against (Exodus 20:1-3, 1 John 5:21).

Many years ago, I came across a little book that had a deep influence on my life. A. W. Tozer's *The Knowledge of the Holy* never talked about psychology or counseling, but it gave me a brand-new awareness of the importance of knowing what God is like. "It is impossible to keep our moral practices sound and our inward attitudes right while our idea of God is erroneous and inadequate," Tozer wrote. He argued that wrong ideas about God lead to doctrinal errors, to ethical failures, and to idolatry—the "monstrous sin" of replacing the true God with one made in human likeness. "That our idea of God correspond as nearly as possible to the true being of God is of immense importance to us."[9]

It is important, too, to recognize that *knowing about* God is not the same as *knowing* God. Before I ever met the woman who became my wife, somebody told me about her. When we met there was no love at first sight. We attended the same classes and knew about each other, but neither of us had much initial interest in getting to know the other. Now, many years later, I know Julie better than anybody else and she knows me because we have spent time together, sharing joys, sadness, and the realities of daily living.

Relating to God can be somewhat similar. We can read the Bible and a host of theology books and know about Him—like a physicist may know about atoms or molecules. But to know Him, we must read about Him in the Bible and seek to apply His Word to our lives with His Spirit's guidance, we must seek to understand His nature and His characteristics, we must make the effort to obey His commands and follow His directives, and we must experience His love as we go with Him through joys, sadness, and the realities of daily living.[10]

HOW CAN A LITTLE MIND KNOW
OR KNOW ABOUT A BIG GOD?

The clearest ways by which God has revealed Himself are through His Word, the Bible, and through His Son, Jesus Christ (John 1:1,14). Nobody has ever seen God (v. 18), but some people did see His Son when Christ walked on earth. By knowing what Christ is like, we get a glimpse of what God is like.

We do have a problem, however. Our minds are too small to comprehend the real nature of God. Even with their training and expertise, counselors often have difficulty really understanding the thinking and feelings of their counselees. If we find it hard to understand other human beings, who in so many ways are like us, how can we know God, who is so different from us and so much greater?

The answer is found in the idea of making comparisons. The Bible refers to some things that we do know and shows how these things are like God whom we want to know. Tozer put this in a sentence that may take a minute to read but that expresses the comparison idea concisely.

When we try to imagine what God is like we must of necessity use that-which-is-not-God as raw material for our minds to work on; hence whatever we visualize God to be, He is not, for we have constructed our image out of that which He has made and what He has made is not God.[11]

To alert us to these comparisons, the Bible sometimes uses words such as "like" or "had the appearance of." At other times we have stories or parables—like the story of the prodigal son that gives us a glimpse of the heavenly Father's caring and forgiving nature. Historical records in the Bible—including the accounts of the life of Jesus in the gospels and the rise of the early church in Acts—give us glimpses into how God has revealed Himself as He relates to human beings.

THE ATTRIBUTES OF GOD

In describing other people, we might talk about their traits or characteristics, but we almost never use the word *attributes*. In contrast, descriptions of God almost always refer to His attributes. According to one definition, "an attribute of God is whatever God has in any way revealed as being true of Himself."[12] Unlike human traits or characteristics that undergo constant change, divine attributes are permanent qualities. They cannot change for the better because God is already perfect; they cannot change for the worse because God is holy and never pulled down by sin. God cannot be separated from His attributes; they are at the core of His nature. For example, the Bible does not say that God has love or that He is characterized by love. It says that God *is* love (1 John 4:8,16).

Love, of course, is only one of God's attributes. Depending on whose book you read, the list of divine attributes can be long and grouped into categories or the list can be short. Several years ago I picked up a weighty volume titled *The Existence and Attributes of God*. The print is very small on the book's 800 pages. The author, a seventeenth-century English cleric named Stephen Charnock, must have spent years in developing his understanding of ten of God's attributes: His eternity, immutability, omnipresence, knowledge, wisdom, power, holiness, goodness, dominion, and patience.

In contrast, we have only one half-chapter left here, so our discussion must be limited to the bare essentials. Following the lead of theologian Millard Erickson, I have chosen to group God's attributes under two broad headings: the attributes that show us God's *greatness* and the attributes that show us His *goodness*.

The greatness attributes are sometimes known as God's natural attributes. These include His power, eternal nature, wisdom, omnipresence, knowledge, and sovereignty. Slightly different are those referred to as the goodness attributes that point to God's being always morally right and just. Often known as the moral attributes, these include God's love, faithfulness, holiness, grace, mercy, and justice. Table 4.1 summarizes seven of God's greatness and goodness attributes.

Don't let charts like this overwhelm you. This is not dry-as-dust theology that we have to pass over before we get on to more interesting things. Nothing in this book could be of greater importance to counselors than an understanding and appreciation for the nature of God. If you are a counselor who wants to know God better, to serve Him with maximum effectiveness, to keep from doctrinal error, and to bring a clear Christian perspective into your counseling, you must dwell frequently on God's attributes and let this growing awareness saturate your mind and sink deeply into the core of your being.

OUR GOD IS A PERSONAL GOD

When I was a student, I once was invited to have lunch in the home of a professor. He suggested that we "say grace" before we ate and proceeded to give thanks to "the great spiritual force" that was supposed to be hearing our prayers. We had that luncheon long before the new-age movement had become popular, but my host had a new-age god.

Sometimes referred to as an "infinite intelligence" or a "divine element in the universe," the new-age divinity is an impersonal force or consciousness that is part of everything. According to this thinking God is in plants, and books, and buildings (philosophers call this "pantheism"), and many would agree with the conclusion that since God is in each of us, then every human being is a god.

How different these views are from the God of the Bible. He is an intelligent, communicating, feeling, moral being who has a name and who interacts with the people He created.

Theologian Floyd Barackman summarized this concisely:

God's personhood is indicated by His having personal
features such as we find in ourselves, including a unique
selfhood with its self-awareness (Exodus 3:13-14; Leviticus
11:44-45; Isaiah 44:6; 45:22; 46:9) and self-determination
(the ability to choose and direct one's affairs in a responsible
way) (Isaiah 46:9-10; Romans 11:33-34; Ephesians 1:11), a
sense of morality with its awareness of good and evil (Proverbs 15:3; Romans 2:5-6; 2 Timothy 2:13), and perpetuity
(Psalm 102:2).[13]

In the Bible we read that God is our Father and that believers
are His children (Matthew 6:9, Romans 8:15-17). He loves us and
showed this love by sending His Son to atone for our sins so we can be
reconciled to the Father (Colossians 1:20, 1 John 4:7-10). God is compassionate toward us, wants to have a relationship with the people He
created, and gives us His Holy Spirit to be a divine counselor and to
help us when we are weak (John 14:26-27, Romans 8:26). Clearly
this personal God has far greater relevance for struggling counselees
and their counselors than the "great spiritual force" that apparently
sustained my old professor.

To help us grasp the nature of God, let us consider one example:
the truth that God is love.

God Is Love

Psychologist John Townsend believes that attachment or bondedness
is our deepest human need. This is true, suggests Townsend, because
love is "the deepest part of the character of God." Since we read in
the Bible that God is love (1 John 4:8), there is reason to believe
that human beings, who are created in His image, will never be at
peace unless they are bonded in loving relationships. We need to be
bonded to God, and we need connections with one another.

Many people, including Christians, don't experience that
bonding. They feel cut off from God and separated from other
human beings. "Just as connectedness is our most basic human need,
isolation is our most injurious state," Townsend wrote. The Devil tries
to cultivate an isolation from God-approved relationships. That is why
the original sin was the pride of self-sufficiency. If we are isolated and
if we "cannot bond to loving relationships, we will bond to something
else that is not so loving. This is the root of the addictive process. It's
also the root of Satan's strategy to sabotage our maturity process."[14]

Table 4.1
SOME ATTRIBUTES OF GOD

GOD'S GREATNESS: His Non-Moral Attributes

Attribute	Definition	Scripture	Significance for Counseling
Omnipresence	God is present everywhere.	1 Kings 8:27 Psalm 139:7-10 Isaiah 66:1 Jeremiah 23:23 Acts 7:48, 17:24	God is aware of all our trials and is always present with us. God's presence can be a restraint on bad behavior.
Omniscience	God is all knowing. He knows everything there is to know about Himself and all things past, present, and future.	Psalm 147:5 Isaiah 46:9-10 Micah 5:2 Acts 15:18 Hebrews 4:13	God knows all of the details and variables of our situations. He even knows how everything will turn out in the end.
Omnipotence	God is all powerful. He is called "the Almighty."	Genesis 17:1 Isaiah 45:11-13 Jeremiah 32:17 Matthew 19:26 Acts 4:24-31 Revelation 4:8, 19:6	Nothing can overpower or limit God. What He says, He will do and He can do.
Immutability	God is unchanging. He does not change in His essence, nature, or will.	Psalm 33:11, 102:26, 103:17 Malachi 3:6 James 1:17	God is always the same— an anchor of stability. We do not have to contend with surprises because He never changes.

GOD'S GOODNESS: His Moral Attributes

Attribute	Definition	Scripture	Significance for Counseling
Holiness (Righteous- ness and Justice)	He is sinless and without fault. He always does what is right. He is perfect and always just.	Exodus 3:1-6 1 Samuel 2:2 Psalm 99:1-9 Isaiah 6:1-13 Revelation 4:1-11	God is completely good and acts out of His good- ness. God hates evil and will eventually destroy it. Ultimately He will bring justice. He has high standards for us.
Love	God has an affection for His creation that causes Him to act in ways that provide for the well being of His creatures.	Deuteronomy 7:6-8 Isaiah 43:4 Hosea 11:1,3-4 John 3:16 1 John 4:8	God wants loving relation- ships with His people. He is forgiving, accepting, compassionate, and a help in times of struggle. Because He is love, He is also merciful and caring.
Truth	Everything that God says and does corre- sponds completely with reality. He is never deceived, neither does He deceive.	Isaiah 25:1 John 17:3 Romans 3:4 1 John 5:20 Revelation 3:7	God is completely trust- worthy and always faithful. We can be sure that what He says is true.

Townsend's theory is insightful and likely to be helpful to many counselors. He has reminded us how the truth of God's love permeates all of our lives and relationships. Nothing can separate us from the love of Christ (Romans 8:35-39). We can resist divine love and look for substitutes, but the truth that God is love remains unchanged.

We must be careful, however, lest we take a clear statement about God and twist it into something that was not intended and is not true.

Shortly after I finished my graduate studies, I felt free enough from the watchful eyes of my professors to read books that said nothing about psychology. One of those books was a best-seller at the time, written by the bishop of Woolwich in England and bearing the title *Honest to God*.

The bishop, John Robinson, started with the truth that God is love, but he turned that statement about God's character into a definition. He concluded that the statement "God is love" means that God is the same as love. According to this reasoning, "God is love" could also mean that "love is God." Anyone who accepts this reasoning probably will agree with Robinson that it makes no sense to believe in the "crude projection" of a God who is "'up there' . . . a God who is spiritually and metaphysically 'out there.'" The bishop concurs with the writer who stated that "the thought of God as a personal being, wholly other to man, dwelling in majesty— this talk may well collapse into meaninglessness in the last analysis."[15] It is not surprising that Robinson put love at the basis of his beliefs about morality. He wrote that any behavior, sexual or otherwise, is right if it is done in love; the only intrinsic evil is a lack of love.[16]

Bishop Robinson made the mistake of building a whole theology and morality on one statement about one of God's attributes. The bishop made two errors, among others, that sometimes characterize counselors. First, Robinson ignored the Bible's other statements about God. Of course God is love, but He is also light and truth. He is holy, just, forgiving, good, and majestic. We must be cautious lest we focus on one divine attribute and overlook the others. Heresies are made from such selective perception.

In a second error, Robinson took a biblical statement, God is love (1 John 4:8,16), and tore it from the biblical context. First John 4 discusses the actions of a personal God who showed His love for us by sending His Son to atone for our sins and to give us new life. When we grasp that biblical kind of divine love, we can rely on the love God has for us, and we in turn can be more loving. This divine love flows from a personal God through His servants and becomes a unique healing balm that Christian counselors can bring to their counselees.

OUR GOD IS AN AWESOME GOD

I suppose there are people with musical abilities who wish they could also be writers. I am a writer who wishes that I could also be a musician. If I had the ability (plus a lot of time and patience), I would learn to play the piano and the drums, become a conductor, and write music that would have a lasting influence. Our lives are greatly enriched by music, including the simple choruses that are sung when Christians get together.

Consider this, for example:

> Our God is an awesome God
> He reigns from heaven above
> With wisdom, power and love.
> Our God is an awesome God![17]

God is awesome, says the song, because of His sovereignty, wisdom, power, and love. But He is more.

God Is Triune

Carl Jung must have been an interesting man. His father and eight of his uncles were clergymen, and Jung's childhood was steeped in the atmosphere of the church. But the Jung home was neither healthy nor happy. His parents did not get along well, and the boy felt that his childhood mission was to help his father make sense of a faith that he preached but no longer believed. Apparently the father lacked the courage or determination to rethink his position so he clung, instead, to the formula that "one must not think . . . one must believe."[18]

Even as a child, Jung thought about theology and reached conclusions that were far from orthodox. For example, he denied that God exists as an external deity apart from human beings. In Jung's view, God could be reduced to "an archetypical image of the Deity," a "God within" who is little more than some kind of vague psychological entity. Jung rejected the idea of the Trinity and proposed, instead, that God is a quaternity that includes the Father, Son, Holy Spirit, and Satan.[19]

I mention Jung because his ideas appear to be growing in popularity among many psychotherapists and theologians, even though the famous analyst has been dead for over thirty years. Most would agree that Jung was an astute observer of human behavior, whose insights about people continue to be relevant. The same cannot be said about his views of God. Based in ancient and Eastern thought and consistent with contemporary new-age thinking, Jung's description of God shows how far human views can be distorted when we cut ourselves loose from the biblical anchor.

The biblical doctrine of the Trinity can be summarized concisely: There is one God who consists of three Persons—the Father, the Son, and the Holy Spirit—who are distinct as well as coexistent and who have always existed. The Bible clearly states that there is one God (Deuteronomy 6:4, James 2:19), but Scripture states with equal clarity that the Father is God (John 6:27, Romans 1:7, 1 Peter 1:2), that the Son is God (Isaiah 7:14; John 1:1,14; Romans 9:5; Hebrews 1:8; 1 John 5:20), and that the Holy Spirit is God (Acts 5:3-4, 1 Corinthians 3:16). At times all three Persons are mentioned in the same text. One example is in John 14:16-17 where Jesus is talking to the disciples before the crucifixion and reassuring them that the Father will send the Holy Spirit to be with them after the Son has gone back to Heaven.

Theologian Millard Erickson has observed that the idea of the Trinity appears to be so unfathomable from a human perspective that nobody could have invented it. Daniel Webster, the orator, was asked how a man of his intellect could believe that three equals one. "I do not pretend fully to understand the arithmetic of heaven," Webster replied. Like Christians throughout the centuries, Webster believed the doctrine of the Trinity, not because we understand it but because the Bible teaches it.[20] The Trinity is so difficult to grasp, cognitively, that scholars through the ages have tried to find analogies to help us understand. All of the analogies fall short, but Erickson suggests a couple drawn from the field of psychology.[21]

The first analogy considers the human personality. Each of us plays a number of roles that are separate but all a part of us. I am a father, a psychologist, and a citizen. These call forth different and unique responsibilities, but they are all a part of me and I can fulfill all three roles at the same time. From a slightly different perspective,

I am a physical being, a psychological being, and a social being—all three in one person.

A second analogy comes from the sphere of genetics and studies of identical twins or triplets. These siblings have the same genetic makeup. Often they look the same and have similar tastes and interests, but they are distinctly separate persons.

These analogies may be helpful, but they can't completely describe the eternal and harmonious union of the Father, Son, and Holy Spirit who are one, but in three Persons. The analogies also fall short in their inability to portray how the three Persons of the Trinity work together in unity. According to the Bible, the Father, Son, and Holy Spirit worked together:

❖ In creation (Genesis 1:1, Psalm 104:30, Colossians 1:16)
❖ In the incarnation (when God the Son came to earth in the form of a man—Luke 1:35)
❖ At the time of Christ's baptism (when the Son came out of the water, the Holy Spirit descended from Heaven, and the Father spoke—Matthew 3:16-17)
❖ In atoning for our sins (Hebrews 4:15)
❖ In the resurrection of Christ (John 10:17-18, Acts 2:32, Romans 1:4)

The three Persons of the Trinity continue to be at work in the salvation of individuals (1 Peter 1:2), and all three continue to be at work within us through the presence of the Holy Spirit (John 14:15-23).

The Christian counselor knows that the God who created us and who cares for us is also a God who is intimately familiar with relationships. The Father, Son, and Holy Spirit related to each other before human beings were ever created. This God of relationships, whose very nature is love, in turn can sustain and guide counselors who work in relationships with their counselees and who help counselees deal with the relationships in their lives. In contrast to the richness and depth of the Trinity, Jung's quaternity of archetypes is empty and pale in comparison.

God Is Transcendent
When I taught undergraduates, I had responsibility for a course in experimental psychology. As part of the requirements, each student

was to work for a semester with a white rat, taking care of the animal and teaching it to run mazes and to demonstrate its capacity to learn.

Even the students who were squeamish about getting close to a rat often developed an attachment to the animals during the course. Sometimes they would talk about what the rat felt, what it was thinking when we put it in a maze, or how it handled the frustration and embarrassment of making a wrong turn. Like little kids with teddy bears, the students were ascribing human emotions and characteristics to those white rats. The dictionary uses the tongue-twisting word *anthropomorphism* to describe this tendency.

Anthropomorphic thinking, of course, goes from our brains down to rats and teddy bears, but it also goes up to God. We can't comprehend God with anything other than our finite human cognitions and experiences, so we assume that He must be a lot like us. That is not completely faulty, because humans were made in God's image and He has allowed us to get a glimpse of His nature in ways that are denied to animals.

But most of us have a view of God that is far too small. We know that He is a friend, so we think that He must be a buddy. We know that He is always near, so we treat Him like a next-door neighbor or a "man upstairs" who is around when we need Him—like a consultant who might be called on to help when a therapist encounters a difficult case. Some among us are like my former professor who assumed that God is little more than an impersonal "force" or an inner part of human nature.

How different all of this is from the biblical view of God as an eternal, unchanging, all-powerful, all-knowing, perfectly holy being who is infinite, unlimited, unbounded by anything or anyone. Nobody has seen God (John 1:18, 6:46), although we have seen glimpses of His eternal power and divine nature in creation (Romans 1:20) and we know that we see Him when we look at Christ (John 14:9). Several times in the Bible, however, we read about human beings who have been in the presence of God and the experience has been overwhelming. Daniel, for example, fell on his face in awe and dread. "I had no strength left, my face turned deathly pale and I was helpless," Daniel wrote. When God spoke, Daniel bowed low with his face toward the ground and was speechless (Daniel 10:8-19).

God is a compassionate and loving friend who helps in time of need, but we must never forget that He is also great and majestic and powerful, beyond any words that we can use or that human minds can comprehend.

God Is Holy

It is mind-stretching for any of us to think of God as being a Trinity and as being transcendent, and our brains also get stretched far beyond their limits when we try to understand what it means for God to be holy. Someone has suggested that holiness is the foundation of God's nature (Isaiah 6:3). The first heavenly song of praise in the book of Revelation is "Holy, holy, holy is the Lord God Almighty, who was, and is, and is to come" (4:8).

This divine holiness involves absolute purity, complete freedom from being tainted with anything that is sinful or unclean, without even a hint of blemish. Because there is no blemish, the holiness of God means that He is perfect in who He is and in what He does.

All of this is made more complex for us by the biblical statements that we are expected to be holy (Leviticus 11:44-45, Matthew 5:48, Romans 12:1-2, 2 Corinthians 7:1, 1 Thessalonians 4:7) and that God expects the Church to be holy as well (Ephesians 5:27). That could lay a heavy burden on all of us and stir up a lot of guilt. But God knows that we as sinful earth-dwellers are in the process of becoming holy. He has given us a high and admirable standard toward which we can strive. He has paid for our sins so that we no longer need to be separated from God, and He has promised to give us help so we need not struggle alone (1 Thessalonians 3:13).

OUR GOD IS AN ACTIVE GOD

When Bill Clinton and Al Gore won the Presidential election and launched a new American administration, commentators were quick to note that a new generation had come to power. These men were baby boomers, the first president and vice-president to be born after World War II. They had campaigned on a platform of change, and they presented themselves as men of action.

Baby boomers are not the only people who like action. Some might argue that we have too much change in our culture, but many of us have active lifestyles and enjoy the diversity of contemporary fast-paced living. If we seek counseling, we look for therapists who can help us get moving in a better direction and who have proven their abilities to help people change. Lying somewhat passively on a couch in some analyst's office does not fit the modern mentality.

This sense of action also applies to religion. In many churches the old hymns are sometimes joined and often replaced by more upbeat music. We look for a faith that is dynamic and able to sustain us in changing times. There is comfort in finding a God who never changes. That fact gives us stability, but it is encouraging, as well, to know that our God is not passively dozing like a grandfather in the sky. God is alive, aware of our needs, and active.

God Is Active as Sustainer of His Creation

The Bible teaches that God created the universe *ex nihilo*—out of nothing (Hebrews 11:3). Some of what He created has changed and developed over time, but the whole of what now exists was begun by God's act of bringing it into existence; it was not a refashioning of something that already existed independently. [22]

What God created was orderly. It was not chaotic, but neither was it rigidly preprogramed so that God could withdraw into retirement and let the world and its inhabitants run along without divine intervention. The same God who created the universe now sustains and holds it all together (Colossians 1:16-17, Hebrews 1:3—see also Ephesians 3:9, Revelation 4:11).

The Bible gives no support for the idea of a rigid determinism that leaves human beings without freedom or dignity. We have a God who is aware of everything in His creation (Hebrews 4:13), who is personally able to sympathize with our weaknesses (4:14-16), and who is on eternal round-the-clock duty, always ready to deal with our needs and to forgive our sins (7:24-26).

God Is Active as Redeemer of His Creation

A redeemer, according to one definition, is one who "buys back or who liberates by paying a ransom price." The modern government that "swaps" hostages in exchange for arms or money is engaging in redemption.

According to some Bible scholars, redemption is the central theme of Scripture. The biblical writers record the intervention of an active God to redeem His whole creation from the results of sin. In the Old Testament, He redeemed His people from Egyptian bondage (Exodus 6:6; Deuteronomy 7:8, 15:15) and from captivity in Babylon (Isaiah 43:1-4, 48:20, 51:11). In the New Testament we read about Christ's death on the cross to pay the moral debt that was due because of our sin and to redeem us (Galatians 3:13, Ephesians 1:7, Colossians 1:14).

Sometimes our counselees act in ways that seem out of character. Conversely God always acts in ways that are consistent with His nature. By sending His Son to redeem human beings and the rest of creation (Romans 8:22-23), God has shown His love, faithfulness, holiness, power, and wisdom (1 Corinthians 1:24). In this one act, God demonstrated His love for humanity and His hatred of sin (Romans 3:26).

A Call to Worship

When we ponder what God is like, what He has done, and what He is doing, we can understand the praise that reverberates through the realms of Heaven in John's vision. God is praised because of His nature and because of His acts as Creator and Redeemer (Revelation 4:11, 5:9-14).

Have you ever wondered why a perfect, self-sufficient, awesome God would have any interest in the praises of sinful human beings like us? Have you wondered, as I have, why God would take pleasure in our imperfect acts of praise?

Almost every parent has the experience of a child who lovingly draws a crayon picture and presents it as a gift. When the kids are small, the drawings tend to be of stick people with big heads, standing in front of a sky with a bright yellow sun. Often the artwork may not be very good and the parents don't need the drawings. But most of us treasure the expressions of love that these pictures represent. The young artists, in turn, feel affirmed and loved when the drawings are received with gratitude.

Perhaps this is how our God responds to us. He reveals as much about Himself as our childlike minds can comprehend, and He treasures our acts of worship and thanksgiving. When we begin to get a glimpse of what God is like, we cannot *not* praise Him.

SO WHAT?

If we ponder what God is like, we cannot fail to recognize His central role in the counseling process.

When Stephen Arterburn and Jack Felton published their book *Toxic Faith*[23] I was reminded how often people's lives are seriously damaged by their inaccurate views of God. People who see God as vindictive, irrational, or inclined to pile on guilt, for example, have difficulty accepting His love or mercy. Others whose fathers have been absent or abusive are inclined to see God in the same way. Sometimes committed believers sit under the teaching of highly influential biblical teachers whose views of God are basic heresy, without realizing that the false teachings are psychologically and spiritually dangerous.[24] Look at almost any cult and you will see that the leaders proclaim faulty views of the nature of God. Is knowing God and knowing about God important for Christian counselors? You bet!

As counselors, we are His instruments to bring change and healing to others. He works through our training and base of knowledge, but ultimately Christian counseling involves a committed believer being an available vehicle through whom the sovereign God of the universe acts.

As you counsel, remember how your knowledge of God can make a difference:

❖ Many people have faulty or erroneous concepts of God. You can help them understand what God is really like and how this knowledge gives cause for genuine hope. We are not "left alone in an impersonal universe, spinning on a planet that is controlled by chance, without any reason to hope, and with no life purpose or ultimate destiny."

❖ We become like the people we spend time with. When we, counselors as well as counselees, spend time with God we get to know Him better and slowly we become more like Him. If we push God aside, we are more easily led into misperceptions and other errors about Him and His creation.

❖ Our God is personal, awesome, and active. He has many attributes. Be careful not to focus on one of these attributes to the exclusion of the rest.

❖ Effective Christian counselors seek to be sensitive to their counselees and constantly look for ways to refine and to improve their therapeutic skills. Good Christian counselors recognize, too, that they serve a mighty God. He is willing to guide our counseling. Seek, then, to be someone who knows God and who brings Him praise. That can make a difference in you and in the life of everyone you meet.

If God really exists as He is described in the Bible, and if He is the Creator and Sustainer of the universe, then the most fundamental question of life is, How can I rightly be related to this God and to the world that He created? (See Mark 12:28-31.) What you or I believe about God will be a core part of the worldview from which we counsel. If your understanding is limited, your knowledge is in error, or your beliefs are fuzzy, your counseling will be much less consistent and more prone to error.

CHAPTER FIVE

❖

Human Nature
and Counseling

IT HAPPENS EVERY SPRING. Thousands of college students from countless campuses crowd into their vehicles and head for the sun. Most have one agenda: to carouse on the beaches and to party in the bars during their annual spring break from classes.

Mark Kilroy joined their numbers in March of 1989 and set off with some old high school buddies for a stretch of sand in a part of southern Texas known as Padre Island. One night, the group decided to make the trek across the Rio Grande from Brownsville to Matamoros, on the Mexican side of the border. They headed for the noisy bistros and brightly lit cabarets on Avenida Alvro Obregon where they partied until 2 a.m.

Then Mark Kilroy disappeared!

The case stumped police on both sides of the border. Everybody suspected foul play, but there were no obvious motives and no suspects. A few weeks later, during a search for drugs at a Mexican ranch, agents unexpectedly found Kilroy's dismembered body, buried in a shallow grave with the remains of several other hapless victims of an international drug cartel. The murderers were involved in black magic and other Satanic rituals that were thought to appease the Devil and to protect the drug traders from detection and arrest. Mark Kilroy had been kidnapped and murdered as an ultimate sacrifice.[1]

While all of this was taking place, a different kind of sacrifice was being offered in an inner-city slum, halfway around the world from Matamoros. A group of unpretentious and courageous Catholic nuns was going about the daily task of caring for the dying, destitute, unwanted people of poorest Calcutta. Led by a world-famous but selfless little woman from Albania, the sisters are living examples of the apostle's call for Christians to "offer your bodies as living sacrifices, holy and pleasing to God—this is your spiritual act of worship" (Romans 12:1-2).

Mother Teresa's colleagues would agree with her view that "the biggest disease today is not leprosy or tuberculosis, but rather the feeling of being unwanted, uncared for and deserted by everybody. The greatest evil is the lack of love and charity, the terrible indifference towards one's neighbor who lives at the roadside assaulted by exploitation, corruption, poverty and disease."[2]

It is difficult to comprehend how Mark Kilroy's murderers could be so cruel and insensitive while Mother Teresa's sisters can be so caring and unselfish. How can human beings be so different? Scientists can measure our differences in knowledge, abilities, intelligence, and physiology, but understanding the basics and uniquenesses of human nature is much more difficult.

For counselors, however, few things can be more important. Counselors are people who work with people, and our views of human nature have a significant impact on how we counsel and on what we seek to accomplish. In your worldview, if humans are assumed to be innately good and living in a universe where there is no God, your counseling will be different from that of the person whose worldview assumes that we humans are the creations of a holy and loving God who has compassion and expectations for His people.

Jay Adams noted that in recent years, "There has been more focus on the nature of the human race and on solutions to human problems than on any other subject." Because of this emphasis, many errors have come into our thinking along with a lot of misleading terminology, all of which confuses our work as counselors.[3]

G. K. Chesterton once wrote, "We have all read in scientific books, and indeed in all romance, about the man who has forgotten his name. The man walks about the streets and can see and appreciate everything; only he cannot remember who he is. Well, everyman is that man in the story." Human beings do not know who they are because they have lost contact with their Creator, the One who gives them identity and meaning.[4]

HUMAN BEINGS ARE CREATURES

To understand what human nature is really like, we need to start with the basics. In terms of physical makeup, human beings are no different from animals. We are born, we grow, our bodies deteriorate, and eventually we die. While we are on this earth, we eat, excrete, procreate, and sometimes suffer because of disease or injury. In biblical terminology, we were created from dust and to dust we will return (Genesis 2:7, 3:19; Psalm 103:14; Ecclesiastes 3:19-20; 1 Corinthians 15:47-48). According to the Bible, both animals and human beings were created by God and we all are distinct from the Creator (Genesis 1:20-31).

In passing, we should note that the physical body and the animal impulses and appetites in human beings are not bad in themselves. God declared that His creation was very good (Genesis 1:31). And when He sent His Son to earth, Jesus Christ took on a physical body (John 1:14).

Starting, then, with the basic fact that human beings are in many ways like animals, we go one step further to recognize that in other ways we are different. We have self-consciousness, language, concern about moral values, the ability to think abstractly, and an intellect that enables us to plan for the future or to see the consequences of our actions. Shakespeare's Hamlet exclaimed, "What a piece of work is man! How noble in reason! How infinite in faculty [capacity]! in form, in moving how express and admirable! in action how like an angel! in apprehension how like a god! the beauty of the world! the paragon of animals!"

We didn't evolve to this position; we were created as something unique. Unlike the conclusions of evolutionary theory, the Bible states that from the beginning, human beings have always been much more than animals. Sometimes, of course, we fall into the "dog eat dog" jungle mentality that leads to the survival of the fittest, the smartest, or the person with the fastest trigger-finger. When people act like Mark Kilroy's drinking buddies or like Kilroy's murderers, they are acting like mere animals. But God had something different in His plans when He created us.

Unlike animals, human beings were made "a little lower than the heavenly beings" and given the privilege and responsibility of having dominion over animals and over everything else that God created on this planet (Genesis 1:26, 2:15; Psalm 8:5-6). Presumably this means that humans also have responsibility to control themselves.

God had no need of us. He wasn't lonely or looking for help. But He created us as a reflection of Himself and to bring Him glory (Isaiah 43:7). And unlike the animals, we human beings were made in God's image.

HUMAN BEINGS IN THE "IMAGE OF GOD"

Many of our secular colleagues in counseling have little interest in the Bible or in learning about the nature of God. These are not the issues that get mentioned in journal articles or professional conventions. But all of us are concerned about human beings. Most of us want to understand why people act as they do, how they can be helped to change, and even why a Mother Teresa would be so different from the men who murdered Mark Kilroy.

How we view human beings is a part of the worldview that guides each of us in our thinking and that determines how we will counsel. Some people believe that we are primarily rational beings, so their therapy is largely cognitive. Others stress the emotional side of human nature and give therapy that is experiential and existential. If you assume that we are controlled by physical drives, your therapy will seek to satisfy and redirect the satisfaction of these drives. Behaviorists have a more mechanistic view of human behavior and have tried to bring change by controlling reinforcement.

What, however, do we do with the biblical statement that we are created in the image of God?

When He had almost completed the act of creation, "God said, 'Let us make man in our image, in our likeness'" (Genesis 1:26—see also 5:1, 9:6). The meaning of this simple statement has caused endless debate among theologians. And if biblical scholars can't agree, where does this leave the rest of us?

Some things we can know for sure.

Relatedness

We can know, first, that we were created by a loving God to be relational creatures who can interact with one another. Mother Teresa's compassionate sisters in Calcutta are far closer to what God intended than are the self-centered, materialistic people who so often come into our lives or parade across the screens of our television sets.

We human beings were not created to be loners or to be self-centered. We are able to have a "loving relatedness" to others that includes intellectual interaction, sharing with a community of people, and the sexual and emotional intimacy of marriage. Each of us was born as the result of a relationship, and most people grow up as members of families. "A Christian view of persons will emphasize family as fundamental to what it means to be human," suggested psychologists Stanton Jones and Richard Butman. "Families are webs of relationships in which we are imbedded throughout life, for better or for worse, in much the same way that God who created us remains in relationship with us, his fallen and wayward people."[5]

Gender

Second, we know that the image of God involves both maleness and femaleness. "God created man in his own image, in the image of God he created him; male and female he created them" (Genesis 1:27). When He created human beings, He used the term *man* to refer to both male and female (Genesis 5:2, Matthew 19:4). Sexuality was present from the beginning. It is an important part of who we are as creatures made in the image of God.

Dominion

Third, our creation in the image of God indicates that we can make moral choices. Of course animals can make choices: the rat in a maze chooses to go left or right, and the pigeon in the Skinner box pecks at a circle instead of a square. But because human beings are made in God's image, our choices are not merely reactions to the events and stimulations in the environment. We are not created to be mechanical robots, programed to react to environmental stimuli or to childhood experiences. Instead, we have minds, wills, and at least a limited capacity to see beyond the present, to weigh consequences, to comprehend the ultimate implications of our moral decisions, to act logically and responsibly, and to decide whether we will even act at all. We have animal impulses and instincts, but we have the capacity to control these inclinations and to act in ways that are disciplined, loving, and consistent with God's perfect standard of morality.

James Sire summarized this as a concise paragraph:

We can summarize this conception of man in God's image by saying that, like God, man has

❖ *personality*,
❖ *self-transcendence*,
❖ *intelligence* (the capacity for reason and knowledge),
❖ *morality* (the capacity for recognizing and understanding good and evil),
❖ *gregariousness or social capacity* (man's characteristic and fundamental desire and need for human companionship—community—especially represented by the "male" and "female" aspect), and
❖ *creativity* (the ability to imagine new things or to endow old things with human significance).[6]

Responsibility

Fourth, our creation in the image of God means that we have a responsibility to rule over the earth (Genesis 1:26). Earlier we noted that the idea of dominion includes the human responsibility to control ourselves, but Scripture suggests something much broader. In an early act of human dominion over the creation, Adam was given the privilege of naming all the animals (2:19-20). We are called to protect, cultivate, and keep the planet on which we live. Human beings have been given the responsibility of being God's landlords over the earth (1:28). We are not free to do as we please with the environment because the earth belongs to the Lord, and He will one day hold us accountable for how we "looked out" for His property. Our challenge is to be like God, who rules over the universe. He rules with justice and kindness. He never ravages or exploits.[7]

I enjoy reading books and articles that critique the societies in which we live and that make predictions about the future. One theme appears repeatedly in these writings: our widespread concern about saving the environment. A congressional aide recently concluded, "Right now, the environment is about ten times more important to our constituents than any other issue."

Saving the planet, reducing pollution, restoring the ozone layer, eliminating acid rain, preventing the garbage glut, recycling whatever can be recycled, saving the forests—these are deep concerns of baby boomers and new-age crusaders. But these must be the concern of everyone who is created in the image of God. Over the centuries we have fulfilled God's instruction to be fruitful and to increase in number, but we have not been faithful in attempting to subdue the earth (Genesis 1:28)—until now.

As God's stewards of the world, all of us are meant to "live out our godlikeness" by taking at least some responsibility for the world in which we live. Jones and Butman make the interesting and plausible contention that this command points to "a human need for purposeful activity in life, a need for meaningful work and the realization of purpose outside of ourselves."[8]

Figure 5.1 summarizes what we have concluded to this point. Human beings were created in the image of God. In many ways we are like other creatures, but we also have been given the ability to relate to others and to God and to have dominion over the earth. In the next chapter we will consider how all of this has been tarnished by sin.

Figure 5.1
THE CREATION OF HUMAN BEINGS IN THE IMAGE OF GOD

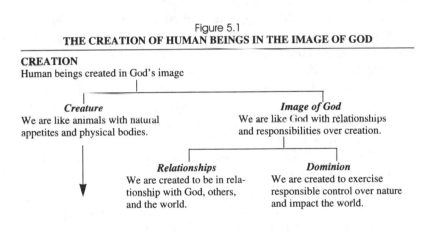

WHY DO WE EVEN EXIST?

I was in graduate school when European-based existential therapy briefly caught the attention of North American practitioners. I had a Viennese professor who tried (with less success than she might have liked) to guide me in an independent study of therapies influenced by people with names like Heidegger, Bingswanger, Dostoevski, Kierkegaard, Nietzsche, Sartre, Buber, Frankl, and Tillich. This was heavy philosophical stuff for a young psychologist who was trained in the principles of behaviorism and cognitive therapy and steeped in the language of operational definitions, testable hypotheses, and the superiority of rigorous empirical investigation.[9]

The existential movement reacted against any therapy that consists mostly of techniques. Existentialists argued, instead, that we should focus on the purpose of life and what it means to be a human being. As we go through life there are times when almost all of us ask questions like "Who am I?" "Why am I here?" "Where am I going?" or "What will I become?" Very often, according to the existential therapists, we encounter meaninglessness in the world, emptiness within ourselves, feelings of loneliness and uprootedness, continual anxiety, or an awareness that life (to use Shakespeare's words) is no more than "a tale told by an idiot, full of sound and fury, signifying nothing." Many counselees are like the person who said, "My fear is that I'll discover I'm a nobody, that there really is nothing to me, and that I have no self. I'll find out that I'm an empty shell, hollow inside, and nothing will exist if I shed my masks."[10]

This hopeless thinking is in radical contrast to the biblical teaching that each of us has been created by God for the noble purpose of bringing Him glory (Isaiah 43:7, Ephesians 1:11-12). The first question in the Westminster Larger Catechism asks, "What is the chief and highest end of man?" The answer: "Man's chief and highest end is to glorify God, and fully to enjoy Him forever." We should seek to live in ways that bring glory to God in whatever we do (1 Corinthians 10:31).

"This fact guarantees that our lives are significant," wrote theologian Wayne Grudem.

> When we first realize that God did not need to create us and does not need us for anything, we might conclude that our lives have no importance at all. But that is certainly incorrect, for Scripture tells us that we were created in order to glorify God, indicating that we are important *to God himself.* . . .
>
> What is our purpose in life? Our purpose must be to fulfill the reason that God created us: to glorify him. . . . We are to enjoy God and take delight in him and in our relationship to him.[11]

All of this seems far removed from the twisted lives that come into our counseling rooms. In an earlier chapter we saw the importance of knowing God. Now we see that humans also exist to bring glory to God. Both of these seem like an impossible dream for those of us who live and work in high-tech environments where people all around seem intent on building careers, marriages, family stability, financial security, and vocational success. Many people seem to have no purpose in life other than survival; they have little time, energy, motivation, or desire for living lives that seek to know God or to bring Him glory. Can't most of us relate better to the frustrations of the existentialist therapists than to the framers of the Westminster Confession who imply that in every period of history it is possible "to glorify God, and fully to enjoy Him"?

The Purpose of Life and the Image of God

It could be argued, perhaps, that the biblical directives to bring glory to God are impossible ideals, far beyond the reach of sinful human beings. But the importance of glorifying God is a scriptural teaching that was given long after the fall of human beings into sin and is made possible because of the work of Christ. Believers can bring honor to God when we eat, drink, work, or engage in other daily activities (1 Corinthians 10:31, Colossians 3:23-24).

Some theologians believe that the image of God in humans was destroyed by the Fall, but most would agree that the image of God was marred and distorted but not obliterated when we fell into sin (Genesis 9:6, James 3:9). Jesus Christ is the only complete and valid revelation of what the full image of God looks like. He came to earth to pay for our sins so that the image of God ultimately could be restored in human beings (Colossians 3:10). Believers are being "changed into his likeness" or image by degrees (2 Corinthians 3:18). This is the goal of our salvation (Romans 8:29), and we know that we will be like Him in the end (1 John 3:2).

How does this apply to us now? Should we value human beings, even ourselves? John Stott gives a concise answer: "Nobody who reads the Gospels as a whole could possibly gain the impression that Jesus had a negative attitude to human beings himself, or encouraged one in others. The opposite is the case."[12]

Jesus clearly saw and condemned human evil, but He proclaimed that people are much more valuable than nonhuman creatures like birds or animals (Matthew 6:26, 12:12). This is not because of what we have done, but because God created us in His image and what He creates has value. In His words and actions, Jesus showed respect for people, including prostitutes and tax gatherers and lepers who were despised by the rest of society. He made friends with the poor and other social outcasts and demonstrated by His death that God loves the human race.

Even while we believers live in a world of sin, the Creator loves us, takes pleasure in His creation, delights in our worship (Proverbs 15:8), enables us to bring glory to Him (1 Corinthians 10:31), and fills us with "an inexpressible and glorious joy" (1 Peter 1:8).

THE ELEMENTS OF HUMAN NATURE

While I was writing this chapter, I took time away to visit a state penitentiary where a friend is serving a six-year sentence for theft and drug possession. He is a bright young man who wrote to me as a stranger following his incarceration and who is determined to "start over" following his release from prison. As these words are being written, my friend's body is behind bars, but his spirit and his hopes, like his prayers, cannot be contained by barbed wire and high fences.

What are we human beings really like at the core of our existence?

Freud believed that we are biological beings with instincts, drives, sexual and psychic energies, and personalities that for each of us consist of an id, ego, and superego. According to the father of psychoanalysis, we are people with behavior determined by basic irrational forces, unconscious motivations, and the influence of psychosexual events that happen early in our lives.

Freud's critics and generations of later writers proposed other perspectives on human nature, including the more recent holistic worldviews. These embrace many elements of anti-Christian Eastern philosophy,[13] but most begin with the laudable idea that the core of each person is the body, mind, and spirit, which are interconnected and constantly influencing one another. According to this view, my prisoner friend's body is confined by the authorities, but his mind and spirit can soar and this, in turn, can influence his health and how he feels physically.

Debates about the essentials of human nature have endured for centuries. Often these reduce to differences over what have been called the tripartite (three part) and bipartite (two part) views of what human beings are really like.

The Tripartite View

Near the end of his first letter to the Thessalonian Christians, Paul wrote about the "spirit, soul and body," suggesting to some readers that we are formed of three distinct parts. The *body* is easiest to define. It consists of everything in human beings that is physical, including our passions. The *soul* is often thought to be somewhat similar to the mind and involves feelings and thoughts, including the will. The *spirit* is the innermost part of human nature, that part of us that is receptive to spiritual input and guidance from the Holy Spirit.

Counselors and other non-theologians (and probably many theologians as well) sometimes find this three-part division to be confusing. Definitions of the soul and spirit tend to differ, in part because these terms are not used in consistent ways by biblical writers. Sometimes words like *soul, heart, mind*, and *spirit* seem to be used interchangeably and on occasion they are used with the word *strength* or *might* (Deuteronomy 6:5, Mark 12:30). Critics of the tripartite view suggest, therefore, that despite occasional references like 1 Thessalonians 5:23, the biblical writers make a real distinction between only two aspects of human nature: the material and the immaterial. This is what one writer has called the distinction between the body and the spirit-soul.[14]

The Bipartite View

The ancient Greeks viewed human beings as having a body and a soul that were at odds with each other and in continual tension. The body was assumed to be an imperfect and often evil container that held the soul. The soul, in turn, was thought to be pure and wanting release from the confines of the body.

In contrast to Greek philosophy, the Bible teaches that all of God's creation, including the body and the soul, was created good (Genesis 1:27,31), although body and soul both suffer from moral corruption and need redemption. When we die, the body disintegrates but the soul continues to live. Human beings, therefore, have a personal existence beyond the grave.[15]

Whether or not you accept a tripartite view of human nature or the more widely accepted bipartite view, it would be wrong to conclude that each of us is carved up into distinct parts, with one added on to the other. Behaviorists and some physiologists might think of humans as being little more than physical machines that can be reinforced mechanically or treated objectively. Some humanists or new-age thinkers might focus on the immaterial side of human beings, stress our union with the cosmos, pay little attention to the physical body, and emphasize subjective experience. But the Bible gives a more balanced view that sees the body and the soul-spirit as unified into one entity. In counseling, we can't treat one and completely ignore the other.

Counseling books sometimes talk about problems that are primarily physical, psychological, and spiritual. For purposes of analysis and discussion this kind of division (corresponding to the body, soul, and spirit) may be convenient, especially if we add the idea that some problems are largely social-environmental in origin. In reality, however, human beings must be seen as unified persons who cannot be split into parts.

SO WHAT?

All of the preceding paragraphs about human nature really do have bearing on how we relate to other people, including our counselees. As we have seen, human beings are biological and relational creatures who have personality, transcendence, intelligence, and the moral capacity to recognize and to act in accordance with what is good and what is evil. We are social creatures who desire and need human companionship and who have the ability to be creative. We have the God-given privilege and responsibility of protecting and caring for our planet. Surely this includes caring for the people God created. And it must include taking care of our own bodies and minds, protecting them from unnecessary pollution and the weakening that comes from physical, mental, and spiritual laziness and neglect.

Human beings are not hollow on the inside, empty selves who hide behind masks and have no purpose for living or no hope for the future except decomposition after death. Instead, we are created in God's image, valuable to Him despite our sinfulness, and challenged to be pure and holy. We can bring honor to God, even in the way we eat, drink, work, or engage in other of our daily activities, including counseling. At death, though our bodies return to dust, each of us has a spirit-soul that continues to live and eventually will be reunited with our resurrected bodies. For believers (as later chapters will show), there is promise of an eternity with Christ, where there are none of the tears that we see in our counseling rooms.

Once again, let us look at the people who killed Mark Kilroy and the sisters who work with Mother Teresa. All have been created in the image of God, and because of the Fall, none is righteous. But their lives and wordviews are very different.

The Matamoros murderers were self-centered and apparently without any awareness of God. Sin had corrupted their relationships. They acted like animals, were unconcerned about self-control, and must have given little attention to the feelings and thoughts of their victims. There was no awareness of men and women as created beings who live to bring glory to God.

Mother Teresa's sisters, in contrast, view all people as valuable to God, created by Him in His image, and worthy of care and respect despite the fact that their lives show some of the most devastating effects of sin. Discipline and self-control are at the core of the lives of these dedicated nuns, along with a desire to serve and to live in ways that bring honor to their Creator. All of this is because of the grace of God in their lives. We might not agree with all the theology of these sisters, but their worldviews and lives reflect an awareness of God's truth about human nature. Their work and "clients" differ from ours, but in many respects their attitudes are models for Christian counselors.

The Bible gives an incredibly rich view of human nature. We who are counselors have the privilege of working with people who may be warped and wounded, like the prostitutes and tax gatherers Jesus knew. But our counselees are loved by God, who takes pleasure in His creation and has shown His love by providing a way for us to be reconciled to Him. My friend in prison acted in ways that put him behind bars, but there is hope for his future. Shakespeare was wrong. Life is far more than a tale that signifies nothing.

With a clear, biblical view of human nature, we can turn now to see how sin influences our lives and the lives of our counselees. Then we can look at the impact of sin and forgiveness on our work as counselors. These issues are the focus of the next chapters.

❖

CHAPTER SIX

Sin and Counseling

OUR FAMILY ONCE lived in a suburb of Philadelphia, where I met a seminary professor who had an interest in counseling. Prior to his teaching career, my friend had spent several years as a pastor. He was (and still is) an expert in preaching, but he had never taken a course in counseling or thought much about it. Then his parishioners began coming to him with serious problems. "It soon became apparent that I was helping almost no one," he wrote later. "And I was wasting valuable time."

To make up for his lack of training and expertise, my friend bought, borrowed, and devoured as many counseling books as he could find. He learned about the methods of Freud, familiarized himself with the work of Rogers, read much of the pastoral counseling literature, and even spent a summer working in two mental hospitals at the side of Dr. O. Hobart Mowrer, a former president of the American Psychological Association. Mowrer never claimed to be a Christian, but he influenced a lot of believers in the 1960s with his criticisms of psychotherapy and his bold suggestion that "evangelical religion [had] sold its birthright for a mess of psychological pottage."[1]

Shortly after this summer experience with Mowrer, my friend

began teaching a practical theology course that included a segment on pastoral counseling. Since he couldn't find a suitable and helpful textbook, he decided to write one—shortly before we first met in Philadelphia. When the work was done, my professor friend loaned me a copy of the manuscript and asked for suggestions that might help with his revisions.

I liked some of what I read. My friend stressed that the Bible says much about counseling people with their personal problems. He stressed the importance of the Holy Spirit in counseling and argued that pastors could and should do counseling, instead of referring most of their counselees to psychiatrists or to other mental-health professionals. The manuscript had a lot to say about Christian love, and the writer acknowledged that many problems have a biological basis.

But in his writing, my friend insisted that except for biologically based difficulties, all problems result from the counselee's own sin. Therefore, the only way to counsel effectively is to expose the sin, confront the counselee with the principles and practices of Scripture, urge the person to confess the sin, and give "authoritative teaching" on how to avoid falling into similar sinful patterns in the future.

I still can remember my reaction to the manuscript. "I am glad for the clear recognition of the role of sin in human problems," I said only to myself, "but the author's approach is so confrontational, so directive, so insensitive, so simplistic and bombastic, that there is never any possibility that this book will ever get published, much less read."

I was wrong.

Jay Adams' *Competent to Counsel*[2] became a best-seller that stirred considerable controversy and did much to stimulate interest in Christian counseling among theologically conservative believers who, to that point, had tended to ignore or resist counseling issues. I suspect that Dr. Adams intended to be provocative with his book—and he was. Despite some of its debatable conclusions, the book boldly focused attention on the role of sin in causing problems and the author proclaimed that Christian counseling has to consider and deal with sin.

THE REALITY OF SIN

Jay Adams was not the only writer to stress the importance of sin in counseling. His one-summer mentor, O. Hobart Mowrer, argued that we should abandon the idea that "neurotically disturbed" people are sick. Then we should admit that most "mentally ill" people are guilty of sin that needs to be recognized and confessed.

> As long as one adheres to the theory that psychoneurosis implies no moral responsibility, no error, no misdeed on the part of the afflicted person, one's vocabulary can, of course, remain beautifully objective and "scientific." But as soon as there is so much as a hint of personal accountability in the situation . . . one might as well . . . use the strongest word of all, *sin*. . . .
>
> Sin, for all its harshness, carries an implication of promise and hope. . . . Just so long as we deny the reality of sin, we cut ourselves off, it seems, from the possibility of radical redemption ("recovery").[3]

Mowrer's writings aroused a flood of controversy, but so did a later book by Karl Menninger, who probably was America's best-known psychiatrist when he wrote *Whatever Became of Sin?* Evil appears all around us, Menninger wrote, and yet "when no one is responsible, no one is guilty, [and] no moral questions are asked . . . we sink to despairing helplessness."[4] Neither Menninger nor Mowrer viewed sin as it is described in the Bible, but both argued that counselees needed to take moral responsibility for their actions and for their rehabilitation.

Despite these and other scattered appeals to take sin more seriously, few counseling books even mention the word. Sin tends to be ignored or dismissed as an archaic concept that has no present-day relevance for counselors. Many would argue that morality is personal, that each of us should establish our own views of what is right or wrong, and that sin is a meaningless concept since it implies violation of an objective moral code that doesn't even exist.[5]

The biblical view is much different. It does not present sin as a misstep, an occasional lapse into unfortunate behavior, or nothing more serious than "any act or thought that robs myself or another human being of his or her self-esteem."[6] Instead, the Bible presents sin as an inner force, an inherent condition, a controlling power that lies at the core of our being. How one views sin, according to Millard Erickson, will have a marked effect on his or her ministry, including counseling, and on how the problems of society are viewed and solved.

On the one hand, if we feel that man is basically good or, at worst, morally neutral, we will view the problems of society as stemming from an unwholesome environment. Alter the environment, and changes in individual humans and their behavior will follow. If, on the other hand, the problems of society are rooted in the radically perverted mind and will of individual human beings, then the nature of those individuals will need to be altered, or they will continue to infect the whole.[7]

An eleventh-century theologian named Anselm of Canterbury was once asked, "Why couldn't God just forgive sin and have done with it? Why all this fuss about sin and the need for Christ to die in order to deal with its penalty and power?" Anselm replied that the questioner had not considered the gravity of sin.[8] It is easy to conclude that the same answer could apply today. Despite death and civil strife around the world and violence on our streets and in our homes, people today do not seem to appreciate the gravity and the reality of sin.

WHAT, THEN, IS SIN?

Most people would agree that something is wrong with our world. But people disagree about the cause of our problems. Consider the different explanations.[9]

Some say there is no problem. We have a few defects here and there, and people can get pretty nasty, but underneath it all, everything is fine.

A few still argue that despite pockets of iniquity, the human race is on the way up and that ultimately things will be better.

A different worldview maintains that human problems can be attributed to the suppression of our potentialities and capabilities. Let human beings express themselves, unencumbered by taboos and repressions, and they will flourish.

A similar view is held by those who see our problems based in negative thinking that needs to be replaced by positive mental attitude and possibility thinking.

The existential view, as mentioned earlier, claims that hopelessness and despair are not surprising since human problems come from our basic alienation and emptiness.

More prevalent today are new-age views that we have problems and limitations because we are not enlightened. Once we know more about ourselves and the universe, we will shed our ignorance and life will be better.

It is easy to see that none of these views seriously considers sin as it is defined and described in the Bible. The biblical worldview gives at least four perspectives on sin.

Sin as a Personal Act of Deviation or Rebellion

In one of David's written prayers, he called to God for mercy following his immorality with Bathsheba. "Cleanse me from my sin," David wrote. "Against you, you only, have I sinned and done what is evil in your sight" (Psalm 51:2,4).

David knew that sin involves a personal act of turning away from God and deviating from His will. Sin is rebellion against God. It is seen in the human tendency to know what God wants but then to do and to approve actions that violate God's directives (Romans 1:32).

Sin involves breaking God's commands (Matthew 15:3-8, Romans 5:14), lawlessness and wrongdoing (1 John 3:4, 5:17), allowing ourselves to go astray or to fall away from divine standards (Hebrews 6:6), and sometimes simply ignoring what God wants. Sin involves doing what we should not do and not doing what we should do. It includes unloving actions against other human beings and even includes mistreating our own bodies (1 Corinthians 3:16-17).

Sin as an Attitude

As described in the Bible, sin is more than an outward act. Sin can also be an attitude or mind-set that may be hidden behind a mask of respectability and piety. Jesus discussed this in the Sermon on the Mount. Any of us can be gripped by lust and be guilty of mental adultery, even if our outward behavior appears to be morally faultless (Matthew 5:28). A person does not need to murder, abuse, or otherwise show violence to be guilty of sin. We can sin when bitter attitudes and a judgmental spirit of revenge are allowed to fester in our minds or to enter our speech (Leviticus 19:18; Matthew 5:21-22, 7:1-5; Romans 12:19; Hebrews 12:15).

When Jesus walked on earth, the religious leaders were outwardly sanctimonious, but He called them hypocrites because inwardly they were filled with greed and self-indulgence (Matthew 23:25).

Basic psychology books often point out that we all wear facades that hide the "real me" underneath. But if we could know what a person thinks and what fills his or her mind, we would have a pretty good idea of what that person really is like. What we think often determines what we do with our behavior when the opportunity arises. There is evidence, for example, that parents who have grown up watching violence on television are more likely to use violence in their own parenting.[10] People who fill their minds with pornography, media sexuality, and sexually explicit novels are more susceptible to immoral behavior when they get into tempting situations. Much of the sin that occurs in our actions has already been rehearsed in our minds.

Sin as a Force

In what *The Wall Street Journal* called a "ground-breaking book," psychiatrist M. Scott Peck wrote about the reality and power of evil. Peck's *People of the Lie: The Hope for Healing Human Evil*[11] suggested that "99 percent of psychiatrists and the majority of clergy" do not believe in the existence of the Devil and most do not believe in evil as a force. But Peck's own investigations and work as a therapist had convinced him that evil is a very present force in this world.

The Apostle Paul expressed a similar idea when he wrote about his personal struggles with an inner "law of sin" that waged war in his mind (Romans 7:23-27, 8:2). This evil force dominates and energizes nonbelievers, and it is a power that affects all of our lives, although the believer does not need to be mastered by it (Romans 6). If we are honest with ourselves, all of us are likely to admit that we encounter the powerful force of sin with some frequency—whenever we are tempted to do what is wrong.

But the forces of sin are far more prevalent and widespread than the temptations that any of us encounter individually. Personal evil beings, described in the Bible as principalities and powers (Ephesians 6:12), utilize the forces of sin to encourage sinful tendencies in individuals and in communities. Sin, as a force, permeates whole societies and that sometimes shows itself in mass movements—like Nazism, Communism, or apartheid—or in deeply ingrained prejudice, self-centered acts of violence, and utter disregard for the rights or viewpoints of others.

Probably I am not the only person who is "turned off" by modern prophets of doom who give alarming lectures or write fear-inducing articles or books describing philosophies and political perspectives that threaten to engulf the world and bring our destruction. Many of these doomsayers are Christians who seem to have forgotten that God ultimately is in control and that no situation is utterly hopeless. But many of the alarmists do have an element of truth in their warnings, and often they recognize that sin is a subtle and powerful force that can lead to the destruction of entire civilizations.

Some alarmists may overreact with their fears of doom, but the attitude of the majority is equally biased and dangerous as they go through life with complacency and ignorance about the potency of sin as a force. Ultimately God is in control, but temporarily He has allowed Satan the freedom to influence the world in opposition to Christ and to everything for which He stands (John 7:7, Ephesians 2:2, 1 John 5:19). It is not surprising that the Bible warns against conformity to the world with its deeply intrinsic sinfulness (Romans 12:2, Colossians 2:8, 1 John 2:15-16).

Sin as a State

All of this brings us to biblical teaching that strongly differs from the views of contemporary thinkers, including counselors. Stated concisely, the Bible teaches that because of the sin of one man, Adam, the entire human race has become corrupted and guilty in God's sight (Romans 5:12-19, Ephesians 2:1-3). At the core, therefore, we human beings are so totally corrupted that in ourselves we have no way of making amends and avoiding the condemnation and just punishment that is coming.

When theologians talk about original sin, they refer to Adam's original sin and its effects on him and on the human race. Biblical scholar Floyd Barackman suggested that this sin has influenced all of us in several ways.[12]

First, Adam's sin caused us all to die spiritually so that we have become alienated from God and naturally unresponsive to the things of God (Ephesians 2:1-3, 4:17-19).

Second, Adam's sin changed human nature and ruined our bodies—so that they experience degeneration, disease, and death—as well as our inner soul-spirit nature. Because of God's grace and our innate morality (Romans 2:14-15), most of us aren't as evil as we can be, but there is evidence that sin affects our thinking (Genesis 6:5, 8:21; Romans 1:21-23, 8:5-8; 1 Corinthians 2:14; Ephesians 4:17-18), our wills (John 8:44, Romans 1:24-32, Ephesians 2:2-4), and our bodies (Romans 8:10).

Third, Adam's sin brought God's sentence of death on the entire human race (Romans 5:12,15,18), although it is clear from Scripture that there is now no condemnation to those who are believers in Christ (John 3:18, 5:24; Romans 8:1; 2 Thessalonians 2:12).

A Timeout

Most athletic events have timeouts so the players can stop the game temporarily to regroup and reevaluate. Maybe books like this one need to call periodically for a timeout as well.

I suggest this because the previous paragraphs have presented some basic theological ideas that are foreign to the ways many of us think and inconsistent with what most people probably believe about the goodness of human nature. Biblical teaching about human sinfulness is the kind of thinking that most of our counseling colleagues would toss aside contemptuously. Before we go further, maybe we need a timeout to ponder the implications of what all of this says about human beings, including us.

Surely nobody wants to believe in the idea of universal human depravity. We can buy the idea that Hitler was controlled by evil. We can agree that serial killers and mass murderers and political leaders like Saddam Hussein are corrupt and even diabolic. Most of us will agree that no one is perfect and we accept the idea that "to err is human."

But it is common to assume that most of us "sin only a little, every once in a while." We all have blemishes and moral failures, but I suspect most human beings look around, see "good people" in their homes and neighborhoods, and mentally toss aside any idea that all of us are corrupt at the core of our being. We can accept the idea that sin and evil might exist at the periphery of most of our lives, but surely they don't penetrate to the core.

R. C. Sproul has dealt with this in one of his books. He noted that every part of us is touched by sin—our minds, our wills, our bodies, our thoughts, our words, our actions. But this idea—which theologians call *total depravity*—does not mean that each of us is as wicked as we could possibly be. Some people are tyrants and ruthless murderers, but that doesn't describe most of us. Compared to the Stalins and Hitlers of this world, we and our counselees are more ordinary sinners, who often do act with kindness and mutual respect.

When we look at Christ, however, we realize that all of us have fallen far short of the ideal, despite our best efforts (Romans 3:10-12,23; Ephesians 2:8). Some are worse than others, but all of us are sinners.

This still leaves us with the objection from some people that it isn't fair to hold modern people responsible for Adam's sin. Why should I be blamed for what somebody did in the far distant past?

To answer we must recognize that Adam's open defiance of God was a sin by somebody who represented the entire human race at the time and whose disobedience set all human beings at odds with God. Because sin entered the human race through Adam, we are all born in sin, innately predisposed to sin, and so much inclined to sin that we actually do sin often during our lifetimes.[13] To use somewhat contemporary language, Adam got the sin bandwagon rolling but none of us is able to resist climbing on board.

THE ORIGIN OF SIN

How did the human race get into this mess in the first place? Where did evil come from originally?

These questions easily stir theological debate, but they aren't easily answered. We know that the Sovereign and Holy God does no evil, and because of His very nature, He could not create sin (Job 34:10, James 1:13). There was nothing evil in the creation when it was created; God Himself declared that what He created was good (Genesis 1:31). How, then, did the universal cancer of evil get into the earth?

For reasons that are largely a mystery to us, God allowed sin to develop in the angelic world. Satan (who is also called Lucifer or "morning star" in the Bible) staged a coup that was designed to replace God as the Sovereign Lord. The coup failed and Lucifer was cast out of the heavens with all of his fellow fallen angels (Isaiah 14:12-15). These evil forces, led by Satan, tempted Adam and Eve to sin, and the power of sin on the earth has existed ever since. As we will see in later chapters, however, the Bible teaches that the Devil is already condemned and eventually evil will be eradicated forever.

Certainly all of this interests counselors, although we rarely think about the orgins of evil when we work with counselees. But sin and the forces of evil exist and continue to influence counselors, counselees, and the work of counseling. If we keep aware of the origins of evil, we are more likely to remember that this evil in human beings is not what God intended. We can best understand our counselees when we keep aware of the impact and the nature of sin in all of our lives.

THE NATURE OF SIN

In a recent book, a professor of both philosophy and psychology described what he calls the "PBC" approach to life. PBC refers to the *p*hilosophy of *b*eak and *c*law. Like the participants in a cock fight, human beings who are ruled by the PBC spend life poking at one another and tearing each other apart. When the PBC exists in business, for example, the competitors use power, influence, and intimidation to chew up and tear into one another so that the victor comes out on top. "When the PBC is active in politics, beaks and claws are made of money and rhetoric and cunning strategy. You 'go for the jugular.' You collect all sorts of corruption in your mouth by researching the other candidate's moral history so you can spit him in the public eye."[14]

Most counselors probably have seen the PBC, so we know that it isn't limited to business or politics. You may think that the above description of the PBC is extreme, but of it we can be certain. Sin shows itself in a variety of forms and makes its influence known everywhere. Sin is complex and not easy to dissect, but its core appears to be summarized in two words: *unbelief* and *rebellion*.

Sin as Unbelief

Genesis 3 records the first temptation that Adam and Eve experienced in the Garden of Eden. The tempter (Satan in the form of a serpent) raises a question about whether God's word can be trusted. "Did God really say, 'You must not eat from any tree in the garden'?" the tempter asks in a way that must raise a question in the mind of Eve. Without giving her much time to think, Satan goes on to state firmly that what God said was wrong. This is reinforced with an alternative viewpoint to cast doubt on the word that had come from God. "'You will not surely die,' the serpent said to the woman. 'For God knows that when you eat of it [the fruit] your eyes will be opened, and you will be like God, knowing good and evil'" (Genesis 3:4-5).

This temptation to doubt God's word was also a temptation to doubt God's goodness. By suggesting that God was keeping Adam and Eve in the dark and withholding knowledge from them, the tempter implied that God was not being good. It was a short step to reach the next conclusion. The person who doubts God's word and His goodness looks for alternatives to God and, in time, begins to think that he or she is like God. New-age thinkers even assume that each of us is a god.

Similar tactics were used when Satan tempted Jesus to turn stones into bread, to jump from the temple, and to worship the Devil (Matthew 4:4-10). By misquoting Scripture, Satan tried to distort the Word of God. The tempter proposed that Jesus would be given food (to meet His physical needs), prestige in the eyes of all who would witness a spectacular religious event (if Jesus would jump over the wall and be rescued dramatically), and power to rule over lands and people. By implication, the Devil was suggesting that God the Father was not good in withholding these benefits.

In a short and thoughtful book, psychologist Larry Crabb wrote that Satan has one central strategy: to distract us from the reality of sin.[15] In doing this, he often causes us to doubt God's Word and His goodness. It is easy for any of us to ignore what the Bible says about God, to focus on our own trials and disappointments (or those of our counselees), and to struggle with the idea that maybe God really isn't good. Accept that idea and you are more inclined to accept the false views of this world that other things are better than God and God's ways—things like excitement, self-satisfaction, "taking charge" of our own circumstances, or being independent. This gets us to the second core word for describing sin. The first word is *unbelief*; the second is *rebellion*.

Sin as Rebellion

Sin is rebellion against God as Lord and against the standards that He has established. One more time we can look to the temptation in the Garden of Eden. By triggering unbelief in the mind of Eve, Satan encouraged her to rebel against God's directives and to be disobedient. Like Adam and Eve, all of us disobey at times, and in so doing we seek to be independent of God. Today, long after the first temptation, we still fall for the tempter's original message: Rebel and you will be like God. The message promises freedom, but it leads to enslavement.

Figure 6.1 summarizes how we have come to this point. Human beings were created in the image of God. We are like other creatures, but we have been given the ability to relate to others and to God and to have dominion over the earth. God's creation became severely tarnished because of the Fall, when we fell into sin through unbelief and rebellion. Because of the unbelief, our relationships have been severely shattered and we struggle to relate to God, to others, and even to ourselves. Because of the rebellion, we have become enslaved by our appetites and unable to take responsibility for ourselves, others, or even the earth over which we are expected to have dominion.

Figure 6.1
THE CREATION AND FALL OF HUMAN BEINGS

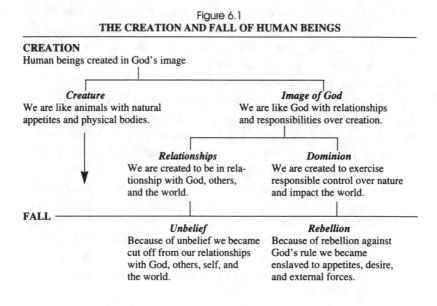

CREATION
Human beings created in God's image

Creature
We are like animals with natural appetites and physical bodies.

Image of God
We are like God with relationships and responsibilities over creation.

Relationships
We are created to be in relationship with God, others, and the world.

Dominion
We are created to exercise responsible control over nature and impact the world.

FALL

Unbelief
Because of unbelief we became cut off from our relationships with God, others, self, and the world.

Rebellion
Because of rebellion against God's rule we became enslaved to appetites, desire, and external forces.

This is not vague theology that has no relevance to our everyday lives. Sin has affected each of us internally, confused our thinking, clouded our viewpoints, complicated our relationships, disrupted the world in which we live, and alienated us from God. Sin has a significant impact on counselors and their counselees, even if the concept of sin never crosses their minds.

THE EFFECTS OF SIN

In talking to her counselor, a young woman recently reflected on the destructive impact of some past moral choices. "I wish I had known at the time how what I did would ruin my life," she said. "I wish I could go back and start over. Since that isn't possible, I wish I could put the past behind me and get on with my life." There are many counseling techniques that would be helpful to this young Christian, but ultimately she will not find permanent healing unless and until she deals with the sin in her life, including the guilt and need for forgiveness that we will discuss in a later chapter.

To better help counselees deal with their struggles and to help ourselves, we need a clear understanding of the ways in which sin has an impact on our lives. Most modern approaches to counseling tend to be optimistic and inclined to ignore or to minimize the idea of sin. Rarely is there any awareness that sin has significant and practical implications in the lives of our counselees.

The Separation of Human Beings from God

Francis Schaeffer, the late philosopher-theologian wrote that sin has led to four great separations. The first of these, the separation of humans from God, has broken our communication and intimacy with the Creator. As we have seen, the almighty and eternal God created males and females in His own image, as the highest of all creatures. God gave us life that He continues to sustain, the freedom to make moral choices, and the challenge of being in charge of the rest of creation. But we human beings disobeyed God's commands, ignored and abused God's creation, failed to treat Him with respect and gratitude (Romans 1:21), and often have rejected His offer of friendship and love. As a result of sin, we have become alienated from God and cut off from the close relationship that He intended to have with us.

Adam and Eve experienced this alienation immediately after the Fall. No longer did they feel the closeness that they had known. Instead, they hid from God, tried to avoid Him, and were afraid of His divine displeasure.

This separation from God has serious and widespread implications. It leads to other separations that we can see easily in our counseling rooms.

The Separation of Human Beings from One Another

Not long ago, a young man from Britain gave me a novel that, he said, had "changed his life." First published in 1890, William Morris' *News from Nowhere* gives a utopian picture of a future in which human beings live together, completely at peace and with shared prosperity, without crime or rebellious kids, and with no divine help or need to depend on God.[16] I knew that the man who gave me the book had gone from bookstore to bookstore in London before he found a copy to give me. I knew that he didn't have a lot of money and that his gift involved a financial sacrifice. Even so, I couldn't share his enthusiasm for a book that was so out of contact with reality and with the real nature of human relationships.

Despite our best intentions, humans are incapable of living in utopian relationships. Instead, we are at odds with one another continally. We see this in wars between nations and in fights between street gangs. But we see it, too, in conflicts between spouses, tension in families, cut-throat competition between business partners, the rejection of authority, bitterness and the failure to show love or respect, and tensions between factions in churches and denominations. Because we are alienated from God, each of us has a never-ending potential for conflict with other human beings. The separation of human beings from one another is seen whenever there are conflicts and tensions.

The Separation of Human Beings from Themselves

I have seen it often in my own life and I have seen it in counselees. We struggle with a problem, look for someone else to blame, and eventually reach a disturbing conclusion: "I am the major cause of my own problems." For each of us it would be accurate to say that "sin permeates to the depths of my own inner being and damages everything that is within me. At times I might be able to spot some of the disorder within, but I find myself unable to fix the core of my human nature that creates some of my own worst problems."

Because of sin, human *intelligence* is impaired. No longer can we gain accurate knowledge of the world in which we live or reason without falling into error.[17] Sin clouds our *perception* ability, so that we cannot know ourselves accurately or perceive and understand others clearly. In terms of our *morals*, sin has hindered the ability to discern good from evil and prevented us from consistently acting in ways that are right. *Social relationships* are handicapped by sin, and as a result, we are inclined to exploit, manipulate, or in other ways bring harm to our fellow human beings. Sin distorts our *emotions* and often leads to emotional disorders such as depression and hyperanxiety. Because of sin, we are prone to let our minds and bodies drift to self-centered, lustful *sexuality* that lacks control and leads men and women to use each other as things to be exploited (James 4:1-3). Human *creativity* still persists, but it is limited by perverted imaginations that prevent any of us from reaching the potential that we were intended to have.

In summary, sin can trap us in enslaving habits and addictions, distort our perceptions of reality, cause us to be insensitive and self-centered, lead to restlessness that robs us of inner peace, and even cause us to deny sin so that everybody is surprised when a psychiatrist writes a book that asks *Whatever Became of Sin?*[18]

The Bible pulls all of this together, especially in Romans 1–2 where the impact of sin is summarized and in other biblical passages that call us slaves to sin (John 8:34; Romans 6:6,16-18). This slavery goes beyond human relationships and even affects how we relate to the realm of nature.

The Separation of Human Beings from Nature

When the Apostle Paul wrote to the Romans, he gave a short and concise course in theology that is filled with interesting insights. In Romans 8, for example, we read that human beings are not the only part of creation that needs to be freed from the effects of sin. Following the sin of Adam and Eve, a curse was put on the ground (Genesis 3:17). As a result, the whole of creation is in bondage to sin, subject to decay, and in need of redemption (Romans 8:19-22).

Since sin has an effect on human beings and on nature, it is not surprising that sin also influences our God-given responsibilities to have dominion over the earth. A flood of recent publications—one book even written by the Vice-President of the United States, most written by people who don't claim to be Christians—have pointed to the fact that we humans have not taken care of the earth. We have polluted, exploited, damaged, and destroyed much of nature. We have contaminated our rivers, dirtied the air, ignored struggling wildlife, and wrecked much of the natural beauty of the earth that God gave us to care for and to enjoy. Because sin has penetrated nature and interfered with our duty to have dominion over the earth, nature itself has come to have control over us—clogging our lungs, withholding its vegetation, blotting out endangered species, and leaving us with filthy rivers and lakes.

There is evidence that only one issue appears capable of pulling together the diverse interests of people today. We are divided over almost everything, but most of us have a concern for protecting the earth. As long as we are bound by sin, our efforts to clean up nature cannot succeed fully. But many of the efforts of modern-day environmentalists appear to be consistent with the responsibilities that God gave us when we were told to subdue and take responsibility for what He created.

SO WHAT?

This discussion of the environment, and some of the theology that appears in the pages of this chapter, may seem far removed from the realities of helping the hurting people who come into our offices. Most of our counseling colleagues aren't much interested in reading or hearing about sin, and even Christian counselors find little time for theology. Juggling our busy lifestyles and facing the continual needs of our struggling counselees, we tire quickly of theological and philosophical debates that appear to have little relevance to our counseling work.

But few topics could be more relevant than the issue of sin. The problems that characterize all of our lives, counselors included, have come because of the pervading and penetrating influence of sin in nature and the environment, in the societies and communities where we live, and in the inner core of every human being. It is worth repeating that the Bible presents sin as an inner force, an inherent condition, a controlling power that lies deep within every person. How we view the issue of sin will have a significant influence on how we counsel and on the effectiveness of our counseling.

As we have seen in this chapter, sin involves unbelief and personal rebellion. It includes distrusting God, ignoring Him or deliberately disobeying His commands, selfishness, involvement in unloving actions against others, and even mistreating our own bodies. Although sin is most easily seen in one's actions, it also involves attitudes and thinking that often are hidden from others. Sin is a force that permeates whole societies and that sometimes shows itself in wars and in other forms of self-centered violence. Sin, too, is a state of being that cuts us off from God, from other people, from ourselves, and from the environment.

Two Extremes

When we consider the role of sin in the lives of our counselees, we sometimes move toward one of two extremes. The first of these is the tendency to assume that whenever a person has a problem, this is the direct result of that person's sinful thoughts or actions. From this, it follows that the only effective method of treatment is to confront the counselee with his or her sin, to help the person find forgiveness, and to challenge the individual to go and sin no more.

Certainly, many problems of the people who suffer come directly from their sinful behavior. Recently, a man in our community shot and killed his eleven-year-old daughter. Now he waits in jail, facing a trial, and (according to newspaper reports) is deeply distraught and in grief because of his daughter's death. Everybody would agree: The man's sin brought on his problems.

On the day following the murder, the girl's classmates and teachers also grieved. Subsequently, some of the kids have become anxious and fearful about their safety and security. Do we assume that their problems are solely the result of their own sin? Their friend's murder was the result of the gunman's sin and of sin that has penetrated the whole of creation. In addition, the grieving of the classmates is made worse because of their own sin. But we would be naive and simplistic to suggest that each of these young students is solely to blame for his or her grief and to suggest that the only effective treatment is to confront and remove the sin in each griever's life.

Jesus spoke to this directly in Luke 13:4, where He emphasized repentance but rejected the idea that personal tragedy indicates that a victim is more sinful than a non-victim.

The second counseling extreme is to assume that problems all come from somebody else's sin. This lets us play the role of a victim, find somebody else to blame, and push aside any recognition of our own sinfulness. As a result, we cast off any notions that each of us must take some responsibility for our actions, and we tell ourselves and our counselors how so many of our problems have come from what others have done.

The recovery movement has been of great benefit to thousands of people. Many have learned how their dysfunctional families, alcoholic parents, abusive childhoods, and other traumatic experiences have caused deep scars that are carried into adulthood. Healing for these people frequently involves facing the past, instead of repressing it, and dealing with the lingering effects of some other person's sin. In doing this, many experience genuine and lasting recovery.

Regrettably, however, some counselees have been encouraged to focus almost solely on the past and on the sins of somebody else. They spend their entire lives "in recovery," never seem to get much better, and rarely ask whether their present sinful thoughts and actions might be prolonging the pain.

If I have a problem, I won't find forgiveness and healing if I take the first of our two extremes, continually berate myself, and assume that whatever comes my way must always be the result of my deliberate sin. But neither will I find healing if I put all the blame on somebody else and deny both my own possible role in contributing to the problem and my present responsibility for making changes.

Two Conclusions

This chapter leaves counselors with two basic conclusions. First, our work involves helping people whose lives have been injured and sometimes torn apart by the effects of sin. Whether or not a counselor recognizes and admits this, he or she is dealing with the influence of sin in the lives of counselees, and the counseling is always hindered by sin in the counselor's own life. This is a strong but valid conclusion: When a counselor ignores sin, he or she will be of limited effectiveness in bringing lasting change to others.

All of this could leave us mired in discouragement, but there is a second and more hopeful conclusion that must be emphasized. Sin has permeated our society; but because of Jesus Christ, people can be changed into "new creations," any of us can find forgiveness, and there is hope for genuine healing. The effects of sin are still with us, but we have the promise that in the future sin's impact will be gone. This challenges all of us, counselors and counselees, to live lives of purity as we anticipate the ultimate destruction of sin from our lives (1 John 3:2-3).

Early in his career, newscaster Paul Harvey established his reputation as a masterful storyteller. For many years he has captivated radio audiences with his fascinating reports of day-to-day events and unknown facts about people whose names often appeared in the headlines. Harvey gave the news but then stepped "behind the headlines" to give us "the rest of the story."[19] In this chapter we have put the topic of sin into the headlines of our thinking. We turn in the next two chapters to the rest of the story.

CHAPTER SEVEN

❖

Christ and Counseling

HAVE YOU EVER HEARD of the "messiah complex"?

This isn't a psychiatric diagnosis or a condition that gets listed in books on abnormal psychology. Instead, the *messiah complex* refers to the tendency for caring people, counselors included, to become rescuers who try to deliver others from their problems and difficult life circumstances. At times, almost all of us want to be like messiahs, saving people from their dysfunctional families, enslaving addictions, or self-destructive lifestyles.

I have a friend who has spent all of his adult life working in a private practice and teaching counseling skills to graduate students. His years of experience have shown that when counselors try to be rescuers, the rescuers almost always end up being hurt. Even so, my friend still is tempted at times to be like a messiah. "It would be nice if I could rescue people from their pain and release them from their problems," he has told his students. "But whenever I am tempted to try taking on that role, I remember how powerless I am and I think about what happened to the real Messiah. He was crucified."

How does the "real Messiah," Jesus Christ, relate to us as counselors? What can we learn from His crucifixion? Do His actions have any practical bearing on our counseling and on our counselees at this present time in history?

Before looking at these issues, it might be helpful to jog our memories about what we have considered so far. We have seen that human beings were created by God from "dust," given the same instincts as other animal creatures, but made in the image of God so that we could have relationships and take dominion over nature. We were meant to bring glory to God, but instead we rebelled and fell into an abnormal, sinful state. The image of God was not destroyed, but it was tarnished. As a result, our creaturely instincts have taken over much of our behavior and self-control has become difficult. Because of the sin of unbelief (not trusting God's goodness) and our rebellious defiance of God's will, we are tainted to the core. Sin has corroded our relationships with God, with others, with ourselves, and with the world. We need someone—a real Messiah—to deliver us from the sinful state in which we are entrapped. This brings us to Jesus Christ.

WHO IS JESUS CHRIST?

Missionaries remind us that the name of Jesus Christ is unknown in many parts of the world, but that isn't true where most of us live. In a recent survey of Americans, for example, 62 percent indicated both that they had heard of Jesus Christ and that they had made a personal commitment to Him even though the researcher was unable to determine how many of these had made "a wholehearted, life-changing submission to the lordship of Christ."[1] Many never make any conscious commitment but apparently still think of themselves as Christians, even though they aren't very interested or involved in religious activities. In addition, others are nonbelievers but they at least have heard about Christ. In U.S. culture, His name is well-recognized.

Despite this familiarity, I wonder how many people really could tell us who Jesus Christ is and what He is like. In one of his books, C. S. Lewis suggested that keeping us in the dark about Christ is one of the Devil's chief tools of deception. Let the people think that He is no more than a great man or an "historical Jesus," the Devil tells his young protege in *The Screwtape Letters*. "We thus distract men's minds from Who He is, and what He did. We first make Him solely a teacher . . . a merely probable, remote, shadowy, and uncouth figure, one who spoke a strange language and died a long time ago. Such an object cannot in fact be worshipped."[2] In sharp contrast, the Bible presents a view of Jesus Christ that is greater than any human mind could imagine. He is both "fully God and fully man."

Jesus Christ as God

Some contemporary new-age thinkers might accept the idea that Jesus is God, but they assume that all of us are gods. Much different is the Bible's teaching that there is only one God (Deuteronomy 6:4, Mark 12:29, 1 Corinthians 8:6, 1 Timothy 2:5) who—as we saw in an earlier chapter—exists in three Persons. Jesus Christ is the "exact representation" of God the Father (Hebrews 1:3), eternal (John 8:58), given the name of God (Titus 2:13), and able to say that anyone who had seen Him had seen the Father (John 14:9).

Theologians use the word *incarnation* (the word literally means "in-flesh-ment") to describe the remarkable event by which God took on flesh and became a human being without giving up His divine nature. The New Testament nowhere implies—as some people suggest—that Jesus Christ came to earth as a human being, like you and me, but then gradually moved from being a purely human Jesus to becoming a divine being. He was the Son of God from the beginning.[3]

All of this gives us further insight into what God is like. He takes sin so seriously that it cannot be ignored, but the Incarnation shows that God's love for us is so great that He sent His Son to pay for our sin (John 3:16; Romans 3:23-26, 5:8).

Jesus Christ as Human

Like every other human being, Jesus Christ was born—even though the birth was supernatural (Matthew 1:18-25, Luke 2:1-7). He experienced hunger (Matthew 4:2), thirst (John 19:28), fatigue (John 4:6), feelings (Mark 3:5, Luke 10:21, John 12:27), loneliness (Mark 15:34), suffering, and death (John 19:30, Hebrews 2:9). Jesus had a physical body that could be seen and touched (1 John 1:1). He had human experiences, including the routine of going to work and the responsibility of caring for His mother (Mark 6:3, John 19:27). Like everybody else, He paid taxes (Matthew 17:24-25) and experienced temptation, so He is able to identify with our struggles and with the temptations that all of us encounter (Hebrews 4:15). In every way, therefore, Jesus Christ was a human being *except* He was without sin (2 Corinthians 5:21, 1 John 3:5).

The Bible sometimes contrasts Jesus with Adam (Romans 5:12-19; 1 Corinthians 15:22,45). The first human being failed to bring glory to God, and instead Adam plunged the world into sin. Jesus Christ then came as the true Messiah, the only possible rescuer. Like the ancient priests who offered sacrifices to atone for human sin, God's Son came as a priest who offered Himself, a perfect sacrifice, to completely make amends for the sins of all people who believe—past, present, and future (Romans 3:23-25; Ephesians 5:2; Hebrews 9:11-12, 24-28, 10:10; 1 John 2:2, 4:10). It is a mystery to us how He could be both God and man, but that was part of God's plan. Jesus Christ was uniquely suited for the task of delivering all of us—that includes our counselees—from sin and evil.

This discussion about who Jesus is sometimes is known as a study of *the person of Christ*. It brings us to the equally important issue of *the work of Christ*.

WHAT HAS JESUS CHRIST DONE, AND WHAT DOES HE DO NOW?

Several years ago, when I was teaching at the Air Force Chaplain School, I met a young Catholic priest, a military reservist whose primary work was to serve as the parish priest in a small community near New York. I was planning to be in that area a few weeks after our class at the Chaplain School, so I accepted his invitation to drop by the rectory for coffee. After a long and relaxed discussion about theology, counseling, and other issues, we went to look at his church's new sanctuary. It was a beautiful building dominated by a large crucifix hanging over the altar.

This crucifix was not like any that I had seen in the cathedrals of Europe or in other Catholic churches I had visited. The crucifix in my friend's church did not have the wood-carved Christ nailed to the cross with His head drooping. Instead, His hands were raised and He was looking upward with an expression of jubilation on His face.

"It is a different kind of crucifix," my priest friend agreed when I asked about it. "Christ came and died on the cross, but He isn't there now. When He rose triumphantly from the dead He defeated death. This is a reminder that His work is done and that He is alive."

That is the message of Good Friday and Easter, but it often gets hidden by our fascination with chocolate bunnies and colored eggs. The human race is so mired in unbelief and rebellion that we cannot pull ourselves out of the muck of sin or clean ourselves off. So God the Father sent His Son, Jesus Christ, who came to earth voluntarily to die in our place, to pay for our sin, to free us from the quagmire of unbelief and rebellion, and to restore the full relationship with God that was torn apart by the Fall (Romans 5:6,10; 6:6-7; 2 Corinthians 5:18-19).

Because He was God, Jesus Christ was sinless, so He didn't have to pay any penalty for His own sin. His sinlessness enabled Him to step into my place and yours and to bear our sins so that justice would be done and we could be forgiven completely.

Because Jesus Christ was human, He was able to make amends for us. Human beings are the ones who have sinned, and in order for unbiased justice to be done, there needed to be a human who would and could pay the price for human iniquity.

In three concise sentences that you may have to read more than once, John Stott summarizes what happened on the cross:

> In order to save us in such a way as to satisfy himself,
> God through Christ substituted himself for us. Divine love
> triumphed over divine wrath by divine self-sacrifice. The
> cross was an act simultaneously of punishment and amnesty,
> severity and grace, justice and mercy.[4]

Because of who He was, both God and man, the sinless Jesus Christ was the only one who could pay the price that would restore our broken relationship with God.

None of us can imagine the shame, scorn, and suffering that He endured (Hebrews 12:2-3). Crucifixion was so cruel that it was never inflicted on Roman citizens. It was reserved for slaves, pirates, criminals, and political or religious rebels whom the authorities wanted to suffer exemplary death. "Tortured by cramped muscles, unable to swat crawling and buzzing insects, hungry, thirsty, and naked before a taunting crowd," the victims were helpless and humiliated. Cicero once termed crucifixion "the cruelest and most hideous punishment" possible.[5] The voluntary sacrifice of Christ on the cross is the supreme example of divine love, grace, compassion, and mercy.

Clearly, the cross of Christ is central to our faith as Christians. Without the death of Jesus Christ on the cross, we would still be enslaved permanently by sin and unable to do anything to save ourselves (Ephesians 2:8). Now, because of Christ's death, we are new creatures who can be reconciled to God (2 Corinthians 5:17-18). The traditional crucifix, with Christ hanging on the cross, reminds us of His suffering and bloodshed.

We must remember, however, that Christ is no longer nailed to a cross. I remember a long discussion that once took place around our dining-room table when a visiting theologian was meeting with some of my students. "The cross is central to our faith," the visitor stated, "but equally important for Christians is the open, empty tomb." Christ died, but He also rose from the dead.

Why does that matter? In the years immediately following the death, resurrection, and ascension of Christ back into Heaven, some critics denied that the resurrection ever happened. In his first letter to the Corinthians, Paul dealt with this "head on": "If Christ has not been raised, your faith is futile; you are still in your sins," and none of us has any hope (1 Corinthians 15:17—see also 12-18).

But Jesus Christ did rise from the dead.[6] His resurrection demonstrates that sin and death have been dealt with, that the forces of Satan are already condemned, and that believers can now be assured of life eternal (John 3:16, Romans 6:5-9, 1 Corinthians 15:21-26). Jesus is in Heaven now, at the Father's right hand, where He always lives to intercede for us and to guarantee that we will be forgiven when we confess our sins (Isaiah 53:12; Hebrews 1:3, 7:24-27; 1 Peter 3:22; 1 John 1:9).

"If anybody does sin," the Apostle John wrote, "we have one who speaks to the Father in our defense—Jesus Christ, the Righteous One. He is the atoning sacrifice for our sins, and not only for ours but also for the sins of the whole world" (1 John 2:1-2).

RESTORATION

The top part of figure 7.1 is something we have seen before. It shows what happened when God created the world and when the human race fell into sin. We come, now, to an added dimension: the changes that occurred when Jesus Christ died for our sins and rose from the dead. Stated concisely, God made it possible for us to be restored to fellowship with Him. In place of unbelief, distrust, and alienation from God and others, we have had a reconciliation. Instead of remaining in a state of rebellion, guilt, and resistance to God, we have been justified and redeemed so that the Holy Spirit can enable us to experience self-control. We still remain creatures with appetites, but we are enabled to appreciate the desires that God has given and to avoid self-centered, lustful behaviors.

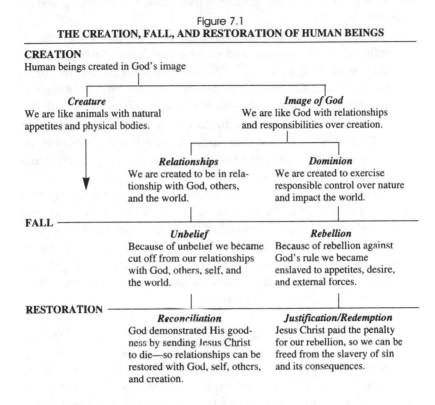

Figure 7.1
THE CREATION, FALL, AND RESTORATION OF HUMAN BEINGS

CREATION
Human beings created in God's image

Creature
We are like animals with natural appetites and physical bodies.

Image of God
We are like God with relationships and responsibilities over creation.

Relationships
We are created to be in relationship with God, others, and the world.

Dominion
We are created to exercise responsible control over nature and impact the world.

FALL

Unbelief
Because of unbelief we became cut off from our relationships with God, others, self, and the world.

Rebellion
Because of rebellion against God's rule we became enslaved to appetites, desire, and external forces.

RESTORATION

Reconciliation
God demonstrated His goodness by sending Jesus Christ to die—so relationships can be restored with God, self, others, and creation.

Justification/Redemption
Jesus Christ paid the penalty for our rebellion, so we can be freed from the slavery of sin and its consequences.

Counselors sometimes use the word *reconciliation* and are less inclined to use words like *justification* and *redemption*. These sound like heavy theological terms, but they take on more meaning when we think of them as images or pictures that give a clearer perspective of the nature of Christ's work. Reconciliation gives an image that points to interpersonal relationships. Justification is an image taken from a court of law. Redemption is a picture that is drawn from the marketplace, especially the old slave markets where human beings were bought, sold, and traded like cattle.

Reconciliation: An Image from Relationships
One of the most well-known parables Jesus told is about a prodigal son (Luke 15:11-32). This kid had an older brother who dutifully worked for his father's business, but the younger son wanted

to get away from home. The young man must have been persuasive because he convinced the father to divide his estate and give half of it to him. He then left home to establish himself in a distant country.

Probably you remember what happened. Young, inexperienced, controlled by his hormones, and ruled by his lusts, the younger son squandered all of the money and ended up without friends, without food, and without any resources. Stated in terms of figure 7.1, the son had broken his relationship with the father, thrown out the father's standards, and decided to do things without any help. As a result, the son was bankrupt, starving, and humiliated. Eventually, he swallowed his pride, returned to the father, and was reconciled and restored to his place as a son.

Some of the parables of Jesus are difficult to understand, but this one isn't. The picture of a sin-saturated child returning to find the father's forgiveness is a model of the restoration that we can have with God. Like the father in the story, God does not force us to return. Each of us must choose either to ignore and reject the divine promise of reconciliation or to return to God, humbly confessing our sins, and asking for adoption into the family.

But this parable doesn't tell us everything about reconciliation. Unlike the father in the parable who waited and watched for the son's return, God was more active. He took the initiative of sending His Son to pay for our debt of sin, and He let us know that the welcome mat is out for our return. Paul understood this so well that he was able to rejoice because "we have now received reconciliation" through Christ (Romans 5:11). The news is so good that believers are charged with the challenge of telling others that reconciliation is now possible, like a free gift, available to any who want it (Romans 6:23, Ephesians 2:8, Colossians 1:19-22).

How does this relate to counseling? Many of the problems we encounter concern strained or broken relationships, so we find ourselves teaching people how to listen, how to communicate, and how to interact without making tensions worse. Christians believe that conflict exists ultimately because we are sinful people, who have turned our backs on God's ways and tried to deal with conflicts on our own. Surely it is significant that Adam and Eve had the first marital tension almost immediately after their fall into sin (Genesis 3:12). Because God has given us minds that think, we can make some progress in resolving tension on our own, but true and lasting reconciliation is found only when we, and our counselees, first are reconciled to Christ. What happens then?

First, we have peace with God (Romans 5:1, Colossians 1:20-22). It is true, of course, that some of our counselees don't care about God, but many do want to know that He accepts them, forgives them, and even allows them to approach Him with confidence (Hebrews 4:16). In times of stress, conflict, uncertainty, and anxiety it can be very reassuring to know that despite the turmoil surrounding us, we can be at peace with our Creator.

Second, we can have peace with others (Galatians 3:26-28, Ephesians 2:14-18). Certainly tensions between people, including Christian people, continue to exist. None of us is perfect. Misunderstandings, disagreements, and self-centered attitudes are likely to be with us for life. But God does enable us to break down the walls that divide us. He can reduce interpersonal tensions and guide as we seek to help others get along better with one another.

Third, we can be at peace within ourselves. Like me, perhaps you have turned often to Philippians 4:4-7 when you feel anxious. Rejoice when there are difficulties, we read (instead of focusing on the negative). Be gentle in what you do, and remind yourself that the Lord is near. We can pray, expressing thanksgiving and bringing our requests. "The peace of God, which transcends all understanding, will guard your hearts and your minds in Christ Jesus." In the midst of our hectic lifestyles and adrenaline-generating circumstances, it can be calming to draw apart (mentally if we can't do it physically) and to experience the peace that comes from God and quiets us within.

Fourth, we can have the experience of helping others find reconciliation—with God, with others, and within themselves. Christian counselors, and all other believers, have been reconciled to God and have been given a "ministry of reconciliation," which involves taking the message of reconciliation to others (2 Corinthians 5:18-19).

Fifth, we can look forward to a time when the whole of creation will be "liberated from its bondage to decay," reconciled to God, and restored to the state of beauty and wholeness that it once had (Romans 8:19-22, Colossians 1:20).

Justification: An Image from the Courts
In an earlier chapter I mentioned a young man who is in prison. During my visits to see him, we have sat across the table from one

another, talking freely and sharing like old friends. We differ in age, education, and past experiences, but we are both human beings with feelings, active minds, hopes for the future, and physical bodies that sometimes get colds and the flu.

There is one very large difference between us, however. When the prison guard shouts, "Visiting hours are over. All rise," my friend goes back to his little cell, but I can freely walk out of the prison and back to my rental car. The laws of the land allow me to be free, but they decree that my friend must remain behind bars and barbed wire fences. He was sent to prison by a judge who pronounced his sentence in a court of law.

The word *justification* refers to the believer's status before God—the only completely fair and unbiased judge. In modern English, we think of justification as something we do to defend ourselves, to "justify" our actions. Computer users talk about "justifying" the right-hand margins of a text so that words are spread out, giving aligned margins on both sides of the page. But in theological talk, justification means that we are in a right status with God.

Once again, Stott gives a concise summary:

> When God justifies sinners, he is not declaring bad people
> to be good, or saying that they are not sinners after all; he is
> pronouncing them legally righteous, free from any liability
> to the broken law, because he himself in his Son has borne
> the penalty of their law-breaking.[7]

My young friend in prison is having to pay for his lawlessness by staying locked up until his term expires or he is paroled. But in God's lawcourt, we have been freed without condemnation, not because we are sinless (in reality, we are all sinful and guilty) but because Christ paid the penalty for our sin. As a result, in God's sight, we are "righteous," accepted, and just. We could never pay for our sin, work hard enough to get God's approval, or be justified by some kind of holy and righteous living. So Jesus Christ took care of the problem. And we are justified when we put our faith in Christ who has already paid for our sin (Galatians 2:16, Ephesians 2:8-9).

I once heard an illustration that clarifies much of this. In a court of law one day, a young girl was brought before a judge who found her guilty and issued a stiff fine, in accordance with the law. The judge happened to be the girl's father and he knew that there was no way by which she could pay the fine. So he took off his robes, came down to stand next to his daughter, reached into his pocket to pay the fine, then went back to his bench and announced that his daughter was free to go. The penalty had been paid and justice had been done. In a similar way, God declared us guilty of sin, sent His Son to pay, and now declares that those who have faith in Him are justified. Case closed! (See Romans 3:23-26, 4:25, 5:1, 8:1-2; Colossians 2:13-14.)

What difference does this make to us and to our counselees? As the next chapter will show, when we know that we are forgiven, we can have an unusual sense of inner peace (Romans 5:1). We can be free from the bondage of guilt and self-condemnation. We can be confident that we are part of God's family. We know that our salvation is assured, and we can be certain that we will spend eternity with Him (Galatians 3:26-29, 4:4-7).

The shelves of my office hold hundreds of books. Many of them deal with complex psychological issues. But nothing could be more liberating to people than this: Christians are not yet perfect (nobody is), but right now and for eternity we are faultless in the sight of God—because Christ paid for our sins on the cross and rose victorious over death. That is true even of my Christian friend in prison. American law and justice has him incarcerated, but in Christ he is already free.

Redemption: An Image from the Marketplace

Sociologist and master storyteller Anthony Campolo has a great ability to use humor and tremendous communication skills to poke at our consciences and make us think. When he addressed the Second International Congress on Christian Counseling, Dr. Campolo reminded his audience of counselors that westerners have a great love of accumulating "stuff," most of which we don't need. We are fascinated with shopping malls, run up big debts on credit cards (with their huge interest rates), and even display bumper stickers that proclaim the joy of being able to "shop 'til you drop." Describing some recent TV commercials, the well-known Christian sociologist observed that "ours is an age in which we dare to say to the people of the world that there are material things that will meet spiritual needs." Often our lifestyles could be characterized by two words: *shop* and *spend*.

All this shopping leaves one universal principle: what we buy has to be paid for. Even if we go into debt, the bill still has to be paid. And the people to whom we owe the money often are neither impressed nor sympathetic if we can't pay. When the debt is huge and our resources are skimpy, our only hope is to find someone with deep pockets who can pay the bills and bail us out of our predicament.

This brings us to the issue of redemption—a theme that is woven like a bright scarlet cord throughout the fabric of the Bible. When the Israelites were penniless slaves in Egypt, they were freed only by the intervention of God. When they fell repeatedly into sin as a nation, God consistently offered forgiveness and freedom. In the New Testament, we read that all human beings are in bondage to sin, following the ways of the Devil, condemned to death, and controlled by the world (Ephesians 2:1-3). But Christ gave Himself to liberate humans and to rescue us from the effects of the Fall.

The word *redeem* means to buy back. In centuries past, Bible readers would have thought about the buying and selling of slaves, but for us a more modern example of redeeming people might come to mind. Within the past several years we have become familiar with groups of international kidnapers who capture some person, hold him or her hostage, and then demand that a government or other "redeemer" pay a significant ransom price to buy the freedom of the imprisoned victim. If you were that victim, held without any possibility of escape, there would be nothing you could do to buy your own freedom. You would be completely dependent on some rescuer-redeemer.

Assume, further, that your abductors decided that you deserved the death penalty. Just before the execution, however, another person volunteered to be executed in your place with the expectation that you then would be released. Your promised release would fill you with tremendous gratitude toward that brave and self-giving person who had agreed to die in your place. Of course, you would have to accept the offer and walk away from your kidnapers, but once free you would always be a person who had been redeemed by the sacrifice of another.

Each of these pictures gives a partial portrayal of what Christ has done for us. The human race has run up a debt of sin. For justice to be done, we need to pay off this debt, but there is no way that we can do so. In His great mercy, therefore, God sent His Son, Jesus Christ, to pay the price of sin and to redeem us, not with silver, gold, or dollars, but with His shed blood by dying in our place (1 Peter

1:18-19). We can ignore the offer—as some people do—but if we accept Christ's freedom plan, we are released from the debt of sin forever, and we no longer are in bondage to sin, to Satan, or to the world (John 15:19; Romans 6:6-7,18; Ephesians 1:7; Colossians 1:13-14, 2:13).

SO WHAT?

As we go through life, we all face what somebody has called "defining moments." Often these come when some event forces us to halt everything and to take stock of where we are and where we are going. We might wait for the birth of a child, for example, but learn that the new baby has a physical or mental deformity that will change our lives forever. A person might lose a spouse in a car accident, learn that he or she has AIDS, or get a call in the middle of the night announcing that a teenage son has been arrested on a drug charge.

Sometimes the life-changing events are more positive. A healthy child is born to a couple who has had several miscarriages. A long-desired promotion comes through, or we get the cherished degree after years of education, only to face the question "What now?" Defining moments like these often lead people to counselors whose task is to give support, guidance, and sometimes a challenge or a gentle shove.

In one sense this chapter is at the core of the book and it points to an issue that is at the core of Christianity. It raises the question, "What do we do with Jesus Christ?" That question brings each of us, counselors and counselees, to a defining moment. How we answer, and even whether we answer, will have an impact for life and for all of eternity.

If we were to visit a shopping mall with clipboard in hand to ask a sample of Saturday shoppers how we can know God, the answers would be diverse. Some—scholars call them advocates of *pluralism*—would tell us that there are many ways to find God and that one route is as good as any other.

But the Bible presents a much different message. It teaches that there is only one way to know God and to find the salvation that we need. Because He is both "fully God and fully man," Jesus Christ is the only one who could represent both God and human beings and bring about our reconciliation. He is wholly unique and uniquely suited for the task of delivering all of us—that includes our counselees—from sin and evil. Because none of us is able to get free of the sin that enslaves us, God the Father sent His Son, Jesus Christ, who died in our place, paid for our sin, rose from the dead, and now offers us the gift of salvation. Like any gift, we can take it or leave it. God's gift remains available as long as we live on earth, but the Bible doesn't even hint that we will have a second chance to make the choice after death.

Later we will discuss the ultimate implications of accepting or rejecting God's offer of forgiveness for our sins and salvation from future punishment. The present implications for counseling are immense. While we live on this earth, both Christians and non-Christians will have problems and experience catastrophes (Matthew 5:45). The Christian has a source of inner peace, knowing that the Spirit is near and that Jesus Christ is in Heaven, at the Father's right hand, where He always lives to intercede for us (Philippians 4:5-7, Hebrews 1:3, 1 Peter 3:22).

Christian counselors have both the opportunity and the responsibility to tell counselees about the inner peace and the interpersonal peace that is available through faith in Christ. It is no less ethical to present a counselee with knowledge about Christ than it is to share information about some effective medication or established counseling method. In all cases the counselee can accept or reject the counselor's guidance. The introduction of Christian concepts (like the introduction of humanistic, new-age, or other ideas) is unethical only when counselees are pressured or manipulated to accept what they don't want to accept. Search the Scriptures and you will discover that no one was forced or tricked into accepting God's free gift of salvation, forgiveness of sin, abundant life on earth (John 10:10), and eternal life in Heaven (John 3:16).

We can avoid words like *reconciliation, justification,* and *redemption,* but often we, as counselors, are in a unique position to be gentle proclaimers of God's plan of salvation and to be a model of how Jesus Christ's life and work enables people to be reconciled to Him, to others, and even to themselves. By sharing and modeling these issues, we present others with types of choices for their "defining moments" and offer healing that no secular therapy can present.

On occasion, my mind goes back to Tony Campolo's speech at the Congress on Christian Counseling. Sometimes we do put too much of our time and energies into activities that have no lasting impact—activities like getting more stuff, exploring people's pasts, or listening while they repeat endless details of their hurts and frustrations. But there are times in life when all of us must bring life to a temporary halt and face life-altering decisions. Often these times occur among our counselees when they are in our counseling rooms. These are times when money or material goods mean nothing, when people in positions of power feel powerless, when the values of our age seem empty. These are times when we need to return to the core of Christianity and help people find Christ.

According to an oft-repeated story, the great theologian Karl Barth once was asked to state the essence of Christianity. The famous man was not inclined to use simple words, but he gave a simple answer—a response that can bring hope and comfort to all of us who live and counsel in this stress-filled world. The core of what we believe is this, Barth said, citing a children's song:

Jesus loves me, this I know,
For the Bible tells me so.

❖

CHAPTER EIGHT

Guilt and Forgiveness in Counseling

I'M NOT SURE when my interest in psychology and religion began, but it probably started with Mr. Nicholson, Mr. Green, and a local psychiatric hospital. Mr. Nicholson taught the introductory psychology course that I took as a freshman, but he mentioned religion only once in his lectures. When we discussed the history of mental illness, the teacher described how religious leaders in the middle ages had tortured emotionally disturbed people, blaming their hapless victims' pathologies on demons that needed to be driven from their minds and bodies.

Mr. Green was my former Sunday school teacher. I doubt that he ever read a psychology book, but he was nervous about my decision to attend a secular university, where he thought I might lose my faith. His fears intensified when he learned that I would be studying psychology. At the time, I wondered if this godly man was overly cautious, but his concerns first alerted me to conflicts between psychology and theology that I would encounter in the years ahead.

As a requirement for my first psychology course, students were expected to make weekly visits to the local psychiatric hospital. This was a smelly, noisy, and sometimes violent place in those days before the invention of psychotherapeutic drugs. I was appalled at the conditions, but fascinated by the people and especially interested in the patients who talked about God. Some seemed to think that they had committed the unpardonable sin, and occasionally a patient would sit at the ward piano and sing from a hymnbook that was identical to the ones we used in our church every Sunday.

Those early experiences aroused my thinking about the links between my Christian beliefs and my growing awareness of the findings of psychology. To my amazement, I discovered that whole books had been written on the subject of psychology and religion. I started buying them, reading them, and adding them to my library.

One of these early books had the intriguing title *Guilt: Where Religion and Psychology Meet.*[1] The author began with a discussion of hypocrisy—the tendency for many people to hide their real struggles, lusts, beliefs, and guilt behind a smiling mask of self-confidence, outward spirituality, and the pretense that all is well. In two sentences that sound remarkably contemporary, the book suggested that "our generation may be characterized as an age of *irresponsibility*. Rather than accepting our guilt for misdeeds, we rationalize our way out, blaming 'conditioned' causes; we attribute our behavior to our environment or heredity, or to our faulty training or lack of need-gratification."[2]

The author, David Belgum—a professor at the University of Iowa—wrote that while some guilty people are apprehended by an officer of the law, others are "caught by their own consciences" and inclined to punish themselves by "various forms of psychic and social misery." These people sometimes become *patients* looking for a therapist who can help them find insight. More often, Belgum wrote, they need to be *penitents* who should seek a minister to help them find forgiveness. We fail in our therapy, the author concluded, if we treat our clients solely as patients and fail to see that many are penitents who need to forsake their hypocrisy, humbly repent, confess their sins, experience God's grace and forgiveness, have opportunity to make restitution, and find encouragement to "go their way and sin no more." The author concluded that we need to do away with hypocrisy, the church's "greatest hurdle and barrier," and to build churches that are genuine fellowships of "the rescued and the rescuing."

If they had read the book, I think Mr. Green would have liked it but Mr. Nicholson might have wondered what all of this had to do with psychology. Looking back at my initial exposure to psychiatric patients, I am sure that some of the people in the hospital could have been helped by a therapy that recognized the role of guilt. I think David Belgum was right: Consideration of guilt really is the place where religion and psychology often meet.

WHAT IS GUILT?

Books and articles describe different types of guilt, but these can be grouped into two broad categories: *objective* guilt and *subjective* guilt. Objective guilt refers to the legal status of a person who has broken a law, committed a crime, or violated some standard. The lawbreaker *is* guilty, even if he or she doesn't feel guilty and even if the guilty person has never been caught. In contrast, subjective guilt refers to the emotions or inner feelings—most often feelings of remorse, regret, or self-condemnation—that come because of one's actions or thinking.[3]

Figure 8.1 shows how objective guilt and subjective guilt can be related. People in category one are guilty and they feel guilty. The drunken driver whose car kills a child, for example, is guilty before the law and often feels great sadness and remorse.

Figure 8.1
FOUR CATEGORIES OF GUILT

Objective Guilt
(What we have done or failed to do)

		We *are* guilty.	We are *not* guilty.
Subjective Guilt (How we feel)	We *feel* guilty.	I	II
	We do *not* feel guilty.	III	IV

People in category two have not done anything to break the law, but they still feel guilty. Sometimes these people appear in our counseling rooms, complaining that they feel shame and self-condemnation even when they know that they have done nothing wrong.

Category three describes people who are guilty of violating

some law but they don't feel any regret or contrition. You will be in this category when you next exceed the speed limit but feel no guilt about breaking the law because "everybody else was going fast."

Category four refers to people who haven't done anything wrong and they don't have any guilt feelings. Most often, counselors see people from the first two categories.

These four groups are important to remember as we now look more closely at both objective and subjective guilt.

THE FACT OF GUILT

Objective guilt—the fact that we have violated some law or standard—can be of several types. As we describe these, the types may seem distinct from one another, but in the lives of people, these types often overlap and sometimes merge.

Theological Guilt

We have seen that God created human beings in His own image so that we could have a relationship with Him and rule over His creation. He didn't make us to be mindless robots or instinct-driven animals. Instead He gave us the freedom to make choices. He instructed the first man and woman to abstain from eating the fruit that hung on the tree of good and evil. But Adam and Eve chose to disobey. They violated God's standards, broke His law, and immediately became guilty before their Creator.

This is *theological* guilt. It involves failure to obey God and breaking His commands. By his or her actions and/or thoughts, the theologically guilty person has pushed aside divine standards, disregarded God's authority, challenged His goodness, rejected His holy will, and dared to defy His truth and wisdom.

Viewed in this way, we can see why sin is so wrong and why guilt before God is so profound. Theological guilt, the result of sin, is much more serious than a reluctance to accept some church doctrinal statement. Theological guilt involves a failure to trust God, a deliberate resistance to His authority, and a decision to make ourselves the center of life and the source of our own fulfillment.[4] By turning against God and rejecting His truth, holiness, and sovereignty, we further breach our relationship with Him and are alienated from Him. Like Adam and Eve—who tried to hide from God following their sin

(Genesis 3:10)—human beings today often turn from God because they fear His reaction.

This description of human rebellion and guilt is not limited to a few theological rebels. According to the Bible, we are all guilty of theological guilt: "There is no one righteous, not even one" (Romans 3:10).

Please look once again at figure 8.1 (page 131). Since we are all guilty, nobody is in the "not guilty" categories two or four. Some of us recognize and feel remorse for our guilt (category one) while others do not (category two), but we are all guilty. As we have seen, the atoning death of Christ on the cross was to pay for our sin and ultimately to release us from theological guilt.

Legal Guilt

Probably this is the easiest type of guilt to understand. It involves a violation of the laws of the land in which we live. People break the law every day, although most offenders never get caught. Technically, these people are legally guilty, even if they never come to trial and despite the fact that they may feel no remorse. When offenders are caught and prosecuted, they can be released from the penalty of legal guilt by paying the cost, often in the form of a fine or prison sentence that a judge imposes in a court of law. Even when they are released, these people have a report of their actions "on their record," and sometimes it stays there for life.

It could be argued that legal guilt really is not separate from theological guilt. Christians are instructed to submit to governing authorities and to pay taxes. When we rebel against this human authority, we are also rebelling against what God has instituted and commanded (Romans 13:1-7). This leaves all of us in a dilemma if the governing authorities pass laws that are clearly in violation of Scripture. In those times, each of us must consider whether or not to submit or to follow the example of those early Christians who disregarded unjust local authorities and insisted, "We must obey God rather than men" (Acts 5:29).

Social Guilt

Following one of His sermons, Jesus was approached by a religious leader who asked Him to identify the greatest commandment in the law. The theologians who gathered around must have thought that they could pounce on the answer and accuse Jesus of error or heresy.

Instead He gave a clear and irrefutable summary: "Love the Lord your God with all your heart and with all your soul and with all your mind. . . . Love your neighbor as yourself" (Matthew 22:37-38—see also vv. 34-40).

The Bible is filled with instructions concerning the ways in which we should love God and love other people. The Ten Commandments, for example, can be divided into two groups—those that give instructions pertaining to God (the first four), and those that tell us how to relate to other people (Exodus 20:2-17, Deuteronomy 5:6-21).

Social guilt occurs when we mistreat and fail to show love to another human being. Sometimes this mistreatment is also a violation of the law. Child abuse, theft, assault, and murder, for example, all lead to social guilt that is also legal guilt. Sometimes, too, the mistreatment ignores scriptural directives concerning interpersonal relations. When we gossip, slander, spread rumors, show favoritism, ignore some person who has a need, refuse to show hospitality, or otherwise mistreat another person, for example, we are guilty of both social and theological guilt (Luke 10:25-37; Romans 1:29-30; 1 Timothy 5:13; James 2:1,16-17; 1 Peter 4:9). David's sexual sin with Bathsheba involved the selfish mistreatment of another human being and led to the death of her husband, but in his prayer of confession, David acknowledged that it was against God that he had sinned (Psalm 51:4). Whenever we mistreat human beings who are created by God in His own image, we are sinning against the Creator.

Very often, social guilt comes because we have broken an unwritten but culturally expected rule. If a person is rude, fails to respond to a formal invitation, or behaves in a socially inappropriate way at a party or business meeting, the offender has broken no formal law and may have no feelings of remorse. Nevertheless, the violator is socially guilty in the eyes of others.

Periodically, I visit other countries to give lectures or to lead seminars. On these trips, I seek to be sensitive to the local customs and expectations. Visitors soon learn, for example, that people bow to one another in Japan, use formal titles in parts of Europe, hug freely in Latin America, and sometimes eat rice with their fingers in India. If I make a cultural blunder during a visit overseas, invariably my hosts are kind enough to overlook my mistake, especially since they know that my errors are not deliberate. Even so, I still am guilty of a social *faux pas*.

If you are a frequent overseas traveler, you probably have cringed as you have watched tourists from your own country, dressed inappropriately, acting inappropriately in the host country, and going about their sightseeing blithely unaware and seemingly unconcerned about the ways in which their actions alienate and sometimes offend local residents. When we act or speak in socially inappropriate ways, we all demonstrate social guilt.

Psychological Guilt

Often a person is guilty of violating his or her own standards. At these times, the person may not have disobeyed God, broken no laws, nor violated any cultural standards, but he or she experiences guilt nevertheless.

Some time ago, my elderly mother accompanied us to our church. She is an alert, up-to-date, flexible lady, but she had some reservations about the idea of wearing slacks to church—even in a congregation where "dressing up" is not considered important. Wearing a pantsuit to a worship service violated no standard except that of my mother, who had always worn a dress to church. She felt guilty about the idea of wearing casual clothes and wondered if this might even be a little disrespectful to God.

Guilt that comes when we violate our internal personal standards brings us to the issue of *the conscience*. The conscience is an inner standard that monitors and enables us to evaluate every thought and action. The conscience directs as we make decisions in the present and as we evaluate what we have done or failed to do in the past. It is a set of guidelines that helps us determine what is good, bad, right, wrong, important, or irrelevant. And the conscience is an inner voice that accuses or excuses us because of what we have done or failed to do, and that sometimes brings feelings of guilt and an awareness that we need to repent.

Psychologist Lars Granberg has given a concise summary of the meaning and role of a person's conscience:

> The conscience aids in discerning what is right and good
> from what is inferior, wrong, and bad; and encourages
> decisions that are right and good or, where there is conflict,
> that follow the higher norm. It [the conscience] is char-
> acterized by a sense of obligation. When its promptings
> are ignored or set aside the person feels guilty, a complex

experience including a sense of judgment, unworthiness, self-depreciation and estrangement from God, others and self (Ps. 32:4); and which is relieved only by forgiveness extended and accepted.[5]

Every counselor knows that the conscience of one person can differ from the conscience of another. Recently, I met with a young Christian college student who had impregnated his girlfriend and was feeling tremendous guilt. My counselee considered himself to be guilty before God, guilty in the eyes of his family and church, and guilty for having violated the purity of his female friend. He was not legally guilty (it is not against the law to get one's girlfriend pregnant), but he had theological, social, and personal guilt all merged together. As we talked, he mentioned that he had ignored his conscience originally and that now his conscience was making him feel guilty because of his sexual behavior.

During the week that the student and I first met, a national news magazine described the behavior of a group of high school boys who had formed an informal pact to see who could have sexual intercourse with the greatest number of different girls. The winner boasted that he had scored sixty-three points and explained that he bought condoms "by the boxload." His parents were surprised but apparently not distressed. When he talked to reporters, this young man showed no evidence that his actions violated his conscience. Probably he would have been surprised at the guilt expressed by my counselee.

How do we account for differences like these? To answer, we must look at both the psychological and the theological explanations about how a person's conscience is formed. Psychological writers have different theories about conscience formation, but most agree that our consciences are shaped mainly by experiences, especially those that come early in life. We learn about right and wrong from our parents. We internalize the standards and cultural expectations of the societies, neighborhoods, and families in which we are raised. As these early experiences become a part of us, we form our own worldviews and we accept certain standards and mores as being the "right way to do things." Later in life these early formulations may be refined and sometimes changed, but each person is assumed to draw from the culture to create and sometimes to remold his or her own conscience.[6]

The Bible presents a different perspective. According to Romans 2:15, God's standards of right and wrong are "written on the human heart." These are built-in, universal, moral absolutes that form the basis of the conscience and that can guide all human beings—even those who know nothing about Christianity—to behavior that is consistent with the laws of God.

This implanted conscience is not pure and unadulterated, however. Like everything else, our consciences have been distorted by the Fall. Presumably through prior learning and repeated disobedience, consciences can become corrupted and so dull that they lose their sensitivity to distinguish good from evil (1 Timothy 4:2, Titus 1:15). Sometimes a conscience can be overly sensitive or so weak that it fails to serve as an accurate guide for behavior (1 Corinthians 8:4-8,10,12). In a person who sins consistently, the conscience continues to deteriorate and eventually it fails to have any impact at all.

But the conscience can also be renewed. The biblical writers spoke about having the guilty conscience cleansed by Christ (Hebrews 10:22), about keeping the conscience clear (Acts 24:16, 1 Corinthians 4:4, 2 Timothy 1:3, Hebrews 13:18), and about having a "good conscience" that is accompanied by a pure heart and a sincere faith (1 Timothy 1:5). Luther once stated that his conscience was "captive to the Word of God." By his consistent study of the Bible, Luther had sought to fill his mind with divine standards so that his conscience was informed and molded by Scripture.

All of this has several practical implications for counselors. First, we can't always "let our conscience be our guide" because the conscience often is shaped by values and experiences that directly violate God's standards. Often the conscience is not clear about how we should react in complex moral decisions. But even with these imperfections, our consciences should not be ignored, because these have been given by God to guide our behavior. If the conscience persuades a person that something is sinful, he or she should avoid that behavior, even if it is never mentioned in Scripture or in the laws of the land (Romans 14:23).

Christians sometimes disagree about what is appropriate or inappropriate behavior. In the early church, for example, there were different opinions about whether or not believers should eat meat that had been offered to idols. "Don't eat it if doing so would violate your conscience," the believers were told, in essence. But what if some who had abstained thought about it or discussed it with a spiritual counselor and concluded that eating the meat was really acceptable after all? On issues that are not specifically addressed in Scripture, our viewpoints, and thus our consciences, can change as a result of reflection or further information.

In our society, Christians don't worry about meat offered to idols, but they do struggle with issues like whether or not one can remarry after a divorce, whether social drinking is acceptable, whether masturbation is always wrong, or whether or not a person should ever seek counseling from a nonChristian therapist. All of this suggests that the conscience can be informed or educated, but the principle of Romans 14 still persists. We should never encourage a counselee to act in violation of his or her conscience.

Finally, we should fill our minds with ideas and biblical truths that lead to a cleansed, clear, and mature conscience.

Once again, Granberg is helpful:

> A mature Christian conscience is furthered by sound instruc-
> tion in the Bible, an open and supportive climate of inquiry
> which encourages honest expression of opinion and thought-
> ful appraisal of experience, good adult models after whom to
> pattern oneself, and a grasp both of the reality of forgiveness
> and the proper fruit of repentance: getting up and going on
> without wallowing in self recrimination.[7]

THE FEELINGS OF GUILT

When guilt is talked about, I suspect that most people think about the uncomfortable feelings that come when we have done something we think is wrong or when we have failed to do something we should have done. Almost everybody knows what we mean by guilt feelings because we've all had them. They can involve a cauldron of self-condemnation, regret, shame, low self-esteem, discouragement, and remorse, often mixed with anxiety, a desire to withdraw, and the fear of punishment.

These feelings can be strong or weak. Usually they are unpleasant, but they aren't always bad. Sometimes they are warnings, alerting us internally to the fact that something is wrong. Often these guilt feelings motivate us to change or to make restitution. Frequently, however, they inhibit us, drag us down, mire us in self-denunciation, and sometimes lead to a "what's the use?" attitude that discourages us from making changes.

Appropriate Versus Inappropriate Guilt Feelings

At times it is appropriate to feel guilty. If I have broken a law, disobeyed a biblical teaching, harmed another human being, acted insensitively in a social situation, or violated the dictates of my conscience, there is nothing wrong with my feeling guilty. This especially is true if the guilt feelings are in proportion to the seriousness of what I have done and if the guilt feelings motivate me to make positive changes in my life.

In contrast to these appropriate guilt feelings, inappropriate guilt feelings are out of proportion to what one has done and often they don't lead to any behavior changes. Serial killers like John Wayne Gacy or Jeffrey Dahmer attract media attention because of their dramatic and horrendous crimes, but reporters notice that repeat offenders often show no sense of remorse and few feelings of guilt. "You had better not let me go free," a convicted murderer said recently. "If that happens, I know that I will kill people again."

In contrast to people who show an inappropriate lack of guilt even after committing terrible crimes, others carry tremendous burdens of remorse and shame following some minor and seemingly insignificant action. Counselors see these guilt-laden people frequently. Their guilt is inappropriately heavy in view of the apparent causes.

Intense guilt feelings may be self-created in people who consistently fail to live up to their own, sometimes impossible, standards. More often, however, guilt feelings come because of the comments or judgments of other people. If a parent repeatedly tells a son that he is stupid, for example, the young man may feel guilty whenever he brings home a B on his report card. If a pastor preaches that "really dedicated Christians" spend at least one hour every day in Bible study and prayer, a whole congregation of people may feel guilty because their schedules won't let them live up to the expected standard.

Healthy Versus Unhealthy Guilt Feelings

Let's assume that you are driving your car along a city street on a winter day and happen to hit an unexpected patch of ice on the road. Your car skids into a parked car and dents the fender. Those of us who live in northern climates call these accidents winter fender-benders. People don't usually get hurt in fender-benders, and everybody knows that often they cannot be prevented. Their major annoyance is inconvenience and the high costs of repairs.

If a fender-bender happened to you, a healthy response would be to acknowledge your frustration with the situation, to apologize to the owner of the other car, and to take whatever action is needed to file the appropriate police report and to initiate repairs. In contrast, an unhealthy response would be to condemn and berate yourself, apologize profusely, tell others how clumsy and stupid you are, and conclude that you are a terrible driver.

Unhealthy guilt feelings leave us wallowing in remorse, self-pity, and self-condemnation. Healthy guilt feelings can also lead to remorse, but in addition, they motivate a person to confess his or her faults, to make restitution if necessary, to find forgiveness, and to move on with life. In 2 Corinthians 7:10, Paul calls this godly sorrow. It is a healthy guilt that motivates us to change. It brings repentance and restoration.

Peter showed this healthy guilt following his denial of Christ (Matthew 26:75). After realizing what he had done, Peter wept bitterly, and surely he felt deep remorse, sincere repentance, and a genuine desire to change. But he didn't stay in the grips of guilt. He confessed his sin, knew that he was forgiven, and experienced freedom from his feelings of guilt.

FORGIVENESS: THE REMEDY FOR GUILT

When Jesus taught His followers to pray, He included the well-known phrase, "Forgive us our debts, as we also have forgiven our debtors." This is the only part of the Lord's Prayer that was followed by a commentary. "For if you forgive men when they sin against you, your heavenly Father will also forgive you. But if you do not forgive men their sins, your Father will not forgive your sins" (Matthew 6:12,14-15). Forgiveness clearly has two sides. We need to receive forgiveness and to extend forgiveness to others.

Receiving Forgiveness
How are most of us inclined to react when we are wronged or treated unfairly? The human tendency, it seems, is to get even, to seek revenge, to insist on our rights, to demand restitution, and failing

that, to bear a grudge and to dwell on the injustice that made us victims. Forgiveness seems low on the human list of alternatives, and it never enters many people's minds.

In sharp contradiction to this, God always is willing to show mercy and to pardon freely. In one of the clearest Old Testament statements on forgiveness, we learn that God's ways are not like ours and neither does He think as we do. Because He is just, He has every reason to reject, disown, and condemn us; but because of His love and mercy, He freely forgives any who forsake their wicked ways, turn to Him, and ask for pardon (Isaiah 55:6-9).

An important digression. In his book *More Than Redemption* Jay Adams raises an important question. If believers have been forgiven for their sins, once-for-all, because of Christ's death and resurrection, why do we need to confess sin and seek forgiveness *again*?[8] In raising this issue, Adams points to the Westminster Confession of Faith, chapter XI, "Justification," section 5:

> God doth continue to forgive the sins of those that are justified; and, although they can never fall from the state of justification, yet they may, by their sins, fall under God's fatherly displeasure, and not have the light of His countenance restored unto them, until they humble themselves, confess their sins, beg pardon and renew their faith and repentance.

When He gave us the Lord's Prayer in Matthew 6, Jesus was talking to people who were already "in a state of justification." They were people who had confessed their sinfulness and acknowledged that Jesus Christ was the Savior and Lord of their lives. These people, in other words, were believers. They had been adopted into God's family and could call God their "Father." (The Father is referred to repeatedly in Matthew 6.) Because they had put their faith in Christ, the people to whom Jesus spoke were eternally forgiven, just like believers today are forgiven once-for-all. Adams calls this *judicial forgiveness*. God, the ultimate judge, forgives believers unconditionally.

This judicial forgiveness differs from *parental forgiveness*. We might call this fatherly displeasure. When we experience judicial forgiveness we are adpoted into God's family as His sons and daughters. But sometimes family members displease a parent and need to say that they are sorry for what they have done. This sin, by a believer, does not get us kicked out of the family[9] but it does lead to strained relationships with the Father until we confess what we have done, express our remorse, resubmit to the Father, and determine to avoid such sin again in the future.

Adams notes, correctly, that there is confusion among counselors when they fail to distinguish between judicial forgiveness that frees us from an eternity separated from God and parental forgiveness that allows believers who have strayed from the Father to find forgiveness and return to full fellowship. "While there are obvious similarities, we must be careful also to observe the great difference between judicial and parental forgiveness," writes Adams. "Few things . . . are more important for biblical counselors to grasp. Their views on this point are altogether crucial for proper counseling."[10]

Once a person has received judicial forgiveness, how does he or she receive parental forgiveness? To answer we must consider three words: *confession*, *repentance*, and *restitution*.

Confession. To confess one's sin to God is to acknowledge honestly what one has done (or failed to do) and to express agreement with God's standards of right and wrong. In the Bible, confession of sin is absolutely necessary before one can experience God's forgiveness and know the sense of psychological and physical liberation that can follow (Psalm 32:3-5, 1 John 1:8-9).

Confession must be to God, but what about confessing to others? When he confessed his sin to God, David presumably was in the presence of another human being (2 Samuel 12), and in James 5:16 we are instructed to confess our sins to one another and to pray together. Historically, the Roman Catholic church has required church members to confess to a priest, but the Protestant reformers resisted this and argued that each person should confess directly to God without priestly or other human intervention.

Only God is able to forgive, and since all sin is against Him, He is the one to whom we must confess. Often, however, there can be great therapeutic value in verbalizing our sins to fellow believers. When we tell somebody else, we often feel less isolated and frequently another person can hold us accountable so that we will be less likely to sin again. When we confess to a person we have wronged, the process of psychological healing can be facilitated when we are forgiven by that other person as well as by God. The man who is unfaithful to his wife, for example, has his relationship to God repaired when he confesses his sin, but that same man is unlikely to sense complete inner healing until he confesses the adultery to his wife and seeks to restore the broken relationship with her.

Repentance. Psychologist Bruce Narramore has noticed that many people go through repeated cycles of sin, guilt feelings, confession, temporary relief, then more sin, and another move around the cycle. Some people, according to Narramore, use 1 John 1:9 as "a kind of psychological spot remover for emotional guilt." There is no determination or expectation that one will change. As soon as the offender experiences the relief of being forgiven by God, he or she feels free to sin again and the cycle is repeated.[11]

This raises an important question: Is confession really genuine if a person does not, at the same time, express sincere sorrow for the sin, determine to change his or her behavior, and resolve to avoid repeating the sin in the future? When Jesus forgave the woman caught in the act of adultery, He instructed her to leave her life of sin (John 8:11). Proverbs 28:13 states that the person who finds mercy is the one who *confesses and renounces* his or her sins.

Some people have suggested that confession and repentance are like two sides of the same coin. One doesn't mean much without the other. Sometimes the Scriptures tell people to confess their sins, and at other times they are told to repent—which seems to mean much the same thing. David's confession was genuine because he repented by expressing genuine sorrow for his sins. He determined to avoid similar sin in the future, he took the responsibility of caring for Bathsheba, and apparently he never again committed adultery.

But what about those people who seem addicted to their sinful ways—people like a young man who is hooked on pornography or a person who gets drunk, feels deep remorse, but then gets drunk again? These people may confess their sins with genuine remorse, and they may determine "never to let it happen again." But if you are a counselor asking if they really think they can avoid a relapse into their repetitious sin, probably both would say no. Based on their past record, repeated sin is likely.

Despite this discouraging prognosis, the confession and repentance of these people can still be genuine, if they really do want to change and if they believe that God has the power to free them from their repetitious sin.

None of us can guarantee that we will be able to confess our sins, repent, then sin no more. We are all sinners, as long as we walk this earth, but Jesus Christ forgives, and over time, He enables us to live lives that are less and less entangled by sinful thoughts, actions, and addictions (1 John 1:8–2:1). When Peter asked how many times we should forgive, Jesus said "not seven times but seventy times seven." In other words, Jesus was saying that we should forgive without limitation (Matthew 18:21-22).

Restitution. Do you remember the story of Zacchaeus, the tax collector who scurried up a sycamore tree because he was too short to see Jesus in the midst of the crowd? When He got to the tree, Jesus stopped, told Zacchaeus to come down, and together they went to the tax collector's house. This simple event got all the local tongues wagging because Jesus had gone to be the guest of a man who apparently was a crook.

The events that followed must have amazed everybody. Zacchaeus repented, gave half of his possessions to the poor, and promised to pay back four-fold all the money he had stolen by cheating (Luke 19:1-10).

Zacchaeus didn't have to pay back these people in order to be forgiven. God's forgiveness is a free gift that cannot be bought. But can you imagine how the local people would have reacted if the tax collector had announced that he was a follower of Jesus while keeping all the stolen money?

Forgiveness always involves a cost to somebody. When you sincerely forgive, you give up all thoughts of getting revenge or of demanding restitution. Your act of forgiveness has cost you something. You have given up the right to get even and have let God take care of bringing justice (Romans 12:17-19). In a somewhat similar fashion, Christ is able to forgive our sin because of the incredible price that He paid when He willingly gave His life at Calvary.

How does this relate to making restitution?

First, if a person has broken the law and is legally guilty, he or she may have no alternative about paying for the offense. The Old Testament law required thieves and others to make restitution for their crimes or failures (Exodus 22:3-6,12; Leviticus 5:16; 6:5; 22:14; 24:18), and murderers were expected to pay by being put to death (Leviticus 24:21). Today, law courts demand that legal offenders pay for their wrongs by going to jail, by paying a fine, or sometimes by being put to death. Forgiveness for sins does not do away with legal justice.

Second, when we have wronged another person who has forgiven us, it is a natural response to express gratitude by making restitution. God does not require this because Christ has already paid for the cost of our redemption. But like Zacchaeus, often the forgiven and grateful person is inclined to make things right. In his criticisms of the Roman Catholic confessional, Luther noted that forgiveness from a priest often avoids the penitent person's deepest problem—a broken relationship.[12] If a man publicly criticizes his business partner but goes to a priest or to God to confess the sin, the man may come away knowing that he has been forgiven by God, but the interpersonal tension remains until the critical man takes some action to make restitution to his partner and to work at restoring their relationship.

Third, it is clear to counselors that making restitution often helps people accept the reality of their forgiveness. Psychiatrist Mansell Pattison has distinguished between what he calls the reconciliation and the punishment models of forgiveness. In *reconciliation*, the forgiven person goes to the one he or she has wronged and seeks to make things right. If I steal your wallet and then seek your forgiveness, I must give back everything I have taken. This is not because your forgiveness depends on my returning the wallet, but because I want to restore what belongs to you, and I know that by making restitution our relationship is likely to be rebuilt.

Sometimes, however, making restitution or demanding restitution become forms of self-punishment. The offender, for example, might continually try to undo or to make up for the wrong that has been done. This is an attempt to make oneself feel better, but often the offender never feels that the debt has been paid—or even can be paid. Sometimes the wronged person is the one who continually makes demands of the offender. The wife who repeatedly reminds her husband of his one act of unfaithfulness, for example, leaves him feeling that he never will be able to make restitution for the wrong that she never forgets or forgives. He keeps trying, but he never feels successful.

This brings us to the issue of forgiveness between people.

Forgiving Others
On the day that he resigned from the Presidency of the United States, Richard Nixon gave a farewell speech to his staff. "Always

remember," the former President said, "others may hate you, but those that hate you don't win unless you hate them, and then you destroy yourself."[13]

Researchers Michael McCullough and Everett Worthington concisely define forgiveness as a complex combination of "effective, cognitive, and behavioral phenomena in which negative affect and judgment toward the offender are reduced, not by denying one's right to such affect and judgment, but by viewing the offender with compassion, benevolence, and love, while realizing the offender has no right to them." In their research studies of forgiveness, McCullough and Worthington were able to demonstrate that forgiveness can lead to restored relationships and to restored peace of mind for both parties. When people forgive, there are decreased feelings of revenge, more positive feelings between everyone involved, and more efforts to bring conciliation.[14] Richard Nixon was right: When you hate others and refuse to forgive, you are the one who really loses in the end. When there is forgiveness between people, the forgiver and the offender both benefit.

It is not surprising that Jesus instructed His followers to forgive repeatedly (Luke 17:4). On another occasion, He spoke with disapproval about the servant who was forgiven a large debt but then refused to forgive the much smaller debt of a fellow servant (Matthew 18:23-35).

Why, then, do we so often refuse to forgive others or fail to forgive ourselves? And why do some people conclude that it is impossible for them to extend forgiveness to others who have hurt them deeply, even though Jesus commanded us to forgive (Mark 11:25)? These complex questions do not have simple answers. The reasons for our reluctance to forgive may be as varied as people themselves, writes Eastern College professor Allen Guelzo. He suggests that for many people the problem is not that they cannot or will not forgive. Instead, the stumbling block is a fear of what the act of forgiving might cost.[15]

When we forgive, we let go of our resentment at being wronged. The person who has been hurt often senses the pain and injustice and then goes through a period of anger, resentment, and hatred. This rarely disappears overnight. More often we can expect the ability to forgive to come only as we spend time in prayer over the hurt, often discussing it with another human being, "patiently pushing aside its incessant demand for attention, and watching it shrink slowly and fitfully into remission."[16] Ideally, in time we will be able to show trust to the offender, as Jesus trusted Peter after he was forgiven for his denials.

Do we extend forgiveness to the person who is not repentant, who does not think he or she needs to be forgiven, or who doesn't care whether you or anybody else offers forgiveness for anything? Luke 17:3 states that if a brother repents we should forgive him, but what do we do if he doesn't repent? When He was on the cross, Jesus prayed that His persecutors would be forgiven even though there is no evidence that they showed repentance (Luke 23:34).

The question of whether to forgive the unrepentant person has led to considerable debate between those who argue that we need to forgive for our own mental health and those who maintain that since God doesn't forgive non-repentant people, we are not required to forgive them either.[17] There are committed believers on both sides of this debate, and each side backs its conclusions with biblical support. Perhaps we could all agree, however, that "if we want to know the power of the Cross, if we want to see whether that Cross still has the power to change lives today, if we want to know what the forgiveness of our sins really means and what it really cost, then we will know those things only as we forgive."[18]

In a file cabinet someplace, I have an old copy of *Time* magazine that shows a picture of Pope John Paul sitting in a prison cell talking with the man who fired the shots in Saint Peter's Square that almost ended the Catholic leader's life. The magazine article described the pope's journey to express forgiveness to the man who had tried to be an assassinator. Apparently the pope genuinely forgave this man, but that did not mean that he was released from prison. In this life, we often have to pay for our illegal and sinful actions, even when we have been forgiven by God and by others and have forgiven ourselves. Only God is able to forgive, pardon, and choose to remember our sins no more (Isaiah 43:25)—all at the same time. But in the light of eternity, God's forgiveness is all that really matters.

SO WHAT?

The recovery movement has reminded us often about the Twelve Steps of recovery that were developed by the founders of Alcoholics Anonymous (AA). The words *guilt, forgiveness, confession, repentance*, or *restitution* rarely appear in Twelve Step statements, but they are all implied. People agree to admit that they are power-less, that they must "turn our will and our lives over to the care of God," that each person must take a "searching and fearless moral" self-inventory, that they admit "to God, to ourselves, and to another human being the exact nature of our wrongs," followed by actions that make amends for wrongs that have been done.

Alcoholics Anonymous began in 1934, and its influence has grown and spread ever since, especially with our recent fascination with issues of recovery, addiction, codependency, and twelve step programs for growth. Believers in recovery programs proclaim the effectiveness and biblical basis of these steps, but critics see dangers and weaknesses along with the benefits. Pattison, for example, has suggested that continued affiliation with AA-type groups can lead to a denial of responsibility, shared group guilt, and continued neurotic attempts to undo wrongs or to engage in rescue fantasies.[19]

Experienced counselors are well aware that many people take good approaches to treatment or valid biblical concepts and distort these. Twelve step programs designed to overcome addictions and to help people handle guilt can turn into neurotic affiliations with recovery groups. Confession of sin, which can accompany repent-ance and bring both restitution and reconciliation, also can become an unhealthy "compulsion to confess" over and over again, so that the confessor sometimes wallows in self-denigration and never bothers to make changes or to experience forgiveness. Some people may freely accept the forgiveness of God, but refuse to forgive them-selves or stubbornly resist forgiving others, all the while continuing to demand that the offenders make atonement in some way. Others become perfectionists who make impossible demands on themselves and on others and who feel guilty or make others feel guilty about the inevitable failures that follow.

Directly or indirectly, all of these issues are tied to misunder-standings or misinterpretations of the issues of biblical and psycho-logical teachings about guilt and forgiveness. To help counselees deal effectively with guilt-related issues, Christian counselors must remember the differences between objective guilt—which is theo-logical, legal, social, and/or psychological—and subjective guilt feelings.

We need to appreciate the impact of the conscience in the lives of our counselees and know the differences between appropriate and inappropriate, healthy and unhealthy guilt. And we need to know how people can be helped to receive forgiveness and to extend forgiveness to others. If we remain unaware of these differences, we are unlikely to really understand or to help the people who come to us with guilt-related issues and who need to find genuine forgiveness.

Surely guilt *is* the place where religion and psychology are most likely to meet, and it is over issues of guilt that theologians and psychologists have some of their greatest disagreements. All of these issues are complex when we discuss them in a book, but they can be even more complicated when we deal with them in our counseling.

Sometimes, however, a recognition of guilt leads to encouraging and remarkable transformation in our counselees. Without revealing details, a counselor recently told me about one of his counselees who had been a victim of severe physical abuse from her father. When she reached adulthood, the young woman harbored intense anger and resentment toward her father. Everybody agreed that she had reason to be angry, but the refusal to forgive apparently was causing a host of physical problems that physicians were unable to treat successfully. One day, in the midst of great frustration, she talked about her situation with a group of Christian friends. They, in turn, prayed with her, helped her to see that her spirit of revenge was creating physical and emotional problems, and encouraged her to ask God to help her forgive. Reluctantly at first, the woman agreed to take a new look at her situation. In time she was genuinely able to forgive her father. In the six months that followed she became symptom free.

Dealing with guilt and learning to forgive are not automatic routes to physical and psychological healing. But my friend's story shows that modern counselees, like King David of old, can find healing and relief when they deal with the sin, guilt, and lack of forgiveness in their own lives. At some time, almost every Christian counselor sees cases like this where an understanding of guilt and forgiveness are of great importance.

In dealing with these and other many-faceted human problems, counselors need the guidance and support of the divine Counselor whom Jesus promised a few days before the crucifixion. This brings us to the Person and work of the Holy Spirit.

CHAPTER NINE

The Holy Spirit and Counseling

DURING THE FIRST YEARS of World War II, the people of Kassel, Germany, lived with a false sense of security. Their city of 250,000 people was located near the mountains, surrounded by green fields, grazing cattle, and flowering trees, but showed little evidence of the gigantic and thriving industrial complex that was hidden underground. Day after day, the Allied bombers passed overhead but not a bomb fell on Kassel.

All of that changed on the night of October 12, 1943. Without warning, one thousand American B-17 bombers flew over the city and dropped their deadly cargo. Twenty minutes later they were gone, but 91 percent of central Kassel was burning or smoldering in ruins. Seventy-four percent of the entire city had been destroyed, and 38,000 lives had come to an abrupt end. Less than two years later, when the U.S. Army swept through Germany near the end of the war, the people of Kassel resisted with vehemence. The ground bombardment was devastating—adding further destruction to the once peaceful and beautiful city.

It is easy to imagine how the people responded when four college kids from Hollywood stepped from a train at the bomb-damaged station of Kassel in the summer of 1950. Deeply committed and enthusiastic Christians, they had come to participate in an international youth camp. This foursome was filled with hope and youthful idealism. They believed with all their hearts that their efforts could bring some help and reconciliation to the ravaged community.

But they were not welcome. Five years after the war, Kassel was inhabited with people who struggled to survive. They had no running water or indoor plumbing, and many still had no roofs over their heads. Their meager possessions included faded photographs of loved ones who had died in the destruction inflicted by Americans—people from the country of these four who dared to walk through the battered city streets.

The little group was headed by a quiet and compassionate man named Ralph Hamburger. He had been born in Germany, but his family had escaped to Holland when Hitler's Brown Shirts discovered that Ralph's father was a Jew. During the war, Ralph worked with the Dutch underground, helping Jews and others escape from Nazi persecution. When he moved to California following the armistice, the young immigrant was filled with hatred for the German people whose leaders had caused such suffering. "I don't know a single person among all of my associates who doesn't hate as I have been hating," Ralph told a friend shortly after arriving in the United States. But Christ slowly released him from this bondage of hatred and turned his heart toward going back to the land of his birth to be available and even expendable as a servant of Jesus Christ in a war-torn land. Could Ralph Hamburger have known, during that difficult summer of 1950, that he would spend his whole life guided by a consuming passion for ministering to the people in Eastern Europe?[1]

I knew none of this when I met Ralph Hamburger in Frankfurt late in 1988. He was to serve as my host and guide on a speaking trip to Novi Sad and Osijek, cities in what then was Yugoslavia. Never before had I met a man with such a servant's heart. His goal was to be available to those of us who would come together on the speaking team. Immediately, I sensed his compassion, sensitivity, and genuine humility, which I would come to appreciate more and more in the days ahead. Here was an unassuming man who nevertheless appeared to be known and respected wherever we went.

I can't prove it scientifically and there are no psychological tests to support my conclusion, but surely only one explanation can account for the transformation of that anger-filled European immigrant who arrived in Hollywood after the war but who spent many of his adult years as a minister to people suffering behind an iron curtain. Ralph Hamburger met God and was changed. The Holy Spirit worked in his life, molding him more and more into a man who, still today, continues to touch others in quiet but powerful ways.

THE IMPORTANCE OF THE HOLY SPIRIT

When I was growing up in Canada, I attended a church where missions were emphasized, where the youth programs were good, and where the Bible was taught. That church was an island of stability for me during some difficult teenage years, but in thinking back, I can't remember anybody ever talking about the Holy Spirit.

Across town, a large Pentecostal congregation worshiped enthusiastically and the church leaders talked often about the Holy Spirit. In our church, we saw these brothers and sisters as fellow believers, but we tended to think that their worship was too emotional so we didn't get together with them very often. In retrospect, I think my early training left the impression that the Holy Spirit was for hand-clapping charismatics but not of much relevance for people like me.

Nothing could be further from the truth. Like God the Father and Jesus Christ the Son, the Holy Spirit is God. He is alive, in the world today, living within each believer (Romans 8:9,11), and one Person of the Trinity who has come to be with us forever (John 14:16,26; 15:26; 16:7). In the original biblical text, the Holy Spirit is given the name *Paraclete*. This term has rich meaning and has been translated as the English words *comforter, helper,* or *advocate.* Others use the word *counselor*, which is the term that we will use throughout this chapter.[2] All of these English words are accurate, although none is broad enough to convey what the original word means or the importance of what the Holy Spirit really does.

Millard Erickson suggested that the Holy Spirit is of special significance to contemporary people. Since He lives and is active within the lives of believers, He is the one Person in the Trinity who is closest to us. God may seem faraway in Heaven, and Jesus Christ may appear to be removed from us by history, but the Holy Spirit is here today, working in our lives, in our churches, and in our world.[3] Since He dwells within each believer, the Holy Spirit guides and transforms us from the inside out.

As westerners, we live in a culture and time of history that stresses participation, active lifestyles, and experience. Hand clapping, enthusiastic singing, and involvement are no longer confined to churches that some would describe as being too emotional. Even in traditional churches, many people innately resist worship that is mostly cerebral, abstract, habitual, and seemingly far removed from real life. Instead, worshipers want to sense God's presence and relevance, and they want to be able to respond with enthusiasm.

From this we should not conclude that most people want an excitement-based, emotional religion overflowing with zeal but lacking logical reasons for believing. We know that emotions change quickly and that feelings can be unreliable guides to truth. But neither do modern church-goers want a dead orthodoxy that has no place for feelings and no recognition that we are people who can know God experientially. God's Spirit enables us to know Him better and to feel His presence. And He enables us to experience the profound joy that comes to the followers of Jesus Christ.

Regardless of our preferred worship styles, all Christians need to know and understand the work of the Holy Spirit, God's divine Counselor. But knowing Him is not easy. The Bible tells us less about the Holy Spirit than about God the Father or about Jesus Christ the Son. The Holy Spirit does not call attention to Himself but, instead, guides and supports believers as we worship and pray to the Father in the name of the Son. To people who live in an age of technology where they are most inclined to believe in what they can see or touch, the Holy Spirit seems vague and hard to grasp intellectually. The result has been confusion, misunderstanding, and sometimes a tendency to go on living as if the Holy Spirit did not exist.

Erickson has written that "on the popular or lay level, the doctrine of the Holy Spirit has been the most controversial of all doctrines" during the period in which we live.[4] To reduce disagreements and conflicts between believers, to clarify our understanding, to facilitate spiritual growth, and to improve our counseling effectiveness, Christians need to know who the Holy Spirit is and what He is doing in our lives and in our world—even as you read these words.[5]

When you think of a spirit or a ghost, what comes to mind? Perhaps you think of a spooky apparition or a fear-inducing phantom creature like the three ghosts that confronted stingy old Scrooge in Dickens' famous *Christmas Carol*. Some may think of a spirit as being some kind of an abstract mystical or impersonal force to influence you or to be largely irrelevant to life. It is easy to hold these kinds of mental images about the Holy Spirit, especially when we remember that He sometimes is referred to as the Holy Ghost.[6]

The Bible makes it clear, however, that the Holy Spirit is neither an apparition nor a thing. The Holy Spirit is both God and a Person.

The Holy Spirit Is God

For four reasons we can conclude that the Holy Spirit is God. First, He is called God (2 Corinthians 3:17-18) and in several places the words *Holy Spirit* and *God* are used interchangeably (compare 1 Corinthians 3:16-17 with 6:19-20, or Acts 5:3 with 5:4).

Second, the Holy Spirit does things that only God can do. The Spirit was active in creation (Genesis 1:2). He brought about the conception of God's Son in the womb of a virgin (Luke 1:35), inspired the biblical writers (2 Peter 1:21), and brings the new birth (John 3:3-8).

Third, the Holy Spirit has divine attributes. For example, He is described as being eternal (Hebrews 9:14), all powerful (Job 42:2), all knowing (1 Corinthians 2:10-11), present everywhere (Psalm 139:7), and holy (Romans 1:4).

Fourth, the Bible uses language that links the Spirit with the Father and the Son. This suggests that all three are equal (2 Corinthians 13:14, 1 Peter 1:2). The best known example of this is in the Great Commission that Jesus gave to His followers before returning to Heaven. He told them, and us, "to make disciples of all nations, baptizing them in the name of the Father and of the Son and of the Holy Spirit" (Matthew 28:19).

The Holy Spirit Is a Person

If we had the time or inclination to look at all biblical references to the Holy Spirit, we soon would conclude that these verses are not describing a vague and hard-to-comprehend entity. The Holy Spirit has the characteristics of personhood.

The Bible shows, for example, that the Holy Spirit has traits that people have. He has self-awareness, referring to Himself as "I" and "me" (Acts 13:2), and He has intelligence (1 Corinthians 2:10-12). We learn in 1 Corinthians 12:11 that He has a will. The fact that we can grieve or bring Him sorrow suggests that the Holy Spirit has emotions (Ephesians 4:30).

The Holy Spirit also does things that people do. We know, for example, that He teaches (John 14:26), convicts people of guilt and sin (John 16:7-9), intercedes for believers (Romans 8:26), and gives testimony (Romans 8:16). In one of his letters, Paul wrote about a decision that "seemed good to the Holy Spirit and to us" (Acts 15:28). By linking the Holy Spirit together with humans, the biblical writer assumed that God's Spirit has qualities and capabilities that are similar to those found in people.

The same conclusion is possible when we see that the Holy Spirit sometimes is treated as people are treated. He is lied to (Acts 5:3), resisted (Acts 7:51), insulted (Hebrews 10:29), and at other times obeyed (Acts 10:19-21).

Even though the Holy Spirit has these marks of a person, the Bible does not describe Him in the same detail that is used to give us a picture of the Father or the Son. References to the Spirit abound, especially in the New Testament, but He is rarely mentioned apart from His ministry and work.

Before we turn to consider this work, however, we must remember that the Holy Spirit, God's Counselor, is one with the Father and Son. Even so, the Spirit lives within us and has an ongoing personal relationship with believers, including those of us who are human counselors. We have the security of knowing that we are not alone or dependent on some faraway God. He is closer than any human being, and as we will see, He guides and helps us, even when we face difficult decisions or must work with hard-to-help counselees.

THE WORK OF THE HOLY SPIRIT

When Jesus was talking with the disciples in the hours before His death, the little group was filled with sorrow at the thought of what was ahead. At that time, some must have struggled to accept the Lord's statement, "I tell you the truth: It is for your good that I am going away. Unless I go away, the Counselor will not come to you; but if I go, I will send him to you" (John 16:7).

How could the departure of Christ and the coming of the Holy Spirit be good and to their advantage—and ours?[7] Jesus answered that question by stating that the Holy Spirit would have an influence in the lives of both nonbelievers and believers.

The Holy Spirit's Work with Nonbelievers
Jesus reminded His followers that many people do not believe in Him, even though He reflected the righteousness of God in His life

and teachings and even though His death, resurrection, and ascension show that Satan was already defeated. But when the Holy Spirit comes, Jesus said, "He will convict the world of guilt in regard to sin and righteousness and judgment" (John 16:8). Stated differently, the Holy-Spirit-Counselor is used by the Father to draw unbelieving people to faith in Jesus Christ (John 6:44). When this happens, the person has the experience of being born again. This new birth comes when one is "born of the Spirit" (John 3:3-5,8).

Nobody can explain how this happens, and neither can we tally all the ways in which the Holy Spirit works. We do know, however, that He is the crucial agent in evangelism. Often He guides and energizes believers as they seek to make disciples in obedience to the Great Commission and as they urge nonChristian people to come to Christ. The Spirit also works in the minds and hearts of nonbelievers, convicting and convincing them of their need for the Savior.

This has great practical relevance for Christians. It is impossible for any of us, on our own, to persuade a nonChristian to believe in Jesus Christ. Nobody can become a believer apart from the work of the Holy Spirit. He releases nonbelievers from their doubt and resistance, and He frees believers to be the human instruments through whom the good news is often presented.

The Holy Spirit's Work with Believers
There are many ways by which the Holy Spirit works within the lives of believers.[8] We will consider five of these, each of which has relevance for Christian counseling.

The Holy Spirit changes believers—for the better. When a baby is born and placed in the nursery, the grandparents and other hospital visitors look through the window and admire the child's tiny features, but nobody expects that this new little life will remain unchanged.[9] From the time of birth the child grows, continuing on the long path to maturity.

God expects something similar in people who experience the new birth. Believers who never mature spiritually are like babies who fail to grow and who need to be fed milk because they have not developed enough to handle anything more solid (1 Corinthians 3:1-2, Hebrews 5:11-14). The Holy Spirit works in the lives of individual Christians to bring spiritual growth through a process that has been given a technical name: *sanctification*.

At the time of the Fall, our relationship with God was broken, and as a result, we humans have experienced inner turmoil and interpersonal tensions ever since. Counselors try to reduce internal stress and restore relationships, but human efforts by themselves can be only partially successful. Because of the death and resurrection of Christ, however, believers become new creatures, indwelt by the Holy Spirit, who begins a process of changing lives from the inside out. *Sanctification is the ongoing transformation of the believer's character so that he or she becomes more like Christ.* Sanctification is intended to "restore God's image by reproducing God's character in his children."[10] Like any other form of growth, this is a continual process. It is a process that we can hinder or squelch, but as a later chapter will show, we also can yield to the Spirit's leading and willingly cooperate as He brings about the changes that make us more Christlike.

As long as we live in this sin-infested world, nobody will be completely perfect; the sanctification process will never be complete. It is easy for all of us to get caught in the self-centered, self-indulgent, self-seeking traits and behaviors of the sinful nature. When we allow the Holy Spirit to fill our lives and do His work of sanctification, however, these old "misdeeds of the body" (Romans 8:13) slowly fade. As the life transformation continues, believers show increasing evidence of characteristics that Scripture describes as the products or "fruit of the Spirit." Nine of these are listed in Galatians 5:22-23—love, joy, peace, patience, kindness, goodness, faithfulness, gentleness, and self-control. When a Christian's life shows no evidence of the fruit of the Spirit, this "indicates that the sanctification process has been stunted and that the Holy Spirit has been spurned" (Ephesians 4:30-32).[11]

The process of sanctification transforms and enriches our lives so that we can have better relationships and more freedom and power to influence the world in which we live. This is seen at the bottom of figure 9.1, where sanctification is added to the chart that you have seen before. Believers are in a restored relationship with God, and as we allow the Holy Spirit to work in our lives, we "are being transformed into his likeness" (2 Corinthians 3:18) so that we are better able to build interpersonal relationships and be at peace with ourselves and with God.

At the same time, the indwelling Holy Spirit gives us increased freedom and spiritual power (1 Corinthians 2:4, 2 Corinthians 3:17, Ephesians 3:16) so that we are enabled to obey God and to have a greater impact in the world.

Figure 9.1
THE CREATION, FALL, AND RESTORATION AND SANCTIFICATION OF HUMAN BEINGS

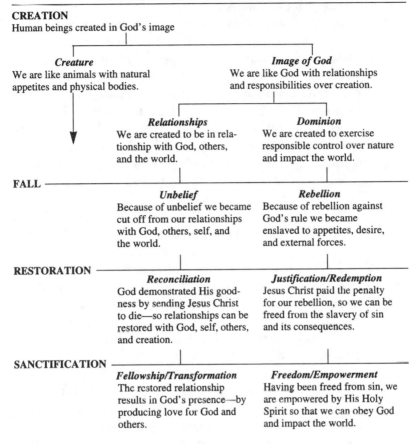

CREATION
Human beings created in God's image

Creature
We are like animals with natural appetites and physical bodies.

Image of God
We are like God with relationships and responsibilities over creation.

Relationships
We are created to be in relationship with God, others, and the world.

Dominion
We are created to exercise responsible control over nature and impact the world.

FALL

Unbelief
Because of unbelief we became cut off from our relationships with God, others, self, and the world.

Rebellion
Because of rebellion against God's rule we became enslaved to appetites, desire, and external forces.

RESTORATION

Reconciliation
God demonstrated His goodness by sending Jesus Christ to die—so relationships can be restored with God, self, others, and creation.

Justification/Redemption
Jesus Christ paid the penalty for our rebellion, so we can be freed from the slavery of sin and its consequences.

SANCTIFICATION

Fellowship/Transformation
The restored relationship results in God's presence—by producing love for God and others.

Freedom/Empowerment
Having been freed from sin, we are empowered by His Holy Spirit so that we can obey God and impact the world.

For the person who wants to look back over the years with satisfaction, nothing could bring greater fulfillment than a life that is yielded to the Holy Spirit's control and work of sanctification. Ralph Hamburger would agree, now that he can look back over his active adult life since that first visit to Kassel. Many of our Christian counseling colleagues and counselees would agree as well.

The Holy Spirit guides. Jesus was led by the Holy Spirit and so were the early Christians (Matthew 4:1; Luke 4:1; Acts 8:29, 10:19-20), but what about those of us who live now? According to the Bible, the Holy Spirit reveals truth to us and guides believers so that we can better understand the Scriptures, more accurately comprehend the message of God's Word, and have a better grasp of spiritual truths (1 Corinthians 2:9-13). People who are the children of God will be led by God's Spirit (Romans 8:14).

Even the most casual reader knows that some parts of the Bible are clearer than others. At times we struggle to understand what the hard-to-grasp passages really mean, but the Holy Spirit helps to make God's Word clear. He inspired the Scriptures and He, in turn, helps us to comprehend the Bible message and put it into practice. Since He guides us into all truth (John 16:13), He often convicts us of what we need to know and keeps us from error. The indwelling Holy Spirit is like an in-built instructor who teaches us and reminds us of what Jesus has taught (John 14:26), who illuminates and clarifies biblical teaching, and who shows us how to live—providing we don't ignore His guidance and squelch His leading.

The Bible makes it clear that God guides His children as they go through life, make decisions, and plan the future (Proverbs 3:5-6; 4:11; 16:3,9). He may do this through different means, but ultimately the Holy Spirit is the one who leads us in the ways that we should go. In our day-by-day activities, therefore, the Spirit is available to clarify our thinking, increase our understanding of the Bible, and give us direction.

The Holy Spirit represents God's presence in the world today. Long before the fall of Communism, our family visited the former Czechoslovakia for a few days of sightseeing. As we drove through the countryside and looked at the tourist attractions of Prague, we constantly were aware that this country was different from any that we had visited previously. Soldiers and the symbols of Communism seemed to be everywhere, always reminding us that we were in the presence of a repressive regime.

God reminds us of His presence in very different ways. In the Old Testament, God the Father was most often highlighted. Later, Jesus most clearly showed God's presence among human beings during the few years that He was on earth. After Christ's ascension, the Holy Spirit came to be God's primary presence among us, and that is the way it is today.

These are more than cold theological facts. The Holy Spirit's current presence among us is a practical and encouraging reminder that no believer is ever alone—even when problems persist and life is tough.

Over three hundred years ago, a devoted French monk wrote a few notes and had some conversations that others recorded. The

Cardinal of Noailles had these published in a little book that has been read by millions—perhaps including you. *The Practice of the Presence of God* by Brother Lawrence[12] has been described as "the simple wisdom of a man who felt the constant companionship of God." Even while he worked in the monastery kitchen, preparing meals among the pots and pans and washing up the plates, this humble believer learned to experience God's presence and "great tranquility" in ways that elude many of us whose lives are much too busy. The Holy Spirit, God's present-day manifestation of the Trinity in our midst, is present and willing to communicate with us, whenever we seek to have communion and conversation with Him. That has practical relevance for the church and for individual believers.

The Holy Spirit creates community. Have you ever wondered how the disciples got along with each other when Jesus was on earth? Mark 10 describes one situation in which two of the disciples, James and John, quietly approached Jesus and asked if they could be seated on either side of Him when His Kingdom was established. When the other ten disciples heard about this request, they became indignant and undoubtedly annoyed.

Nonbelievers are concerned about prestige, about where people will sit, and about who will be greatest, Jesus told the Twelve—perhaps in an effort to calm a tense situation—but that kind of status seeking should not characterize Christians. Instead, we should come together as humble people who are willing to be servants (Mark 10:35-45), working together instead of playing games of one-upmanship. Shortly before His death, Jesus prayed that believers would be one, as the Father and Son are one (John 17:11,21-22). Of course human beings have different personalities and perspectives, but God intended that we should serve, worship, and work together in community.

This happened dramatically when the Holy Spirit came into the believers on the day of Pentecost. Shortly thereafter, the Christians began to eat together, serve together, pray and worship with one another, and do whatever they could to meet each other's needs (Acts 2:42-47, 4:32-35). They were a new community of Christ's followers.

That isn't what we see in many congregations today. Most of us know about churches that are places of back-biting and self-centered hypocrisy, sometimes headed by leaders who are manipulative, insecure, and self-centered. These tensions between believers are evidence that the Holy Spirit is not in control there. Instead, the people are being divided by the Evil One, who always seeks to destroy unity and disrupt community.

The Holy Spirit, in contrast, breaks down walls of partition between people so that we have unity in the Church and are all one in Christ Jesus (Acts 4:32, Galatians 3:28). Racial, socioeconomic, sexual, and other differences are swept away. Believers with different gifts and abilities are able to work, worship, and serve together—distinct people working with one another in community.

Psychiatrist M. Scott Peck has become an advocate for what he calls *community making*. The modern church has not been a very effective community, according to Peck. Instead, many congregations prefer to be a "pseudo-community where everything is all smiles and politeness, all sweetness and light," but where in-fighting goes on behind closed doors. Church members want to maintain their individualism, Peck writes, so few are willing to make commitments. But the "process of community-building begins with a commitment—a commitment of the members not to drop out, a commitment to hang in there through thick and thin, through the pain of chaos and emptiness. Such commitment has not generally been required by the Church. Now the time has come to require it. For without that commitment community is impossible."[13]

Dr. Peck has seen the lack of community in the church and has rightly concluded that community rarely comes without commitment. But even with persistence and positive mental attitudes, true community comes only to people who are bound together by the Holy Spirit. "We live in a world that relentlessly destroys community by creating and emphasizing differences and inequalities," wrote Gilbert Bilezikian. Guided by the Holy Spirit, the church "is God's answer to the community-shattering forces loose in the world." It is called to establish and to model community by minimizing differences and by striving for equality among its participants (2 Corinthians 8:13-15).

The Holy Spirit empowers believers so we can serve. The Holy Spirit empowered Jesus for His ministry (Matthew 3:16, Acts 10:38) and He, in turn, promised that His followers would be given power to impact the world with the gospel (Luke 24:49, Acts 1:8). Throughout the book of Acts we see how power from the Holy Spirit did, indeed, change lives and lead believers to activities that "turned the world upside down."

The New Testament describes how the Holy Spirit currently works in Christians and gives us power to serve most effectively. The answer is that God gives one or more special gifts to each believer.

These gifts, which are listed in four different Bible passages (Romans 12:6-8, 1 Corinthians 12:4-11, Ephesians 4:11, 1 Peter 4:11), include supernaturally given abilities to teach, serve, evangelize, heal, give aid, show mercy, or fill the role of pastor or apostle. Since the four lists are not all the same, many Bible scholars conclude that the listed gifts are examples and that others also may be bestowed on selected believers but are not cited in Scripture. We do not know if the gifts are endowments from birth or if they are special abilities that come later in life. Perhaps they are a combination of the two.

We do know, however, that spiritual gifts were given to build the community of believers and to empower the Church, but they also have been steeped in controversy that has divided believers. Especially intense debates have surrounded discussions of the more spectacular gifts, such as healing, speaking in tongues, or working miracles, and there is disagreement about whether the gifts were for New Testament times only or whether they apply to us today.

These differences may be of more interest to theologians and biblical experts than to those of us who are counselors, but of some things we can all be certain.

- ❖ The gifts were given to individual believers for the purpose of building up the Church (1 Corinthians 12:7; 14:5,12). Gifts are not given primarily for the personal enjoyment or enrichment of the persons who receive and possess them, although many people find fulfillment in developing and using their gifts in ways that will strengthen the Church.
- ❖ No one person has all the gifts, and neither is any one of the gifts possessed by everybody (1 Corinthians 12:14-21,28-30).
- ❖ Some gifts are more conspicuous and more attractive than others, but all gifts are needed and all are important (1 Corinthians 12:22-26). There is no evidence in the Bible that any gift is given based on the fact that the recipient is more worthy than somebody else.
- ❖ We are encouraged to eagerly desire, cultivate, and excel in spiritual gifts (1 Corinthians 12:31; 14:1,12), but we must realize that the Holy Spirit determines who gets which gift (1 Corinthians 12:7,11). Nobody is justified in thinking that some of the gifts—or the people who

possess these gifts—are unimportant and not needed
(1 Corinthians 12:14-25).

❖ Spiritual gifts are of limited effectiveness unless they are
accompanied by genuine love (1 Corinthians 13).

COUNSELING AND THE SUPERNATURAL

Is counseling one of the spiritual gifts? Certainly *counseling* is not
included in any biblical listing of spiritual gifts, but we could conclude that gifts such as teaching, healing, discernment, or showing
mercy all have relevance for counseling.

In Romans 12:8 we read about the gift of encouraging. The
Greek word from which this is translated means more than slapping
somebody on the back and saying "Hang in there!" The term implies
activities such as admonishing, exhorting, urging others to make
worthwhile changes, supporting, comforting, and encouraging people to face the future. All of this sounds very much like counseling.
All of this is implied in a gift given by God to a select group of
believers for building and strengthening the Church.

From this it does not follow that only a select few are competent
to counsel and neither do we conclude that counselor training is irrelevant. Consider the gift of teaching. Some believers are spiritually
gifted as teachers, but all of us are responsible to teach our children.
Similarly, some believers have the gift of evangelism, but all of us
are called to be Christ's witnesses. The same is true of counseling.
All believers are to encourage and help one another with the Holy
Spirit's help, but some have a special spiritual gift of encouragement-
exhortation-counseling. Whether or not we have this gift, all people-
helpers can profit from training—even as gifted teachers and evangelists
can become even more effective when they have education. Ultimately,
the Holy Spirit gives gifts and guides counselors who sharpen their skills
with training and who then become the best helpers.[14]

Miraculous Counseling?

Jesus once was approached by a government official whose son was
close to death and who begged for healing. Before He healed the boy,
Jesus made an interesting statement that summarized the thinking
of some who were in the crowd. Unless these people "see miraculous signs and wonders" they will never believe, Jesus said (John
4:48—see also Hebrews 2:3-4).

Debate over miraculous signs and wonders has continued from that time until the present, and the topic appears to have come into new prominence during the past few years. Many believe that their spiritual leaders, including counselors, should have ministries that are characterized by miraculous spiritual and psychological healings. Some suggest that counseling might involve "a word of wisdom," "a word of knowledge," or a special ability to distinguish between evil spirits and wrong human spirits. All of these are included in a biblical list of spiritual gifts (1 Corinthians 12:8,10), but counselors are among those who differ in their opinions about when and whether these should be used today.[15]

We who hold a Christian worldview recognize that God works in many ways to accomplish His purposes. The Bible is clear that He can intervene in sensational ways, and certainly He has done so in the past, but we also know that He can and most often does work in ways that are much less dramatic.

Christians tend to fall into one of two groups in their views about the more prominent spiritual gifts—including healings, working miracles, giving supernatural words of knowledge, or speaking in tongues (language that is unintelligible to the speaker).

In one group are those who maintain that too many Christians have ignored God's supernatural power and have stifled His Spirit by an overemphasis on rationalism. All of us need to be more open to manifestations of the Spirit's "miracle-working power," according to Christians holding this view. Then we will see miraculous evidences of His signs and wonders—even in the lives of people whose problems are emotional and relational.

In a different group are those who argue that miraculous signs were given to authenticate the ministry of Jesus and the apostles, but the Bible gives no indication that these would continue after the time of the early church. People who hold this view dismiss the more spectacular gifts and point out that signs and wonders are not necessarily the work of the Holy Spirit. Many segments of the new-age movement, for example, emphasize miracles, spirit visitations, and other experiences that certainly are spectacular and that easily could be termed supernatural even though they are not from God.[16]

Christians on both sides of the debate would agree that the Devil, who is the great deceiver, is able to perform counterfeit miracles that can fool even believers (Matthew 24:24, 2 Thessalonians 2:9-12). Speaking in tongues, for example, occurred in ancient pagan temples and reportedly is common in nonChristian religious circles today. In addition, there is evidence that tongues-speaking (known technically as *glossolalia*) can be learned and produced psychologically. All of this gives added reason for any believer to "test the spirits" (1 John 4:1-2) lest he or she conclude that something is from the Holy Spirit when it is not.

An overemphasis on the miraculous or an uncritical acceptance of signs and wonders can encourage a quick fix mentality and a tendency of many Christians to undervalue that which is natural and ordinary. "There are just too many people who want every problem to be solved by an immediate miracle, a display of the supernatural, a wonderful providence that will change everything," wrote J. I. Packer. This is a sign "not of great faith, but of great immaturity."[17] This same kind of immaturity leads people to rush from one miracle conference to another, but to avoid such growth-producing disciplines as Bible study, meditation, or serving others humbly and consistently.

Even Jesus cautioned against an overemphasis on the spectacular. After going on a preaching mission, the disciples returned with great enthusiasm, telling about the sensational and thrilling things that had happened, including the subduing of demons.[18] Jesus turned their attention away from the dramatic experiences and told them not to "rejoice that the spirits submit to you, but rejoice that your names are written in heaven" (Luke 10:17-20). He appeared to be less interested in sensational ministry experiences and much more concerned about ongoing relationships, especially one's relationship with God.

A Balanced Perspective
Packer gave a thoughtful and balanced perspective when he wrote,

> A line of thought about evangelism discussed recently seems to say that public preaching of the gospel is not all it should be, unless it is accompanied by a particular kind of physical manifestation (signs, wonders, miracles). These, it is implied, give the message credibility that it could not otherwise have and trigger a "power encounter" that the verbal message alone would hardly induce. By biblical standards, however, it seems to me a gross overstatement and indeed a real error. Also, it sets those who proclaim the gospel in

public on a very slippery path. The temptation to manipulate people and situations to make it appear that the power of God is producing the desired manifestations is likely to prove irresistible. . . .

It is true that the New Testament regularly views the "signs and wonders" as the Father's authentication of the ministry of Jesus and his apostles (Acts 2:43, 5:12, 14:3, cf. 10:38, 19:11; Romans 15:19; 2 Corinthians 12:12; Hebrews 2:3). There is no clear promise that these manifestations will continue after the apostles' ministry is over. But there is no denial that they will either. The New Testament leaves open the possibility. . . .

The supreme sign and wonder, giving the fullest credibility to Christianity, will thus always be the changed life of the believer. . . .A Christianity that is prepared to go on cheerfully without any signs of God's supernatural transforming power in people's lives shows a very unbiblical spirit.[19]

Has this discussion taken us too far from counseling? It hasn't if we realize that new-age emphases on unusual experiences are permeating much of the current counseling literature. And our discussion is of great relevance when we consider how resistance to supernatural influences as well as an overemphasis on presumed spectacular supernatural influences both affect our Christian counselees and some of our counseling colleagues.

It would seem that Christian counselors are like many other believers who live their lives without many thoughts or expectations of what God can and does do. "It is right to bring the supernatural into prominence and to raise Christians' expectations with regard to it," wrote one theologian, whose comments surely apply to most Christian counselors. "Generally speaking, our expectations with regard to seeing the power of God transforming people's lives are not as high as they should be."[20] When we lack a daily awareness of the Holy Spirit's presence and power, we fail to reach our greatest potential as Christian counselors.

Once again we are faced with the issue of worldviews. Some of my Christian friends are convinced that "signs and wonders" are evidence of the Holy Spirit's continued presence in our midst and that believers should actively seek and be open to supernatural occurrences and events. Others of my friends believe that these signs and wonders have ceased in our age and that we should neither seek nor encourage dramatic evidences of the Holy Spirit's power. Both of these groups would agree that there are extremes, both in people who are carried away by emotional experiences that may have nothing to do with the Spirit's power and by those who are so cognitive in their Christianity that in their minds they have stripped God of His ability to work in supernatural and surprising ways.

Sincere and competent biblical theologians will continue to disagree and to debate these issues. Each of us should determine what we believe, to the best of our abilities under the guidance of the Holy Spirit, but we should be cautious about condemning or dismissing the worldviews of other believers with whom we might disagree.

SO WHAT?

I have a friend who works in the counseling center of a large and influential state university on the west coast. My friend is a committed Christian but his job description does not allow him to bring the name of Jesus Christ into his counseling sessions. As a dedicated believer, my friend does not want to push spiritual things aside, but neither is he free to violate the requirements of his employer. Can this man be a Christian counselor where he works?

"When I started this job, I learned some things very quickly," my colleague said when we discussed his work recently. "I learned not to view my nonChristian clients and colleagues as enemies. They may have beliefs and lifestyles that are clearly unbiblical, but they are people who have hurts, pains, and insecurities. They need a Christian associate or counselor who will befriend and help them, not somebody to attack and to alienate them."

My friend has learned, too, that the people with whom he works notice that he is different. His life reflects the fruit of the Spirit, and when others ask why—as they often do—he is free to answer.

Frequently in a conversation or counseling session, my friend senses that the other person needs to talk about spiritual issues. Is this inner conviction the prompting of the Holy Spirit? Whenever it comes, the counselor friend will describe a biblical event—like the parable of the prodigal son or the good Samaritan. Invariably these descriptions lead to discussions of spiritual issues that frequently are at the core of the counselee's problems.

None of this can be effective until the counselor has shown that he can be trusted and the counselee feels safe to discuss painful experiences. Many people who come to that secular counseling center have been wounded by their experiences with the church, but they find healing of these spiritual wounds in the presence of a man who is sensitive to the Spirit's leading and available to be used.

Since he lives within each believer, the Holy Spirit knows us well and can work through us to influence counselees in a variety of ways. Consider again what the Holy Spirit does and think how this applies to counselors.

First, we have seen that the Holy Spirit changes believers for the better. Perhaps He does this even when we are unaware of His presence and influence. To be of maximum effectiveness, however, the transforming process of sanctification must involve the believer's cooperation. With His guidance and empowerment, we are to pull away from attitudes and behaviors that are unlike Christ. And we must develop moral qualities and lifestyles that are characterized by holiness and Christlike love (Ephesians 4:17-5:20, Colossians 3:8-14). This is an ongoing process, but it is not a hopeless task. God's Spirit develops fruit in our lives and changes us as we seek to live in accordance with Scripture and yield obediently to His promptings, instruction, and discipline (John 17:17; Romans 8:2-4; Galatians 5:16,22-23; Hebrews 12:10).

In what appears to have been their first arrest, Peter and John were seized, sent to jail for the night, and brought the next morning to appear before the local religious leaders. The two apostles gave an eloquent defense of their beliefs and clearly they amazed the "rulers and elders of the people" who had gathered to listen. "When they saw the courage of Peter and John and realized that they were unschooled, ordinary men, they were astonished and they *took note that these men had been with Jesus*" (Acts 4:13, emphasis added).

Ultimately, others will notice the changes for the better that come into our lives when Christians—counselors included—take the time and effort to be with Jesus.

Second, we know that the Holy Spirit guides us. Probably we can't comprehend all of the ways in which He does this, but we do have some understanding. The Spirit uses the Scriptures, with their commands, guiding principles, and examples, to indicate what God wills (Psalm 119:11,105; 1 Corinthians 10:11; 2 Timothy 3:16-17).[21] A careful reading of the book of Acts and the epistles

170 The Holy Spirit and Counseling

indicates that the Holy Spirit also leads through circumstances, people, events, and inner impressions or promptings that are consistent with biblical teaching.

How can the counselor experience this kind of leading? To begin, we must be filled with the Spirit (Ephesians 5:18). This is an ongoing process that involves a willingness to be under His control "not in an absolute sense so that we are passive and our personal faculties cease to function, but in a relative sense in which we cooperate with Him by doing our part and by depending upon Him to do His work (cf. Acts 2:4; 4:8, 31; 6:3, 5, 8-11; 11:24 . . .). This cooperation allows Him to energize us and to do through us all that He desires."[22]

Then, we need to avoid those behaviors that stifle the Holy Spirit's leading. We must not quench or grieve the Spirit by resisting His control, engaging in willful sin, ignoring His promptings, or refusing to cooperate (Ephesians 4:30, 1 Thessalonians 5:19). And we must not test the Spirit by lying (Acts 5:9) or resist Him by refusing to obey His directives (Acts 7:51).

The Christian counselor who seeks to be guided by the Holy Spirit will be led in every area of life, including what we do or say in counseling. This does not make training of no importance. The Spirit works through our training and our personalities to change the lives of our counselees, even when they and we are unaware of His influence.

Third, we have seen that the Holy Spirit represents God's presence in the world today. This is a practical reminder that no believer is ever alone, even in the midst of a difficult counseling situation. Brother Lawrence learned to experience God's presence and tranquility in the midst of the pots and pans of an old monastery kitchen. We can experience something similar in our counseling rooms when we willingly invite God's Spirit to be in control.

Fourth, the Holy Spirit creates a new community of believers, a community that ideally is characterized by care, sensitivity, sharing, and oneness. When the Christian counselor is not an active participant in a local church, he or she misses this support and sense of community that God wants for all believers.

It is no secret that many counselors, including Christian counselors, have been stung by past experiences in church. Many of our counselees bear the wounds of their involvement with dysfunctional churches or their years of sitting under the teaching of manipulative, guilt-inducing leaders. It is not surprising that these experiences push people away from the church and sometimes away from God.

But we must not ignore the church that God created solely because it has imperfections. Of all people, counselors should be the most willing to accept imperfect people and to see value in churches where walls of partition are broken down and where people can find support, acceptance, and encouragement. Christian counselors who are guided by the Holy Spirit will not ignore or isolate themselves and their counselees from the local church. Spirit guided counseling must work in partnership with the church community, not in opposition.

Fifth, the Holy Spirit gives us spiritual gifts so we can serve Him better, in ways that will build the lives of people in the church. Many times we do things on our own and often we are successful. But the Spirit-guided Christian counselor has been specially gifted by God for the work that he or she is doing. We must never forget that He is the one who gives us the strength, the health, the insights, and the special giftedness to bring genuine and lasting help into the lives of our counselees.

Each reader of this book must decide, before God, whether he or she will rely on the so-called miraculous gifts to bring change in people's lives. Make your decision based on a careful study of the Bible and with a willingness to learn from God and from mature believers who can help you make a decision. If you are a professional counselor, do not overlook the possible ways in which this decision might influence your state license to counsel. And recognize that we will all be influenced, at times, by the Devil, who is the father of lies and the great deceiver.

Before we look at supernatural forces in the next chapter, however, one conclusion is clear to the Christian who is indwelt by the Holy Spirit and sensitive to His leading. Whatever resistance and difficulties we might face, we can always remember the words of 1 John 4:4—"The one who is in you [the Holy Spirit] is greater than the one who is in the world [Satan]."

❖

CHAPTER TEN

Supernatural Agents and Counseling

ON JUNE 25, 1947, Seattle businessman Kenneth Arnold was flying his private plane near Mount Rainier in Washington when he encountered a startling sight. Nine large disk-shaped objects appeared to be skipping above his little aircraft at fantastic rates of speed. The incident marked the first reported sighting of unidentified flying objects (UFOs), and before long the public imagination was captured. By the end of the year, 800 people reported that they too had seen "flying saucers," and since that time the reported sightings have been in the millions.

In a recent Gallup poll, almost half the respondents agreed that UFOs are real and not just a product of human imagination. Fourteen percent of the respondents claimed to have seen a UFO.[1] Dozens of organizations have been formed to study UFO phenomena, thousands of books have reported and analyzed mysterious sightings, and unknown numbers of scientists and others have attempted to explain the UFO mystery.[2] Even Carl Jung got into the debate and appeared to endorse the reality of UFOs in a book that he titled *Flying Saucers.*[3]

It is not surprising that reports of flying objects led quickly to speculation that extraterrestrial beings must exist to pilot and to ride on board the UFOs. By the mid-1970s, stories were circulating that extraterrestrials had begun abducting human beings. Two decades later, in the summer of 1992, over 100,000 American mental-health professionals received a free sixty-three page booklet titled *Unusual Personal Experiences*,[4] written by researchers from Temple and Eastern Michigan Universities, and endorsed by the former head of Harvard's department of psychiatry. Based on a national survey conducted by the Roper Organization, the authors concluded that "a massive weight of evidence" supports their conclusion that as many as 3.7 million people have been kidnapped temporarily by aliens and returned to earth where they now suffer from "UFO abduction syndrome." Most of these people have no recollection of their experiences, according to the authors, because they have repressed all memory of their encounters with the alien kidnapers.

Hundreds of investigators have attempted to document UFO sightings and reports of abductions by extraterrestrials. These studies give virtually no solid support to the existence of UFO phenomena, but many people have little interest in what the scientists think. In one of her books, Shirley MacLaine described a conversation with a channeller who concluded that we are free to believe whatever makes us feel good, even if there is nothing to indicate that our beliefs are true. Without giving any evidence to support his conclusions, new-age author David Icke wrote that "extra-terrestrials are arriving on earth in such large numbers to help us. . . . They are here to guide us through tremendously difficult times with love, wisdom and understanding, and we ignore them and reject what they say at our cost."[5]

More recently, some popular writers have concluded that the extraterrestrial alien forces really are angels who protect us and are able to guide our lives. We can make contact with them through "divination tools" such as "Angel Oracle Cards," according to the authors of one popular book that urges readers to get in touch with "celestials" by aligning with "angelic energy fields."[6]

Our world has come a long way since Mr. Arnold saw his flying saucers several decades ago.

CELESTIAL BEINGS AND WORLDVIEWS

Why do large numbers of modern people seem to believe so freely in abductions by extraterrestrials, in the idea that truth is equated with what feels good, or even in angelic energy fields and angel oracle cards? To answer we must look briefly at how western thought has changed, not only during the past half century but in the centuries since the time of the philosopher Descartes.

When Descartes was born in 1596, people in the west generally agreed that God's revelation was the real source of our knowledge about the truth.[7] Human reason was assumed to have been created as part of the image of God, and even as one person can communicate rationally with another, so God communicates rationally with us. "Revelation, in the Judaeo-Christian sense, was not an intuitive, private, mystical, non-rational or 'right brain' activity—it was a rational communication between one infinite Person and his creation, man, who was infinite."[8]

Descartes' theory of knowledge changed some of these ideas and moved from thinking of God as the source of knowledge to the idea that human beings are the ultimate source. Many years later, a further move away from belief in divine revelation came with the suggestion that perhaps reason couldn't even be trusted. Over time, there was a gradual dethronement of reason (left-brain logic) and a growing fascination with more mystical, "right-brain, private, esoteric experiences" that could not be supported by reason or science and that many people had no interest in supporting. More recently, new-age advocates have come to distrust and often to reject reason. For these people it makes perfect sense to "unlock the mysteries of the universe" through aligning with angelic energy fields, feeling "intense communication with your higher self," or even seeking religious experiences through sex.[9]

Some of this diversity of thinking might have been anticipated by C. S. Lewis in a book about demons that was published five years before Mr. Arnold saw those first flying saucers. In what probably is the most familiar and frequently quoted phrase from all of his writings, Lewis warned that we can fall into "two equal and opposite errors" in our views of supernatural forces such as demons. "One is to disbelieve in their existence. The other is to believe, and to feel an excessive and unhealthy interest in them."[10] Lewis called these the *materialist* and the *magical* perspectives. The highly rational, left-brain, materialist view is in danger of rejecting supernatural agents that cannot be analyzed with scientific logic. The highly subjective, intuitive-emotive, right-brain, magical view develops an excessive and unhealthy interest in extraterrestrial spirit forces and feels free to believe "whatever gives us good and comfortable feelings, irre-spective of whether or not it is true."[11] Both of these extremes are seen in the church. Both are in error. Both, wrote Lewis, bring equal pleasure to the Devil.

These two extremes are also seen in the worldviews that many people hold today. In chapter 1 we discussed the importance of worldviews and suggested that every person operates in accordance with his or her assumptions about what the world is like. Worldviews are like sieves that help us determine what is true or false, what needs to be discarded, and what should be retained as truth. Psychological researchers, rational-emotive counselors, or behavior therapists, for example, tend to hold a strongly rational (materialistic) worldview. Ideas that can be proven empirically are kept, but views that can't be analyzed scientifically—including belief in supernatural beings—are tossed aside as being unlikely or untrue. In contrast, many in the new-age movement, counselors who utilize methods based on East-ern religion, and the followers of something called constructivism hold an intuition-based (magical) worldview that says objectivity is impossible. They maintain that reality is all in the mind, that all truth is relative, and that therapy is a vague process of conversation that is not tied to values or to absolutes.[12] These people have little interest in objective scientific data or in what God's Word says is true.

Whenever people are divided into two camps, most of us tend to fall someplace in the middle. We all bring our worldviews into counseling, and it is likely that every helper has a perspective about supernatural agents and their influence in the lives of our counselees. When these worldviews tend to be near one of the extremes—disbelieving in supernatural beings or believing with an excessive and unhealthy interest—there will be radically dif-ferent approaches to understanding and dealing with counselee problems.

It becomes important, therefore, for counselors to have a clear and accurate understanding of what God has revealed about both angelic and evil beings.

ANGELIC FORCES

Most of our ideas about angels probably come from the centuries-old paintings of medieval and Renaissance artists or from Christmas card illustrations showing the manger in Bethlehem or the shepherds keeping watch over their flocks in the fields. *Angel* comes from a Greek word that simply means "messenger." Angels are God's messengers, and this explains why they sometimes reflect divine glory and majesty and arouse fear when they are seen by humans (Luke 2:8-9).[13] The hosts of Heaven are not always visible, however (2 Kings 6:15-17), and when angels do appear, sometimes they look so much like ordinary people that they aren't even recognized as supernatural messengers (Genesis 18-19, Hebrews 13:2).

The Nature of Angels
Somebody has suggested that angels "poke their celestial heads repeatedly into the scenes of Bible stories," but the Scriptures don't dwell on telling us what they are like. We know that angels are supernatural, heavenly beings, but they never are worshiped or aggrandized. What, then, do we know for sure about angels?

* Angels are created beings (Psalm 148:2,5; Colossians 1:16).
* Angels are spirit beings that have individual names but no physical bodies, although they sometimes appear in forms that are visible to human beings and occasionally they look like people (Daniel 10:11-14; Luke 1:19,28-35; Hebrews 13:2).
* Angels have superior intellect and wisdom (2 Samuel 14:20), are powerful (2 Kings 19:35, Acts 5:17-32), sometimes show superhuman strength (2 Peter 2:11), are unrestricted by physical boundaries such as walls (Acts 12:7), and can communicate eloquently (1 Corinthians 13:1).

Some of us might be inclined to dismiss these facts as interesting but largely irrelevant for our work as counselors. Recent surveys have shown, however, that interest in angels has been increasing—especially among baby boomers and people who are younger. This, of course, is the age group that is most likely to seek counseling. An upsurge of popular books and seminars about angels has led many people to the false idea that angels can be consulted as spirit guides to help humans make decisions. Angels "provide a temptation for those who want a 'fix' of spirituality without bothering with God himself," wrote Timothy Jones. "Some prefer shuffling a deck of

'Angel Oracle' cards over reading the Bible or listening to sermons. They prefer God in celestial soundbites."[14]

The prevalence of misunderstanding and error about angels is special reason for us to know what God's angel messengers are really like and what they actually do.

The Activities of Angels

During World War II, Gestapo agents came to a house in Holland and dragged the occupants off to prison. Only one of the family members survived that horrible prison camp experience, but Corrie ten Boom later traveled around the world, telling about God's provision and protection.

When Corrie and her sister arrived at the dreaded Ravensbruck camp, all possessions were to be taken by the Nazi guards. Corrie hugged the little Bible that she hoped to smuggle past her captors and she prayed, "Lord, cause now Thine angels to surround me; and let them not be transparent today, for the guards must not see me."

Calmly, Corrie walked in line to the place where every person was being checked, "from the front, the sides, the back. Not a bulge escaped the eyes of the guards. . . . They felt over the body of each one who passed. I knew they would not see me, for the angels were still surrounding me. I was not even surprised when they passed me by; but within me rose the jubilant cry, 'O Lord, if Thou does so answer prayer, I can face even Ravensbruck unafraid.' "[15]

At the beginning of her greatest life crisis, Corrie ten Boom recognized the protective role of angels. But that is only one of several angel activities.

Angels worship God. This appears to be their primary function. Whenever a human being offers praise to God, he or she is joining celestial beings who praise him continually (Revelation 5:11-12).

Angels communicate messages from God (Acts 7:53, Revelation 1:1). They give warnings, for example (Matthew 2:13), and sometimes they make announcements, as when Gabriel appeared to Zechariah and to Mary, announcing the coming births. At other times angels give direction, as when the angelic messenger told Joseph to flee to Egypt with Mary and the baby Jesus. Angels were active in communicating the laws of God (Acts 7:53, Hebrews 2:2), although it is clear that no angelic message ever contradicts the Word of God.

Angels give guidance and instruction. Do you remember when

Abraham's servant was sent to find a wife for Isaac? He left on the journey with an assurance that God would send His angel to give guidance (Genesis 24:7,40). This angelic leading appears in both the Old and New Testaments (see, for example, Genesis 28:12-15; Exodus 14:19; Acts 10:3-5, 8:26).

Angels minister to the needs of God's people. Although there is little scriptural support for the idea that each of us has a personal guardian angel,[16] we do know that angels protect believers (Psalm 91:11, Daniel 6:22), guard us (Daniel 3:28, 6:22), deliver us from danger and difficulties (Psalm 34:7, Acts 12:7), and give strength and encouragement, as when they ministered to Jesus following the temptation (Matthew 4:11) and to Elijah during his time of depression and weariness in the wilderness (1 Kings 19:5-7). Maybe, too, they influence human actions, as when they apparently stopped the Nazi guards from spotting that bulge under Corrie ten Boom's dress.

Angels carry out God's justice. Sometimes God executes judgment directly, but often He works through angels. This is seen repeatedly throughout the Bible, and there is frequent reference in the book of Revelation that the final battles of history will involve divine angels powerfully and fiercely inflicting the judgment that awaits those who have rejected or rebelled against Christ (2 Kings 19:35; 1 Chronicles 21:15; Matthew 13:41, 25:31; Acts 12:23; 2 Thessalonians 1:7-8).

Modern Angels?

Periodically, some person will write a book or preach a sermon that describes an angelic visitor who has given a special message. The visited person often shares this special message with enthusiasm but with nary an awareness that the message might have come, not from God, but from the speaker's imagination or even from the Devil. How do we evaluate reported angelic visitations, and how can our knowledge of angels be useful in counseling?

Let us begin by acknowledging that angels are active today, whether we notice them or not. Angels seem to appear more frequently around pivotal events in the history of God's people. Their presence was clearly seen, for example, when Christ came to earth, when He rose from the dead and when He ascended to Heaven (Matthew 28:1-8; Luke 1:11-20,26-37; 2:8-14; 24:1-7; Acts 1:10-11). Nothing in the Bible would suggest that angels aren't at work now as they have been in the past and as they will be in the future.

But let us acknowledge, too, that the angels people see are not always angels from God. Paul warned that Satan himself sometimes masquerades as an angel of light, bringing deceptive messages that appear to be truth (2 Corinthians 11:14). These false messengers may even quote the Bible out of context, but overall the bogus messages are intended to lead people away from biblical truth.

In common with other Christians, as counselors we should keep four conclusions in mind when they consider the influence of angels in the lives of modern people. First, remember that if you hear about some angelic message that in any way deviates from the teachings of Scripture, then the supernatural messenger really is a deceitful spirit who is not from God (Galatians 1:8). If any message presumes to give a new revelation about God, His nature, His purposes, or His plans, that too is not from God.[17] Believers are cautioned against believing every spirit and are instructed, instead, to test the spirits to see if they come from God and if they communicate messages that are consistent with the Word of God (1 John 4:1).

Second, remember that some people have the spiritual gift of discernment, a gift that enables them to determine whether a spirit is from God or from Satan. This gift is not given to everyone, of course, but when it is guided by the Holy Spirit it enables some people to discern whether or not an angelic messenger is really divinely sent and whether the message is genuinely valid.

Third, remember that the visits of angels were rare and usually grouped around significant pivotal events, even in Bible times. Scripture puts more emphasis on the continuing presence of angels than on their visits. When he wrote a book titled *Angels: God's Secret Agents*, Billy Graham acknowledged that angels are active in our century, usually working as the undercover agents of God. Surely Corrie ten Boom was right in praying to the Lord, asking that angels would be sent to protect her in a time of danger, but she never asked for a vision or for an angel visit. Expecting, looking for, or hoping for angel visits is never encouraged in the Bible, but we can and should rejoice in the guidance, protection, and other ministries of angels—God's special messengers.

One final observation is worth noting. When angelic visitors appeared in the Bible, they never appeared as teachers giving long discourses about what people should believe. Angels made brief and pointed announcements that called for obedience. The Holy Spirit is the one who teaches and leads us into truth—primarily by illuminating the Scriptures; angels minister and bring messages that are consistent with biblical teaching (Galatians 1:8).[18] Be very skeptical, then, if a counselee describes some new idea that is assumed to have come from angels.

In our work as counselors, we are concerned about the ministries of God's holy angels, but we also must have a concern about what have come to be known as the fallen angels: Satan and his demonic hosts.

EVIL FORCES

I once listened to a tape made by a pastor who claimed to be an expert in knowing about the nature and impact of demons. The speaker gave numerous facts that he had learned in his work as an exorcist. He told us about the names of demons and the nature of their power—all of which he had learned through what the demons had told him during many "counseling sessions" with people who appeared to be demon-possessed. The tape was fascinating, including excerpts of the speaker's loud and angry confrontation with demons who were living inside some of his parishioners.

As I listened to the tape, one idea kept coming into my mind. Satan, the one who leads these demonic forces, is a great deceiver and the father of lies. How, then, could the speaker on the tape be so sure of the facts that he proclaimed with such enthusiasm? He had accepted what he heard without question, had assumed that the demons he encountered were telling the truth, and had never given any apparent thought to testing what he heard against the Bible to see if what he proclaimed so eloquently was really valid.

None of this is meant to discount the reports of people who have had dramatic encounters with demonic forces. D. L. Moody, the renowned evangelist, once stated that he had two reasons for believing in the existence of Satan. One was that the Bible says he exists; the other was that "I have encountered him. I have done business with him."

Whether we realize it or not, all of us have frequent encounters with Satan and his forces (Ephesians 6:12). The very act of counseling is an encounter with Satan's destructive influences in the lives of human beings. No Christian counselor can be of maximum effectiveness if he or she is ignorant of Satan and his schemes (2 Corinthians 2:11).

The Existence of Satan

The Bible pictures Satan as a celestial spiritual being who was created by God and clothed with great splendor but who rebelled against his creator and even decided to make himself "like the Most High." As a result, Satan lost his exalted position and was cast from the presence of God. Apparently, Satan took one-third of the angelic beings with him (Isaiah 14:12-15; Ezekiel 28:11-19; Revelation 12:3-4, 7-9) and has been at odds with God ever since. The biblical accounts of the Devil's temptation of Jesus show us clearly that God's Son was personally acquainted with the reality of Satan (Matthew 4:1-11, Luke 4:1-13).

The Character of Satan

Even a casual reading of the Bible shows that Satan in no way resembles the cute little kids who come to our doors on Halloween, dressed in red devil suits with horns, a long tail, and a pitchfork.

The name Satan is derived from a Hebrew word that means "adversary" or "opponent." Satan is the powerful adversary who opposes God and the people of God. Frequently he is called the Devil—a term that means "accuser" or "slanderer," but the Bible gives him a variety of other names. Together they portray a being who is strong (but not stronger than God) and who presents us with a mighty adversary. Satan, says Scripture, is a tempter (Matthew 4:3, 1 Thessalonians 3:5), enemy or adversary (Matthew 13:39, 1 Peter 5:8), evil one (Matthew 13:19,38), deceiver (2 Corinthians 11:14-15, Revelation 12:9), liar and murderer (John 8:44), and a being who is the ruler of evil and darkness (Ephesians 6:12). Sometimes he appears as an angel of light, looking harmless and beautiful, but his activities are malicious as he attempts to uproot good and sow evil.

The Activity of Satan

Satan uses a variety of methods to carry out his evil work, but none is more common than temptation. He who tempted Adam and Eve, and who later tempted Christ, is active in tempting human beings. Sometimes he uses direct suggestion, as he did with Judas Iscariot (John 13:2,27). At times he works through a person's own weaknesses (1 Corinthians 7:5), attacking at the most vulnerable points. Often he uses deception, seeking to lead us away from truth and into sin and rebellion against God (1 Thessalonians 3:5, 1 Timothy 3:6-7, 2 Timothy 2:24-26). If we do not use discernment, he is able to fool us by his ability to duplicate miracles and to counterfeit God's work (2 Corinthians 11:13-15).

Stated concisely, Satan draws us away from the will of God (Galatians 5:16-17), the Word of God (Matthew 16:23), and the worship of God (1 Peter 5:5-11). The Devil's activities are directed at destroying our dependence on God (John 15:5), our confidence in God (John 15:7), and our obedience to God (John 15:8-10).[19]

Demons: The Accomplices of Satan

Satan doesn't work alone. He has a host of accomplices who, like the Devil, are fallen angels working together to oppose the purposes of God. Presumably, this fall occurred before the world was created, leaving Satan and some of his cohorts available to contaminate the human race almost from the beginning. Some of the fallen angels have been imprisoned, but others clearly are free to join Satan as he prowls around the world, seeking people to devour (1 Peter 3:19-20, 5:8; Jude 6).

Fallen angels are evil and active. They are involved in spreading false doctrine, creating physical ailments, causing mental problems, actively opposing God's purposes, and disrupting the spiritual progress of God's people.[20] Satan and his demons greatly influence the world, and they are able to inhabit human bodies (Matthew 4:24, Mark 5:9). Together, they tempt humans to doubt God's goodness, to rebel against God's rule, and to yield to lustful appetites that can be enslaving (1 John 2:15-17).

In his work as a psychiatrist, Dr. Scott Peck initially concluded that Satan and demons did not exist. Then he began to look more closely and the famous doctor changed his opinion. In a book that we mentioned earlier,[21] Peck wrote about evil and stated his firm belief in the reality of the Devil and his demonic cohorts. The psychiatrist has been joined in recent years by a flurry of new people who acknowledge Satanic rituals and other forms of demon-inspired abuse.

Many of our counseling colleagues still dismiss the demonic as a remnant of middle-age superstition, but regardless of their personal opinions, the Bible clearly presents Satan and his accomplices as destructive beings who are active and deceptive in the world today, even as they were in New Testament times.

The Destiny of Satan

Every believer is in an ongoing struggle, not against flesh and blood but against powers of darkness and spiritual forces of evil

(Ephesians 6:10-20). The battles will continue as long as we live on earth, but the outcome has already been determined. Because of Christ's death and resurrection, the power of sin and of Satan has been broken. He already has been defeated, even though he continues to struggle and to go about his work. Erickson summarizes this concisely:

> The decisive battle in the war between good and evil was fought and won by Christ in the crucifixion and resurrection. Satan has been defeated, and although he continues to fight on desperately, his fate has been sealed. The Christian can take comfort in the realization that he need not be defeated in any of his specific encounters with Satan.[22]

The Devil and his demons continue to attack, deceive, tempt, and accuse us, and at times we yield to their influences. But the Holy Spirit who lives within believers is greater than the evil, demonic forces in the world (1 John 4:4), and Satan cannot tempt us beyond our power to resist (1 Corinthians 10:13). Jesus came into the world to destroy the works of the Devil (1 John 3:8). By His death on the cross and His resurrection, He disarmed and triumphed over demonic forces (Colossians 2:15). They already are defeated.

SPIRITUAL WARFARE

When you took your training as a counselor, did you ever have an instructor who talked about the role of spiritual warfare in your counseling work? Most of us probably would answer *no* to that question. Even many Christian counselor-training programs ignore or appear to be oblivious to the role of evil forces in the development and continuation of personal problems and interpersonal conflicts. In contrast to the majority, a few Christian counselors appear to be obsessed with the demonic and so involved with spiritual warfare and "power encounters" that they seem to know more about the Devil than they know about Christ.

What do we need to know? Like any general leading his troops into battle, Satan has an overall battle plan and a great variety of specific weapons. When we know the overall tactics and are familiar with his weapons, we are better able to resist demonic onslaughts and be more effective in helping our counselees resist.

Satan's Tactics: The Overall Battle Plan for Attack

In Ephesians 2:1-3, Paul gives an indication of the Devil's overall, three-part battle plan that he uses against all humans, whether or not they are Christians. First, the Evil One works externally in the world, disrupting societies and individuals from without. Second, he works internally, through the flesh, causing our thoughts and cravings to pull us into sin. Third, he works supernaturally, able to do evil by going beyond those of us who are earthbound. Stated concisely, we are influenced by the world, the flesh, and the Devil.[23]

The world. Think about the world and the society in which you and your counselees live. Think about the media, the schools, the work places, the entertainment industry, the political environment, even many of our churches. While we live in this world, we are surrounded and bombarded by influences that are strongly at odds with biblical values. Principalities and powers work through individuals, societies, and social institutions—including governments, unethical business corporations, repressive religious bodies, and revolutionary movements—to bring exploitation, conflict and ideological confusion.

Unless we are hermits without access to the media or to other human beings, we are in constant contact with people whose actions and values can pull us toward evil. Poverty, hunger, unemployment, political turmoil, crime, inner-city violence, family dysfunction and abuse, varieties of addiction, a glorification of immorality, and the widespread cultural values of self-centered materialism and pleasure-seeking—all of this gives a familiar picture of a world infested by Satan and pulling individuals further and further into sin and destruction.

The flesh. The influences and allurements of the world are not the only temptations that people face. Often the source of our problems lies within. When the New Testament refers to "the flesh," the biblical writers are describing those inner inclinations, drives, and cravings that pull us toward actions that violate God's standards. These are the tendencies that lead us to sexual immorality, attitudes of bitterness and revenge, uncontrolled anger, envy, pride, gossip, greed, obscenities, and a host of other behaviors that are self-centered and show a lack of self-control.

The Devil and his hosts undoubtedly know where each of us is weakest, and that is where the inner temptations are focused. Most often, it seems, these temptations start in the mind (2 Corinthians

11:3). Like the serpent who tempted Eve to doubt God's Word, the Devil comes into our thinking today, causing us to doubt and to violate God's moral precepts.

The Devil. Because he is a supernatural agent and a spirit, Satan is not confined to a physical body or bound by gravity. He is called "the ruler of the kingdom of the air," who can move about freely in his work of stimulating disobedience. The powerful supernatural work of the Devil and his demons may be directed against individual Christians, whole societies, and the Church. Even when the Devil chooses to work through the world and through the flesh, we should realize that it is still Satan who is at work, using a variety of methods.

Satan's Activities: The Methods Attack

It would be foolish and dangerous to go into battle completely ignorant of what the enemy might use against us. If you know nothing about the military, think about sports or business. I live in a part of the country where professional sports are big news and where almost everybody is interested in the home teams (especially when they are winning!). The sports writers talk often about the coaches and players watching films of their opponents and developing strategies to win the next game. Business people and political candidates do something similar.

The Christian should be like the Apostle Paul who was aware of Satan's schemes so that the Devil "might not outwit us" (2 Corinthians 2:11). What are Satan's schemes that he uses on us and on our counselees?

Temptation. This appears to be the Devil's major tactic—the tactic he used successfully in the Garden of Eden and the tactic that he used without success when he tempted Jesus in the wilderness. Evil spirits tempt both believers and unbelievers to doubt God's goodness and to rebel against God's authority. Demonic forces often work through our natural impulses, intensifying a desire so that we give in to our urges and fall into sin—which always is self-destructive. Whenever a person gives in to a temptation repeatedly, the resulting behavior becomes a habit, resistance gets weaker, and Satan's forces get a foothold in our lives (Ephesians 4:26-27).

It is obvious that we can fall in a number of areas. Some of these areas are summarized in Galatians 5:19-21. Satan's forces tempt us to engage in moral sin (impurity, debauchery, corrupt sexuality), religious sin (including idolatry and witchcraft), and personal-social sin (such as hatred, discord, jealousy, rage, selfish ambition, dissension, factions, envy). All of these attitudes and behaviors are lacking in love or self-control and are destined to hurt both the person who sins and other people.

Deception. Satan delights in deception, leading people to believe what is contrary to divine truth. The biblical epistles to the early churches were filled with references to false teachers who deceived the early believers. In 2 Corinthians, for example, a group of people who called themselves apostles and missionaries had come into the church with teaching that was doctrinally unsound. These people may not have known that they were the dupes of Satan, but they claimed to be true and righteous in what they taught and they must have been persuasive. Apparently they were eloquent speakers, critical of Paul, and so effective that they were in danger of leading Christian minds astray and away from sincere and pure devotion to Christ (2 Corinthians 11:3-6,13-15).

Within recent years, a handful of critics have written books and articles attacking people who are Christian counselors, especially those of us who are psychologists and other professionals. Some of the critics appear to be angry—more prone to launch written attacks than to follow the guidelines of Matthew 18:15-17 for expressing grievances. Some of the critics use arguments that might be considered distorted and facts that are sometimes inaccurate. As I read their criticisms, however, I recognize that much of what they say is right.

They argue that Christian counselors too often ignore Scripture, show ignorance of basic biblical teaching, uncritically accept the theories of secular psychology, and use therapeutic techniques that may be at odds with sound Christianity. Are some of the psychological teachers and therapists who have instructed us much like the deceptive teachers in Corinth, pawns of Satan but masquerading as sound and morally upright people? Without sliding into paranoia, it is wise for any of us to ponder what teachers or theories might be guiding us into untruth and how Satan is using influence-molders in our midst to deceive.

Physical influence. In the New Testament we have illustrations of Satan producing disease, deafness, the inability to speak, blindness, convulsions, paralysis, and lameness. It would be simplistic and inaccurate to conclude that whenever you get sick, physically or mentally, demons are at work sending germs and disease. Sickness and death came into the world when human beings fell into sin. In this respect, we could attribute all sickness to Satan, recognizing that most illness comes from the natural consequences of having imperfect bodies in a corrupt world. But sometimes physical ailments do come directly from the power of the Devil (Acts 10:38), like the thorn in the flesh that came to Paul, clearly from Satan but with the permission of God (2 Corinthians 12:7).

Demonization. This brings us to one of the most controversial topics among Christians and to an issue that has great relevance for Christian counseling.

To begin our discussion, let us assume that we live in a universe that is divided between two forces in which the Kingdom of God and the kingdom of evil are in conflict. From a biblical perspective, there is a conflict between God and His angelic Kingdom and Satan with his demonic kingdom. God, of course, could end this conflict at any time—and some day He will do so in divine victory (Revelation 20:9-10)—but at present He has allowed the conflict to persist. Christians wrestle against the demonic forces of error and deception (Ephesians 6:12), but we human beings are not pawns in the battle. We are presented with a choice: to submit to the authority and Kingdom of God or to yield to the influence of the Devil and his angels.

As long as we live in this world, human beings will be influenced by demons who attack, tempt, deceive, and seek to disrupt us mentally and physically. There are differences in the extent to which people are affected by these demonic forces, and because we each have unique personalities, it may be that no two people are influenced in exactly the same way.

Do some people come under so much demonic influence that we could say they are demon possessed? If so, is demon possession reserved for nonbelievers only or can Christians be possessed as well? These are very controversial questions that bring conflicting opinions from biblical scholars and Christian counselors.

Demon possession is a term that appears in some English translations of the Bible, but it never appears in the Greek text. The Greek New Testament speaks of people who "have a demon" (Matthew 11:18; Luke 7:21,33; 8:2,27,29) or who suffer from "demonic influence," but it never uses language to suggest that demons actually possess or totally control a human being. This conclusion has led many recent writers to abandon the term *demon possession* and say instead that people can be "demonized."[24] According to Ed Murphy, author of the massive *Handbook for Spiritual Warfare*, a major reason for rejecting the term demon possession is that,

> The state of being completely, continually, and totally possessed or controlled by demons would be very, very rare, if it even exists at all. Such persons would be totally unresponsible for any of their actions since the demons would possess and control them at all times. Scriptures never place total responsibility for human evil upon Satan and his demons. Persons are always held responsible for their actions. However, persons severely demonized over a long period of time by extremely powerful demons find it difficult to maintain self-control when the demons are in manifestation, leading to what psychologists call "diminished capacity." Mark 5 is a case in point.[25]

Murphy suggests a six-part "continuum of sin" that illustrates how Satan's forces progressively entrap believers. First come *thoughts* in which our minds dwell on ideas that are sinful and opposite to thinking about what is true, noble, right, pure, lovely, or admirable (2 Corinthians 10:3-5, 11:3; Philippians 4:8). Next comes *choice*. Thoughts can lead us to choose behaviors that can become *habits* that lead to increasing *loss of control*. In time we can be involved in *bondage*, and eventually we can reach a state of being under *almost total control*.[26]

Why do some people make this downward slide more easily than others? Murphy suggests that six conditions make some people more susceptible than others. First comes generational sin that moves through family lines. If you grow up in a family or are part of a household that is steeped in sin and rebellion against God, you and future generations can be affected and more likely to slide into a state of increased demonic bondage.

Second, victims of abuse, especially child-abuse victims, are susceptible to demonization, according to Murphy. These people have been subjected to human and supernatural evil from which they are unable to defend themselves. Often, they develop malicious and hate-filled attitudes that can open them to demonic attack.

This brings us to a third avenue for demonic involvement—the harboring of anger, bitterness, rage, and unwholesome talk. When we deliberately engage in sins such as these, we give the Devil a foothold in our lives (Ephesians 4:26-31).

Sexual sins are a fourth opening to demonization that we can all understand. The fifth category is much less familiar: curses that are pronounced against us. Finally, says Murphy, involvement in occult practices can open someone to excessive demonization. This is a reason for Christians to avoid horoscopes, Ouija boards, psychic healings, involvement with seances or mystical religions, music with immoral lyrics, and most new-age practices.[27]

"These sin areas do not automatically lead to demonization, and where it does occur, it can range from mild to severe," wrote Murphy. Deliverance and freedom from the grips of individual sins "can vary from the instantaneous, in which, for example, one is totally freed at the moment of conversion, to the prolonged. In the latter case, the victim may need to practice self-deliverance (spiritual warfare focused on breaking the demonic strongholds within one's own life) over a period of time or seek the help of other believers."[28]

Deliverance, exorcism, and counseling. Surely it is of significance that the Bible gives no commands or instructions regarding deliverance or exorcisms. But we are given three basic guidelines for dealing with Satan and his hosts: practice godly living, submit to God, and deliberately resist the Devil. Each of these must be applied to our own lives and can be used in our counseling.[29]

Godly living involves putting on "the full armor of God so that you can take your stand against the devil's schemes" (Ephesians 6:11). This involves standing firmly in biblical truth, living righteous and obedient lives, praying consistently, and keeping our minds alert to harmful influences.

Submitting to God for the unbeliever involves acknowledging one's sinfulness and receiving God's salvation that comes through belief in Jesus Christ. For the believer submission involves consistent obedience, confession of sin, commitment of one's ways to Christ, and seeking to be filled with the Holy Spirit. All of this is an active yielding of one's will, attitudes, and personal conduct into conformity with the will of God. Since the downward-continuum slide into sin begins in the mind, it is important to fill the mind with ideas, thoughts, and musical lyrics that are pure and Christ honoring. Submission to God also involves consistent times of personal prayer and Bible study, accompanied by worship with fellow believers.

Resisting the Devil involves deliberate efforts to avoid tempting situations and companions, refusal to engage in sinful thoughts or behavior, and change of sinful habits. The Devil is powerful, and his influence will not be resisted successfully without the support and help of the Holy Spirit. The resister also needs to be involved in a supportive community of believers, and often he or she needs the prayers, support, and encouragement of a fellow believer or counselor to whom one is accountable.

I have found that an effective way to resist the Devil is to verbally tell him, "Satan, in the name of Jesus Christ, I resist you and command you to leave me alone because I have been redeemed by the blood of Jesus Christ." Often I say this out loud or at least verbalize the resistance with my lips because the Devil is not omniscient; he can't always know what I am thinking. Of course, Satan has no inclination to pay any attention to me on my own. Believers do not confront evil forces on our own authority, but we can resist Satanic onslaughts because we know who we are in Christ. We are instructed to resist him, knowing that he will flee from the believer who stands firm in the faith, who is indwelt by the Holy Spirit, and who as a Christian is redeemed because of the shed blood of Christ (James 4:7, 1 Peter 5:8-9).

SO WHAT?

On a visit to the Philippines several years ago, I met an American missionary who had developed a fascination with demon possession. My new friend appeared to be a genuinely committed believer, and in our occasional contacts since our first meeting, I have never had reason to doubt his dedication.

But I have questioned his approach to counseling. This man, who now pastors a church in Canada, tends to see a demon behind every problem that his parishioners encounter. His approach to counseling almost always involves "calling up the demons" and casting them out in the name of Christ. Sometimes there are prolonged sessions of exorcism that leave everybody drained and the counselees more confused than helped.

This man's experiences suggest that understanding the facts about good and bad angels is very relevant to the counselor's work. As this chapter shows, we do our counseling in the midst of a conflict between two powerful supernatural forces, one godly and one Satanic. While some of our counseling colleagues develop an over-fascination with denomic influences and others counsel as if the Devil no longer existed, we must be people-helpers who take Satan seriously but who also remember the Bible's clear teaching that the Devil and his forces already are defeated.

But the primary focus of Scripture is not on angels, demons, or exorcisms. We are not told to focus on UFOs, extraterrestrials that might look like heavenly creatures, or even on demons or the angels of God. Instead, we are to focus on the Lord and to make choices that enable us, and our counselees, to grow in godliness, in grace, and in the knowledge of our Lord and Savior Jesus Christ (2 Peter 3:18). Spiritual warfare involves both resisting Satanic forces as they work through the world and the flesh and allowing our minds to be transformed by God's truth.

In this period of history, when increasing numbers of people are interested in spirits and occult phenomena, counselors need a clear concept of the truth about supernatural beings.

It is comforting to know that powerful and numerous unseen holy angelic agents are available to help and to minister both to us and to our counselees in the midst of our needs.

It is sobering to realize that even angels have given in to temptation in the past and have fallen; we too must take heed lest we fall (1 Corinthians 10:12).

It is very important to recognize that powerful and subtle Satanic forces can deceive, tempt, attack, and disrupt our lives. We must not take the Devil lightly, but neither should we be overwhelmed by his activities. The Holy Spirit who is in us is greater than the Devil who is in the world (1 John 4:4). That same Holy Spirit will not let any of us be tempted beyond the point of endurance (1 Corinthians 10:13).

It is reassuring to know that Satan's activities are limited and that his ultimate defeat is certain.[30]

For centuries, mental-emotional disturbances and behavior disorders have been explained in religious terms. Until the rise of naturalism in the late nineteenth century, most mental disorders were explained in terms of demonic influence. Even today some believers are like my pastor friend who assumes that when people have problems this must be the result of the Devil and demons.

Christian counselors work on a different premise. We assume that the conflicts and struggles of our counselees often come from the natural consequences of living in a sinful world where mental illness and physical disease are common. But we assume, too, that demonic influence also accounts for some of the problems we see in our counseling. Since the symptoms of demonization and mental disorders often are so similar, we can't clearly distinguish one cause from the other and neither can we come up with two different and separate treatments.

The effective counselor realizes that people are complex and that problems often have a mixture of biological, psychological-social, and spiritual components. Just as it is irresponsible to overlook physical and psychological influences in the lives of our counselees, so it is irresponsible to ignore the spiritual, including the demonic. Christian counselors who keep this broad perspective in mind ultimately are likely to be more effective than their colleagues whose understanding of supernatural agents is either nonexistent or at the level of misunderstanding of those who look for extraterrestrial beings or spirits riding in UFO spaceships.

❖

CHAPTER ELEVEN

The Church and Counseling

IN 1909, A YOUNG graduate of Yale University wrote a letter to the governor of Massachusetts. "I take pleasure in informing you that I am in the crazy business," Clifford Beers wrote, in an early effort to alert public officials to the mistreatment and inhuman conditions that prevailed in many mental institutions. Beers had endured several severe mental breakdowns and had written about his experiences in *The Mind that Found Itself*, a book that documented the brutal and sadistic treatment that mental patients endured in the hospitals and "insane asylums" throughout the country. I'm not sure how the governor of Massachusetts responded to the letter from Clifford Beers, but the book attracted worldwide attention and led to the founding of what is now the National Mental Health Association.

While Beers was campaigning for the fair and humane treatment of mental patients, another young man was suffering through the first of several psychotic episodes that led to three hospitalizations for a "schizophrenic reaction, catatonic type." Like Clifford Beers, Anton T. Boisen had been born in 1876, had experienced the trauma of mental breakdown and dehumanizing hospital stays, and later made significant contributions to the improved treatment of psychiatric patients. But Boisen wanted to work through the church. Liberal in his theology and "at best mediocre in his functioning" for the first two-thirds of his life, Boisen's career finally focused when he at last became symptom-free at age sixty. For the next thirty years he wrote books, did research on the psychology of religion, served as chaplain to psychiatric hospital patients, worked to bring seminary students into contact with mental patients, and sought to link church leaders and mental-health professionals with each other. Boisen felt that the church had neglected the mentally ill, and he was determined to bring change.[1]

It could be argued that the church has made significant contributions to the care and counsel of needy people—including people with mental problems. Through what have become known as the "four pastoral functions" of healing, sustaining, guiding, and reconciling, the Church of Jesus Christ has ministered to millions of physically ill and mentally distraught people throughout the centuries.[2] But according to one psychiatrist, that same Church also has created religious addiction and dysfunctional religious behavior. "In my practice I have seen people burdened beyond their ability to cope, with guilt placed on them by their church or an unbalanced minister," wrote Dr. Michael Douchette.

> I have seen them become compulsive in their church work
> and attendance. They have attempted to work their way
> toward perfection and favor with God—sometimes leading
> themselves into psychosis . . . because of such an ill-defined
> faith. . . .
>
> Egos, desire for power, searching for a quick fix for
> pain and the need to manipulate have produced a generation
> of faithful followers whose faith is toxic.[3]

How, then, does the Christian counselor evaluate the Church? When is it a toxic producer of mental abnormality, and when is it a healing balm in the lives of our counselees? To answer questions like these we need to look at the nature of the Church and at its divinely ordained ministries. When we understand the ideal that Jesus Christ established for the Body of believers, then we can appreciate the unique and significant therapeutic role of the Church, and we can better grasp why and how churches sometimes fall short of the standard that God intended.

THE NATURE OF THE CHURCH: WHAT IT IS

When you think of the Church, what comes to mind? For many people, thoughts of Church bring images of tedium, irrelevance, mediocrity, close-mindedness, rigidity, and hypocrisy. Others may think of buildings, like the places where the family "went to church" in earlier years or where they "go to church" now. A few might think of Church in terms of denominations, like the Catholic church or the Lutherans, while others have thoughts of seminaries, mission boards, pot-luck suppers, youth programs, publishing houses, committees, or stained glass windows. Less complex is the New Testament word for church, *ekklesia*, which refers to a gathering of people who come or are called together for a meeting.

As defined by one recent writer, the Church "is the community made up of those who believe in God as revealed in the Scriptures and who unite for worship and service to him."[4]

Bible scholars often think of this community in two ways. The *universal Church* is the entire Body of believers, coming from diverse denominations and from all over the world, including those who are alive and those Christians who have died. The universal Church grows whenever another person puts his or her faith in Christ and joins the company of the committed. The *local church* is the group of believers who gather in one place for worship, mutual growth, and service. True believers who are part of local churches are also part of the Church universal.

The Bible does not present the Christian life as a solo experience, marked by rugged individualism and a make-it-on-your-own mentality (Romans 14:7). God, Himself, is a Trinity of Father, Son, and Holy Spirit—three distinct Persons in oneness. When the human race was created, in God's image, we were made of two sexes that were intended to be "one flesh." Whenever Satan has had his way and sin has taken control the oneness has been broken and replaced with fragmentation. God's ultimate goal is to rebuild community and to "bring all things in heaven and on earth together under one head, even Christ" (Ephesians 1:10).

This oneness in Christ is not like the new-age goal of obliterating all individuality into an undifferentiated *monism* where there are no boundaries or lines of demarcation separating you from me, from God, from a plant, or from the furniture in a room. God didn't merge everything together. In contrast, He separated light from darkness, the sky from dry ground, various kinds of plants and animals from the others, people from one another, and each of us from Himself. Every human being is a unique person, living in a universe marked by diversity, but where God has always planned to have all of creation under His control and lordship.

When He prayed to His Father prior to the crucifixion, Jesus asked that believers would be one, as God is one (John 17:11,21-23).

Paul reminded the early believers that from God's perspective every person in His new community has equal access to God regardless of ethnic, social, and sexual differences; each is unique but all are one in Christ Jesus (Galatians 3:28).[5] Near the end of the Bible, we read of a day when the disruptive forces of Satan will have been defeated forever, and all believers, from the time of creation, will be together with God Himself—individual people, together in unity and community (Revelation 21:1-4).

Most of us know Christians—some among our counselees and colleagues—who are sincere and dedicated but who see no purpose in getting together to worship with other believers. Often these non-church-goers have become disillusioned or frustrated with the church and prefer to worship on their own or in small groups that are separated from larger bodies of believers.

The Bible specifically teaches, however, that we should "not give up meeting together, as some are in the habit of doing" (Hebrews 10:25). Building the Church is the most important thing that God is doing, suggested Gilbert Bilezikian. According to Scripture, the Church is the only "earthly reality that will survive time and last throughout eternity."[6] We who are individual believers must be involved in a local church—even when that church is like Noah's ark "where the stench inside would be unbearable if it weren't for the storm outside."[7] There is certain to be disappointment in people who expect their local churches to be places of perfection. We are people on the way to perfection. We aren't there.

To help us understand the nature of the Church, the Bible uses a number of images. Three stand out in particular and remind us of the Trinity. The Church can be viewed as the people of God, the Body of Christ, and the temple of the Holy Spirit.[8]

The Church as the People of God

All of us have had the experience of being with a group of people and feeling that we didn't fit. We can handle this as long as we know of at least one place where we do fit. But what happens when a person feels that he or she doesn't belong anywhere? People who lack a sense of belonging feel isolated, lonely, unwanted, and often unable to trust. We see this in some of our counselees, in members of minority groups, in people who are alienated from their families, or in those whose addictions, dysfunctional backgrounds, or deviant behaviors have cut them off from the rest of society. Cult recruiters, unethical business people, and even some religious leaders prey on these alienated individuals and exploit their strong need to belong.

In contrast, the Church is the place where Christians already belong. God the Father adopts us into His family forever, so that we become part of a community where we fit and where we can feel wanted, welcome, and free to trust (John 1:12-13; Romans 8:15-16, 9:24-25). This does not mean that you or I will feel equally at home or accepted in every church we might enter. God's people are not perfect, and too often we snub or exclude strangers, including fellow believers who are "not like us." If you have had opportunity to visit different churches, you will know that worship styles differ broadly and that even when visitors are welcomed warmly they still may feel awkward and out of place. Despite these differences, God accepts us into His family and it is His desire that believers, as His people, will strive to be like Him and to accept and welcome others with whom we are united in Christ.

The Church as the Body of Christ

The New Testament likens the Church to a living organism, a Body in which Christ is the Head and all of the extremities are important and interconnected body parts (1 Corinthians 12:12-30, Ephesians 1:22-23, Colossians 1:18). As parts of the Body, we belong to each other, we need each other, and we affect each other. We have different gifts, places of service, experiences, and needs, but God has put us together as parts of a Body. Each of us is called to be obedient to the Head, Jesus Christ, and to work together with the other body parts.

John Winthrop, the first governor of the Massachusetts Bay Colony, may have had this in mind when he spoke to his fellow colonists shortly before they set foot in the new world in 1630. "We must delight in each other, make other's conditions our own, rejoice together, mourn together, labor and suffer together, always having before our eyes our community as members of the same body."[9]

These words to the early settlers could apply equally well to the Church as the Body of Christ.

The Church as the Temple of the Holy Spirit

Early in the book of Acts, we see the first biblical example of church growth. Empowered by the Holy Spirit, Peter spoke to a large crowd, built a sermon around three Old Testament Scriptures (Psalm 16:8-11, 110:1; Joel 2:28-32), and saw about three thousand new believers added to the Church (Acts 2:14-41). Many years later, Peter wrote that believers are like living stones who form the building blocks of a "spiritual house" (1 Peter 2:5).

Paul used a similar picture. "Built on the foundation of the apostles and prophets, with Christ Jesus himself as the chief cornerstone," the church is like a building that is "joined together and rises to become a holy temple in the Lord. And in him [Jesus Christ] you too are being built to become a dwelling in which God lives by his Spirit" (Ephesians 2:20-22—see also 1 Corinthians 3:16-17).[10]

In Old Testament times, the temple was a building set in a place where believers worshiped, made sacrifices, and served. Today the people who are part of each local church may meet in a building, but the Church should not be thought of as a structure set on a corner. The Church is not made with wooden beams and stones but built of people who bond together in community to create a stable structure where God is worshiped and believers are empowered for service.

THE MINISTRIES OF THE CHURCH: WHAT IT DOES

I have a good friend who has served on the staff of a local church for several years but who has been struggling with the purposes and effectiveness of his congregation. "We are very good at doing busy work in our church," he told me recently over lunch. Then he described the immorality in some of the church leaders. "Where have we failed?" my friend asked. For a long time the church was led by people who appeared to be dedicated and committed to Christ but whose acts of debauchery and disobedience were hidden.

As my friend talked, I listened (like a good counselor) and later made a comment: "I guess all of this makes you wonder if there are others who might still be looking pious and committed but who are leading double lives, engaging in sin that nobody in the church knows about!"

My friend nodded in agreement.

The Church that Jesus established was not created for busy work or for hypocrisy. Instead, the Church exists to continue Christ's ministry in the world. Guided and empowered by the Holy Spirit, the Church is a community of believers who unite for worship and for carrying out Christ's mission of building up believers and reaching out to make disciples of all nations. Stated theologically, the Church exists for worship, edification, and evangelism. Counselors might prefer to think of the Church as a group of people who exist to praise God, to build people, and to make a difference in the world where we live.

Worship: The Church Exists to Praise God

In this age of change, technology, pressing demands, and ever-present stress, worship of God is not likely to be high on the priority lists of many people. Even among Christians, I suspect, worship tends to get equated with a Sunday morning "church service" that might put more emphasis on programs and activities than on the quiet and reverent adoration of God.

It has been said that worship is more easily done than defined,[11] but even the doing of worship is difficult. For many years I attended a large church where the "worship leader" was really a "cheerleader" who presided over the music with enthusiasm and with mannerisms that drew most of the attention to himself. Even more distracting, for me, are the thoughts that even now flood into my mind whenever I set time aside for worship. I can sing songs of praise with enthusiasm and never once think about the familiar words. I can be present while the words of Scripture are being read, but find my mind actively engaged in thoughts about my work, my finances, my schedule, my family, my personal insecurities, or even my sexuality. Sometimes I determine to shove out the distractions and to worship only God but realize that at the core of my life, I really worship career success, productivity, and quality performance. Surely worship is a discipline that must be developed with determination and effort.

True worship involves expressing our love to God in specific and thoughtful ways. If we fail to do this, then we haven't really worshiped, regardless of what might have transpired in church or in a private time of devotion. Worship is saying "thank You" to God. It includes remembering what God has done in the past—sometimes with the aid of bread and wine that give tangible reminders of the

Lord's death and resurrection (1 Corinthians 11:23-26) or with our presence at the public baptism of new believers. Worship includes the expression of one's determination to become more obedient and Christlike in the future.[12] We worship by singing, praying, expressing praise, listening, meditating, and giving. In worship, we praise God not only for what He has done but for who He is. By using words, thoughts, rituals, music, and symbols, the worshiper focuses on the greatness, beauty, goodness, mercy, and other attributes of God.

But true worship goes further. It permeates into all of life so that we commit ourselves to loving God, knowing God, obeying God, and becoming more and more like God. In a world that seeks to squeeze us into its mold, worshipers seek to present their bodies and minds to Him in willing sacrifice. This pleases God and is described as a "spiritual act of worship" (Romans 12:1-2).

When Jesus was asked to give the greatest commandment, He replied, "Love the Lord your God with all your heart and with all your soul and with all your mind," then He talked about loving our neighbors. The divine priority appeared to be worship first, service second. Even among the Old Testament priests, their first priority was to worship, coming near to God to minister to Him, before they turned to other tasks (Ezekiel 44:15). We worship, therefore, because God commands it and because He is pleased when we express our praise to Him (Psalm 29:1, Ephesians 5:19-20, Hebrews 13:15-16).

This does not come naturally, but the Church encourages, stimulates, and guides our worship. Often we worship privately, although this personal adoration and prayer is to be balanced by community praise. God takes delight in communities of believers who come together to offer Him praise (Hebrews 13:15).

Worshipers also benefit. "There is something about being together, blending our hearts and voices together in praise, that lifts us away from our own concerns and focuses our eyes on Almighty God," Howard Snyder suggested. When we look at God and ponder His attributes, "we find our own lives turned around, healed and prepared for service in the world."[13]

David Watson was a British pastor whose writings included a poignant diary of his struggles with the cancer that eventually took his life at age fifty. In the midst of his pain, Watson developed a growing appreciation of the personal benefits of praise and worship.

It is a sad commentary on the life of the Church in this
country today that worship is often sterile and dull, and at
the same time the level of faith to be found in many congregations is dismally low. The two factors almost inevitably go
together. . . .

All too often our faith is earth-bound and we find it
hard to believe that God can do anything that our minds cannot explain. It is only as we spend time worshipping God,
concentrating on the nature of his Person, especially his
greatness and love, that our faith begins to rise. Like a plane
soaring through the dark rain clouds into the fresh beauty
of the sunshine, so our faith rises, stimulated by the worship
and by the new vision of God that worship brings, until
we begin to believe that God can work in ways that may be
beyond our present understanding.[14]

Community: The Church Exists to Build People

In a *Time* magazine cover story about baby boomers, "The Generation that Forgot God," Catholic theologian Avery Dulles complained
that just about everything in the United States, religion included,
"succeeds to the extent that it can arouse interest and provide entertainment." The article describes people who dropped out of church
twenty years ago but who are returning in the midst of their middle-
age crises. Many are shopping from church to church or faith to faith,
sampling creeds, shopping for a God and a local congregation that
will meet their needs. Many sense the vacuums in their lives and their
lack of religious moorings as they try to pick up their broken lives
or "raise children in a society that has lost all connection to God."[15]
Churches that arouse interest, provide entertainment, and meet needs
are the churches that attract contemporary seekers.

This conclusion has led to warnings and sometimes protest from
those who see dangers in the church's overemphasis on meeting
needs. It is possible, the critics suggest, that we can shift from the
adoration and glorification of God to the entertainment and gratifi-
cation of human beings. How, then, do we reach out to excessively
busy nonbelievers or marginally religious people and pull them into
churches where biblical truth has not been abandoned and where
Christians are still called to obedience? Surely much of the answer
is found in the role of Church as a community of believers who are
dedicated to encouraging and building up one another. In a society

204 The Church and Counseling

where there is widespread isolation, loneliness, self-centered career building, and broken relationships, people need the kind of community that is found only in the Church.

Shortly after Peter's famous sermon on the day of Pentecost, the believers devoted themselves to "the fellowship." The Greek word is *koinonia*, a term that refers to a group of people who are in community or communion, having things in common and bound together by what they share. The early believers must have met together publicly, in the temple courts, but they also "broke bread in their homes and ate together with glad and sincere hearts, praising God and enjoying the favor of all people" in small-group settings (Acts 2:46-47). These people met every day, shared what they had with one another, prayed and learned together, and undoubtedly built up and encouraged each other.

The word *edification* isn't used much in our day-to-day conversation and it rarely appears in the Bible. But this word summarizes how the early Christians interacted and how we should relate to other believers today.

Edification refers to the community building and people-helping ministries of the Church. To be the Christian community means that we acknowledge our need for one another and "take responsibility for the welfare of Christian brothers and sisters in their social, material and spiritual needs."[16] Spiritual gifts have been given to all believers "for the common good" and for edifying and building up the Church (1 Corinthians 12:7, 14:12; Ephesians 4:12). Within the Body, believers care for one another and share together in a mutual desire to help each participant become more like Jesus Christ.

Sooner or later, all of us discover that Christian communities are not places of Heaven on earth where there is perfect love, compassion, self-sacrifice, giving, encouragement, joy, and praise. Often there is disappointment, disillusionment, and discouragement among believers who undercut one another, gossip, criticize, and battle for power or influence. But even when we miss the ideal, Christian communities can be and often are places of genuine caring, sharing, and support. Genuine fellowship comes when Christians stop relating to one another as people who have already arrived, instead interacting with each other as imperfect people who are in the process of transformation and best able to grow when we are related in a community.

How does the Church build community and edify believers? The Bible gives several guidelines.

Edification comes through teaching and preaching. Before He went back into Heaven, Jesus instructed His followers to make disciples, teaching them to obey everything that He had commanded. As we have seen, the early believers "devoted themselves to the apostles' teaching," and some must have been spiritually gifted to teach, even as some believers today are divinely equipped to be teachers (Romans 12:7, Ephesians 4:11). In one of his letters to Timothy, Paul gave a model for teaching and Christian education. He wrote, "The things you have heard me say in the presence of many witnesses entrust to reliable men who will also be qualified to teach others" (2 Timothy 2:2). One role of teachers is to train others to be teachers too.

None of this implies that teaching should be boring or irrelevant to modern audiences. My friend Lee Strobel is a speaker who seeks to translate the historic Christian message into language that twentieth-century people can understand. This does not need to be teaching that is related only to meeting needs or to gathering crowds around leaders who push aside sound doctrine and say what the itching ears of their students want to hear (2 Timothy 4:3-4). Biblical teaching involves giving training and encouragement that is relevant and practical, but it also includes rebuking people and correcting their errors (2 Timothy 3:16–4:2). This kind of teaching might scare away some fickle church-hoppers, but many others are likely to respond with enthusiasm to the kind of teaching that challenges listeners to commitment and obedience without watering down the biblical message.

Teaching is an activity that might use a variety of methods, including instruction, modeling, giving people learning experiences, or helping them learn through interaction and discussion. Preaching, in contrast, is a form of teaching that involves proclamation of the Word of God. Jesus did it, and so did many others. Paul commended it, and Timothy learned to do it (2 Timothy 4:2). And it doesn't have to be dull.

Edification comes through sharing, giving, and loving. The counseling literature often makes reference to love and stresses the importance of loving relationships. These therapist-writers assume that human love will bind people together and remove some of the tensions that divide us. That is not a bad idea except that it isn't easy to love and often we fail in the effort. "Human love, for all its powerful out-flow of emotions, is basically self-centered and self-seeking," according to a recent writer.

It desires to have, to possess, to capture; it does not serve and give. Human love is reluctant to release the object of that love for the good of the whole. Human love manipulates people and situations to achieve its end. It is restless, insatiable, and destructive of true fellowship. . . .

When Christians open their hearts to one another, and love and serve one another *in their human strength*, the result is that natural desires are awakened, vulnerability and emotional entanglements soon follow, and suspicion, jealousy and resentment are aroused. What may have begun as a genuine work of the Spirit ends in the flesh, bringing confusion and disaster.

Unfortunately, the natural reaction from those who have been hurt, is to back away from deep relationships altogether, to withdraw to a safe distance, to erect defenses to prevent further wounds. This fleshly reaction is another way of destroying the community of love that Christ longs to see in his church.[17]

As a counselor you might be more likely than others to accept this somewhat negative appraisal of love that is based solely on human effort. In contrast, love that is guided by and dependent on the Holy Spirit is different. It is love that is sincere and without manipulation or deceit. It is generous and from the heart, marked by the sacrificial giving of time, money, energy, and gifts to people in need. It is a forgiving love, sensitive to the needs of others, an upbuilding love that avoids backbiting or putting people down, a unifying love that works to heal divisions and restore relationships, and a positive love that believes the best about others and doesn't focus on the negatives.[18] This is a love that involves the sharing of experiences and burdens. If one part of the Body suffers, "every part suffers with it; if one part is honored, every part rejoices with it" (1 Corinthians 12:26).

Think about how your counselees could benefit from this kind of love and support. Sadly, many have never seen it and neither, I suspect, have some of us who are counselors. But this ideal is both realistic and possible.

Edification comes through burden-bearing and confession. Within the Church there must be mutual caring and support, especially in times of stress and need. "Bear one another's burdens," we read in Galatians 6:2. James 5:16 tells us to confess our sins to each other and to pray for each other so that we will experience healing. Psychologist and former APA president O. Hobart Mowrer was so impressed by this that he built his whole therapy around confessing our sins to one another, even though he neglected most other parts of the Bible.

On a regular basis, I meet with a group of four men, all of whom are believers who met in the same church. We share our needs and struggles, hold one another accountable, pray together, and rejoice together when one of us experiences something good. We build up each other, forgive one another, genuinely care for one another, and make ourselves available to bear one another's burdens. And there are times when we confess our failures to one another and encourage each other to do better.

During the time that we have been together, the members of our little group have bonded together like brothers. We have discovered that our commitment to confession, mutual prayer, and accountability makes a difference in how we live. As a result, we all have grown. That is at the basis of Christian community.

Edification comes through mutual submission. Christians are instructed to submit to God (Hebrews 12:9, James 4:7), to legal authorities (Romans 13:1,5; Hebrews 13:17; 1 Peter 2:13), and to employers, even when they are unfair (1 Peter 2:18). But we also are instructed to submit to one another, even to the point of serving others and considering others to be better than us (Mark 9:35, 10:43-45; Ephesians 5:21; Philippians 2:3).

This is a radical idea that rubs against the "look out for yourself" mentality that is widely accepted in our culture. Nevertheless, if we are to be built up in the community, we need to learn from one another, listen to what God may be saying through others, and be willing to be mentored by more mature members.

Edification comes through discipline. Within the past several years, there have been occasional reports of churches being sued because they have sought to exercise discipline on members who violate biblical standards, show no evidence of repenting, and resist the efforts of congregations to bring correction. Every parent knows the pain and lack of control that follows when children are not disciplined, but Christians are inclined to overlook misbehavior among fellow believers. Perhaps we ignore the offending behavior because we don't want to be sued, but more often we probably want to avoid embarrassment or tension. The Bible is clear, however, that offending believers need to be confronted and sometimes excommunicated, not with the goal of kicking them out of the community forever but with the motive of eventual restoration to the Body (Matthew 18:15-18, 2 Thessalonians 3:14-15). Without this cleansing, the local church body often is destroyed and its members are deeply wounded.

Edification comes through Communion. Christians have different names for the Lord's Supper, the Eucharist, or Holy Communion. Whatever it is called, believers can bond together and build up one another when they come together to remember Christ through the taking of bread and the cup. Too often this becomes another ritual and routine part of the church service. Instead we need to put special emphasis on this significant and Christ-ordained way of remembering Him together, in community (Matthew 26:26-29, 1 Corinthians 11:23-30).

Outreach: The Church Exists to Make a Difference

In reaching out to nonbelievers in ways that will make a difference in their lives, the Church has two responsibilities: evangelism that wins people to Christ, and social action that does something to alleviate suffering and deal with the problems of the needy.

Jesus instructed His followers to go into the whole world to make disciples, and He promised that the Holy Spirit would provide the power (Matthew 28:19, Acts 1:8). This was a command; it was not an optional proposal that believers could choose to accept or to reject. We aren't all called to be evangelists, but every believer is called to evangelize. Francis of Assisi had a good perspective: "Preach the gospel all the time; if necessary use words." Think about that the next time you go into the counseling room.

But Jesus also commanded us to be involved in social action. After telling about the good Samaritan who went to the rescue of a man who had been abused, Jesus instructed His followers to "go and do likewise" (Luke 10:25-37). He was compassionate, sensitive, caring, and people-oriented. He applauded those who fed the hungry, gave drink to the thirsty, clothed and cared for those who were needy or sick, took in people who needed a place to stay, and visited prisoners. And He criticized those who failed to meet social needs and did nothing to follow His example (Matthew 25:31-46).

The book of James reprimands those who are hearers of the Word of God but not doers, and we read that a faith unaccompanied by compassionate action is useless (James 1:22, 2:14-20). In the book of Galatians, we are given clear instructions for helping others by doing good. "Let us not become weary in doing good, for at the proper time we will reap if we do not give up. Therefore, as we have opportunity, let us do good to all people, especially to those who belong to the family of believers" (Galatians 6:9-10).

The Need for Balance
Worship, edification, outreach, praise, giving, people building, difference making—have you ever noticed how many of us are good in one or two of these but weak in the others? Some churches have great worship services and effective programs for building believers, but they have little involvement in evangelistic outreach or in social concern. Others are highly involved in social programs that seek to reduce poverty, house the homeless, or feed the hungry, but they have little concern for evangelism or the church members are made to suffer through weekly rituals of dry-as-dust worship services. In contrast, the community of believers should seek to be balanced, keeping worship, people building, and outreach all in perspective.

This isn't easy and the struggle to keep the balance is likely to be a continual challenge. But I must agree with Erickson's conclusion that "evangelicals, concentrating their medical, agricultural, and educational [and evangelistic] ministries in countries where the needs are most severe, have outstripped their counterparts in the mainline churches in worldwide endeavor."[19] Christians, especially evangelicals, often are criticized in the media, but God continues to work through the Church to change lives. That should interest every Christian counselor, especially since we are in the people-changing business.

SO WHAT?

Charles Colson is not a theologian and neither would he claim to be a therapist. Colson and his coauthor Ellen Santilli Vaughn are master storytellers. Their book *The Body* captivates the minds of readers with arresting accounts of churches that have made a significant difference in world history and in single human lives. Theirs is one of the most interesting and well-written volumes on the theology of the Church, but in the process, they have expressed some disturbing opinions about therapy.

In a chapter titled "Gimme That Hot Tub Religion!" Colson and Vaughn condemn religion that focuses on making people feel better about themselves. This is described as a "dreadful heresy," a "feel-good, restore-your-self-worth, therapeutic gospel" that seeks to fulfill emotional needs but has little interest in doctrine, commitment to authority, or obedience to Christ.

Christian counselors would agree that this kind of religion is currently popular but far removed from the biblical teaching on the Church. But most of us would disagree with Colson and Vaughn when they set up an artificial dichotomy and imply that therapy and the gospel are at war with each other.[20] It is true that therapy, divorced from the Church, often "works from the outside in to restore self-esteem by enabling us to adjust to our circumstances; carried far enough, it can lead us to feel good about being bad." We would agree, as well, that the gospel "is designed to transform our lives and circumstances; it works from the inside out." But it is not true that therapy alone is concerned with changing behavior while the gospel changes character. Working in partnership with the Church, guided by the Holy Spirit, and in submission to the teaching of Scripture, Christian counseling can have a powerful impact. It can be used by God to change both behavior and character, to help meet real needs, and to work from the outside in and from the inside out to help people grow into greater Christlikeness.

In the pages of this chapter we have acknowledged the weaknesses of self-centered and hot-tub religion and have conceded that many churches are places of busy work, boredom, and bickering. But we also have seen what God intends His Church to become. The Church of Jesus Christ is not an optional adjunct to counseling, a possible referral source that might help some people who need extra support and encouragement between counseling sessions. The Church exists to bring people together into a community that worships God, builds individuals, and reaches out to make a difference in people's lives. Can we be Christian counselors and ignore such a powerful institution, despite its weaknesses?

Have you ever noticed that the Bible rarely mentions the word *religion*? When the book of James uses this word, however, we see religion in a clear perspective: "Religion that God our Father accepts as pure and faultless is this: to look after orphans and widows in their distress and to keep oneself from being polluted by the world" (1:27). In this sentence we have the core of Christian counseling. We are to be involved in people-helping and in developing personal holiness. By seeking to build people and to reach out to make a difference, we become genuine people-helpers. By worshiping God in private and with other believers, we grow in personal holiness.

Counseling is not Christian when it ignores the Church and when it is done in isolation from the community of believers. The counselor who bypasses the Church might help people, but the help will be of limited value and the helper might spend life somewhat like Clifford Beers, working without God "in the crazy business." When we ignore the Church, we are not helping people to be what God intended them to be: individuals who identify with a community of believers for the purpose of worship, edification, transformation, and service.

❖

CHAPTER TWELVE

The New Age in Counseling

THERE ARE THOUSANDS of them spread throughout the country; perhaps tens of thousands. They work—usually for a fee—in shopping malls, at church bazaars, in dingy offices, at psychic fairs, in the living rooms of their homes, and sometimes in fashionable business places. Many wear neat business suits and seem far removed from the beaded curtains, blinking neon signs, or crystal balls that sometimes are associated with their craft. Nobody knows how many fortune tellers, tarot readers, astrologers, occult practitioners, or professional psychics (they go by different names) ply their trade, but many report that interest in their services has never been greater. Business is booming for publishers of "divination system" card decks. New-age bookstores are increasing in numbers and in the volume of their sales to clients who want books, cards, crystals, and other paraphernalia that will help them make life decisions and predict the future.

"It's a poor man's way of going to a psychologist," says one University of Oregon professor. "There's nothing to it." But adherents are willing to pay $125 and more for guidance about their decisions and for predictions of what their futures may hold. According to psychic readers themselves, many people have lost faith in government, religious institutions, and their own families. So they look to non-traditional institutions, Eastern mysticism, native Indian cultures, new-age spirituality, readers of divination cards, and sometimes to tea-leaf readers in an effort to find stability and hope. Caught in the modern quest for "religious consciousness" and spirituality, many people appear to be overlooking or forsaking biblical doctrine and turning to more flexible, popular, and immediate ways of predicting the future.[1]

The Bible forcefully condemns divination, sorcery, the interpretation of omens, consulting mediums or spiritists, and other psychic practices, blatantly calling these sin and "detestable to the Lord" (Leviticus 19:26, Deuteronomy 18:10-14, 1 Samuel 15:23, 2 Kings 21:6, 2 Chronicles 33:6, Acts 19:18-19). But the Bible does not keep us in the dark about the future. None of us can know, for sure, what our individual lives will be like tomorrow or in a year, although the Bible paints a broad perspective on where we all are going. It points to the ultimate destiny of human beings, gives an accurate indication of where the world is headed, and gives all believers, and their Christian counselors, genuine reason for hope—even in the midst of present pain and conflict. And the Bible points to a new age that is far different from the dreams of Shirley MacLaine or the most sophisticated advocates of the new-age movement.

TWO PERSPECTIVES

According to new-age writer David Spangler the coming "new age" will be "a culture in full harmony and attunement within itself, with nature, and with God: a culture in which the divine perspective of love and wholeness can find full expression."[2] Christians would agree that this is an accurate picture of the future new age, but we part company with new-age thinkers when we consider how this goal will be reached and what it will be like to be part of that future culture.

All new-age thinkers agree that we are moving to an era of global harmony, and most would agree that we realize this goal by becoming enlightened regarding our divine potential. New-age advocates widely assume that the problem of humanity is ignorance and a lack of knowledge about our own potential. The solution to the problem is a change of consciousness so that we are enlightened and enabled to realize that we are all divine.

Christianity also affirms that we need a change of consciousness, but the followers of Christ believe that the problem of humanity
is not ignorance. Our problem is that we have rebelled against a Holy
God and against His moral law. The solution to our problems is not
enlightenment; Scripture teaches that the only way out is through
repentance and faith in Jesus Christ, God's Son, who came to redeem
and restore us.[3]

The biblical writers make it clear that history is going someplace
and that God has a specific and detailed plan that will move us to an
eternity where He alone is sovereign and where human beings will
live together in endless harmony. This brings us to an issue that
Christians have discussed for centuries but that Christian counselors
have tended to ignore. It is an issue that has tremendous relevance
for people-helpers: the issue of the Kingdom of God.

THE KINGDOM OF GOD

When they see a new client, counselors often take a case history to
help them understand how the person's problems got started, how
they developed, and how they might be dealt with in the future. To
understand how we human beings fit into the whole of God's plans,
we need to look at a different type of case history. It is a case history
of the human race. It considers how our problems got started and
developed and how they will be dealt with in the future.

In earlier chapters, we have seen how the Sovereign God created
the universe that included human beings made in the divine image. It
was God's desire that we would reflect His character in our relationships with Him, with other people, and with ourselves. And He gave
us the privilege of being the caretakers of His world.

But human beings rebelled and fell into sin. Tempted and
spurred on by Satan and his demonic forces, we have resisted God's
sovereignty. Beginning with Adam and Eve, we have defied God and
attempted to manage our lives and determine our destinies apart from
divine rule.[4]

Throughout history, however, God has been moving to reassert
His supremacy. A prominent theme running through the Old Testament is the promise of a Deliverer who will restore harmony to
creation and establish a new Kingdom where God alone is supreme.
When Jesus was on earth, the Jewish people were waiting for the
promised Messiah and expecting that something spectacular would

happen on a single day—the Day of the Lord—when they believed God would deliver them from the yoke of Rome and dramatically assert His reign on earth. The atmosphere must have been charged with wonder and excitement when John the Baptist arrived on the scene and proclaimed that the people should "repent for the kingdom of heaven is near" (Matthew 3:1-2). Jesus began His ministry with the same message (Matthew 4:17, Mark 1:15). It appeared that a new age was about to begin.

The preaching of Jesus did not conform to the expectations of the people, however. When the religious leaders asked when the Kingdom of God would come, Jesus did not reply with talk about an imminent political revolution. He said, instead, that the Kingdom might not even be visible at first because "the kingdom of God is within you" (Luke 17:20-21). Even so, He talked about future times when the Kingdom of God would come with power (Mark 9:1). This suggested that some Kingdom events were still ahead. In the Lord's Prayer, the words "thy kingdom come" would not have meant much if Jesus did not have something future in mind.

It could be argued that preaching and teaching about the Kingdom of God was at the center of Jesus' earthly life and ministry.[5] Even so, it appears that some of the Jewish leaders who listened to Jesus, and even some of His own followers, misunderstood His teaching about the Kingdom (Luke 24:21). They failed to recognize that the Kingdom of God is *both* coming in the future and present now.

The Kingdom of God Is in the Future

Perhaps it was more common a few decades ago, but many churches and Bible colleges still have "prophecy conferences" in which they discuss the past and future, sometimes with dire and speculative predictions about events that are coming. While many of these conferences are built around messages that emerge from careful study of Scripture, sometimes the speakers give dramatic conjectures about present-day events. Whole "ministries" have developed, giving information about the end times. These sometimes are . . .

supported by TV shows, radio programs, innumerable books and pamphlets, specialized magazines, study Bible notes, and a legion of "prophecy" speakers, all competing to titillate the public with the most sensational and the most exotic

predictions of the End. They make their million, then wait
for the next international crisis or the next war in the Middle
East to revise their charts, face-lift their books, readjust
their timetables, and fleece the gullible public out of another
million.

Partly in reaction to such excesses, many Christians
refuse to commit themselves to a specific line of belief on
the doctrine of the end times. . . . Yet they yearn to know
what the Bible teaches on this subject.[6]

Unlike the lengthy and detailed charts of some prophecy speakers, figure 12.1 is a concise illustration of the present age in which
we live, and the new age that ultimately will be seen in its future
fullness.

In this diagram, the section between A and B refers to the period
of history from the time of the creation to the coming of Christ. B
to C is the time frame when Jesus was on earth, and the section
between C and D is the time in which we presently live. At some
time in the future (marked by the letter D), this present age will
end and there will be a new age that lasts for eternity. Much of the
emphasis in prophecy conferences and many of the debates about last
things concern the events that take place at the end of this age. While
these events will be of infinite importance, they are only a part of the
whole picture.

Figure 12.1 indicates that there is overlap (the section on the
chart between B and D) between the present age and the new age
to come, between what we can call the kingdom of this world and
the Kingdom of God.

Figure 12.1
TWO OVERLAPPING KINGDOMS:
THIS AGE (THE KINGDOM OF THIS WORLD)
AND THE AGE TO COME (THE KINGDOM OF GOD)[7]

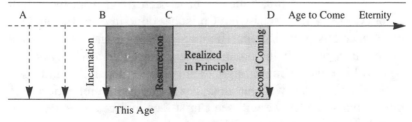

When Jesus came, at the time of His incarnation (B in figure 12.1), He launched a new age that is described in Scripture as the Kingdom of God. The Kingdom did not come in its fullness when Jesus came to earth, and it is not fully here yet, but at present God is pulling more and more people into His family. Together, believers can anticipate the time when there will be no more tears, temptations, or tendencies to run our own lives on a course of rebellion and isolation. Throughout all His ministry, Jesus pointed to the future when His new age of divine rule would be experienced in its completeness (see, for example, Matthew 24–25, Mark 13, Luke 21). Until Christ returns, Christians probably will differ in their views of when and how this new age will be ushered in, but we can agree that someday we will be like Christ and will spend eternity with Him.

The Kingdom of God Is Present
The Old Testament shows that God intervened in human lives long before Christ was born in the manger of Bethlehem. He created us and frequently influenced individuals and nations, often at crucial times in history.

When Christ came, however, and the much awaited Kingdom of God began, God intervened to redeem us and to start the process of bringing His Kingdom to its fullness. Since the time of Christ's death, resurrection, and ascension, individual believers have lived as part of two worlds. We are still in this present age with its pain, suffering, turmoil, and stress. But the future age of the Kingdom of God has started within us, because of our faith in Christ. We live in a world of sin and rebellion, but when we repent and believe that God is reconciling the world to Himself through Jesus Christ, we are no longer under condemnation as we were in the past (Romans 8:1). Instead, we live with Christ, as Savior, Lord, and King of our lives. We begin to get a taste of what the future Kingdom experience will be like. When we are born again we get a glimpse of the future Kingdom (John 3:3).

In this present life, believers have been freed from their guilt before God. We have seen what Christ has done in our lives, and we experience His presence and His impact. But we know that we are not yet made over wholly into the new creatures with heavenly bodies who will live with Him through eternity. Even our understanding is limited. Right now we see what looks like a poor reflection in a mirror, but someday we will see Christ face to face and understand completely (1 Corinthians 13:12).

"But I'm a Counselor"

Knowing that we live our lives in two overlapping kingdoms might appear to be of limited interest to Christian counselors. You might be among those who would think that this theology probably is significant and worth knowing about, but you're a counselor, faced every day with the nitty gritty issues of people's lives. How can knowledge about the Kingdom of God have any relevance to the counselor's work?

To answer, let us begin with the reminder that at times all of us can benefit by seeing beyond the present and getting a bigger picture of where we are going. Counseling often focuses on the past, looking at prior ordeals and pain that must be faced, handled, and resolved before counselees can put aside their background experiences and move on to recovery.

Too often, however, counseling is stuck in the past. Counselees are encouraged to wallow in the memories of their dysfunctional backgrounds. As a result, they play the role of victims, focus attention on blaming others, and avoid taking responsibility for the future. Certainly this is not true of all counseling. Most counselors agree that present problems often have their roots in the past and that helping people deal with their prior experiences can be a long process.

But ultimately the Christian's goal is to forget the things that are behind and to press on to what God has called us to be in the future (Philippians 3:13-14). This is not a call to suppress all memories of the past and to pretend that the past hurts never happened. Instead, we are to recognize that past events occurred, to face them honestly, and then to move into the future without excessive dwelling on our prior experiences. Anthony Campolo suggested that "Christian counseling should focus more on helping clients define their futures and not pay exaggerated attention to the past."[8]

The New Testament has a future perspective. It spends more time looking ahead than it does looking back. It reminds us that God is in control, that the future belongs to Him, and that some day we will understand His ways and will experience happiness that is far different from the pain, despair, and confusions that we might live with now. Even now, we are to be in the process of becoming more Christlike, transformed into the image of Jesus Christ (1 Corinthians 15:49, 2 Corinthians 3:18, Colossians 3:10, Ephesians 4:24).

The Christian doctrine of "the end times" is not an irrelevant addition tacked on to what we have discussed in earlier chapters.

What God has revealed about the future has profound implications on how we live and counsel in the present. The Christian faith is ideally suited to provide the forward-looking and hope-filled counseling that people need. Because we have insight into the coming Kingdom of God, we have hope and can give hope to our counselees, even in the midst of trials. We accept the fact that suffering will come while we live in this world, but we know that in time God will bring an end to suffering, injustice, and evil when His Kingdom comes in its fullness. Even now, we and our counselees can begin to experience the peace and joy that will be ours in abundance in the future (Romans 14:17). We can even develop a fresh perspective on death.

WHAT ABOUT DEATH?

Several years ago a student gave me a copy of Ernest Becker's Pulitzer prize winning book *The Denial of Death*. Inside the front cover, my student wrote that this book had made a profound impact on his understanding of how Christianity and counseling are related. Becker wrote that the "idea of death, the fear of it, haunts the human animal like nothing else; it is a mainspring of human activity— activity designed largely to avoid the fatality of death, to overcome it by denying in some way the final destiny of man."[9] Long before Becker wrote, Freud observed that belief in life after death is "the oldest, strongest and most persistent wish of mankind." It is found in nearly all religions, ancient and modern. And it even permeates the new-age ideas of people who believe in reincarnation and have a fascination with NDOBEs—near death out of body experiences.[10]

All of this points to the human desire to deny the reality of death. No longer do we talk about old people dying or about undertakers who bury bodies in cemeteries. Instead, we think of becoming senior citizens, who live through the golden years, until we pass away and are laid to rest in a memorial park.[11] This is far removed from Paul's description of death as an enemy (1 Corinthians 15:26).

As everybody knows, death is the cessation of life in our physical bodies. When we die, our breathing ceases, our hearts stop beating, and our bodies decay and return to dust. Modern medicine might delay death, and morticians might partly hide its appearance, but eventually every physical body give out and dies (Ecclesiastes 12:7,

3:19; Hebrews 9:27). According to the Bible, however, we should not think of death as being equivalent to nonexistence and conclude that life is the same as existence. Instead, we should think of death as the transition from one type of existence to another. Death is not the same as extinction or complete annihilation.[12]

In addition to physical death, the Bible talks about spiritual death. This is the state of being separated from God because of sin. It is a state of deadness that applies to every person, including some who look very much alive but who are walking in the ways of Satan and the world (Ephesians 2:1-2).

When Adam ate the fruit, he died spiritually on the same day—even though he stayed alive physically for a few more years (Genesis 2:17—see also Ezekiel 18:4,20). Since the time of Adam's sin, all human beings have been born dead in their transgressions and sins (Ephesians 2:1). When people who are spiritually dead do not repent of their sins, they are condemned to spend eternity in endless punishment and separation from God. This has been called eternal death or the second death (Revelation 21:8).

This second death is avoided by people who put their faith in Christ, who is the giver of life (Revelation 20:6). God sent His Son to redeem us through His life, death, and resurrection, so that those who believe in Him would have everlasting life. The person who has the Son has eternal life (John 3:16,36; 5:24; 6:40; 20:31; 1 John 5:12-13). When he or she experiences physical death, that person is away from the body but present or "at home" with the Lord and assured that the dead earthly body will someday be transformed into a glorious heavenly one (1 Corinthians 15:40-49, 2 Corinthians 5:8, Philippians 3:21).

Gorbachev's Fable

On his last day as president of the Soviet Union, Mikhail Gorbachev was accompanied by American newscaster Ted Koppel. It was Christmas Day in Moscow, and the television cameras recorded the president's stroll outside of the office that he would soon vacate. He reminisced about a visit to Washington in which he had met with spectators and appreciated their "spontaneity, their openness, their frankness." He telephoned President Bush to send Christmas greetings and to say goodbye. And he responded to the newscaster's question about the future.

"There is a fable I learned years ago," Gorbachev told the television audience. A young ruler wanted to succeed as a leader but he never had the time to read the teachings of the wise men. When he was at the point of death, the declining leader was visited by the chief wise man who came to summarize the wisdom of the ages.

"All that is here can be summarized in a single formula," he said. "People are born, people suffer, and people die."[13]

Unlike the "wise men" in Gorbachev's fable, the Christian does not see life as nothing more than a time of suffering that ends in death. Period! We recognize that death is an enemy, but it is a conquered enemy. When we die and leave the body, we who are believers go to be with Christ, and that is far better. The Christian view of death is unique, because it enables us to see both life and death in the perspective of God's coming Kingdom.

WHAT HAPPENS NEXT?

A Christian doctor once stood by the bed of a dying man who wanted to know something about the place where he would be going after he took his last breath. While the physician fumbled for an answer he heard his dog scratching at the door of the room.

"Do you hear that?" the doctor asked his patient. "It's my dog. I left him downstairs, but he has grown impatient, and has come up and hears my voice. He has no notion what is inside this door, but he know that I am here. Isn't it the same with you? You don't know what lies beyond the Door, but you know that your Master is there."[14]

We don't know, for sure, what life is like immediately following death. Several Scripture passages suggest that we experience an intermediary state between life here on earth and the final state of eternity in Heaven or hell. When we are absent from the body, we are present with the Lord, Paul wrote (2 Corinthians 5:8-9). In the parable of the rich man and Lazarus, both had died but were in a conscious state, separated from each other by a gulf that could not be crossed (Luke 16:19-31). When he repented on the cross, the thief was told that he would be with Jesus in paradise on that very day (Luke 23:43). There are no detailed accounts of what this intermediate state will be like, but "it appears that believers will experience the actual presence of the Lord, in other words, heaven, but not as fully as will be the case after the resurrection." Unbelievers, in turn, will be in hell, but this will be less fully experienced than it will be after the final resurrection.[15]

There is much about the future that we don't know. But some things are both clear and generally accepted by almost all Christians, even when they hold strongly different views about the sequence of events that will end this earthly kingdom and usher in the Kingdom of God in its fullness. Where do we agree, and what do we know with certainty?

Jesus Christ will return to earth (John 14:2-3, Acts 1:11, 1 Thessalonians 4:13-18). We don't have many biblical details about this return, but two things appear to be certain. First, the return of Christ will be without warning. It will come as a surprise, so each of us needs to be ready, waiting diligently in anticipation (Matthew 24:36, 25:1-13). Second, we know that Jesus will be visible, personal, in a body, and recognizable, as He was when He ascended into Heaven (Acts 1:11, 1 Thessalonians 4:16). There is no biblical support for the idea that Jesus already has returned secretly or that the second coming was really what occurred when the Holy Spirit came at Pentecost.

The dead will be raised to life (Daniel 12:2, John 5:28-29). Immediately, however, there will be a separation into two groups. Those who believed in Christ will meet Him and will be joined by Christians who have not yet died. All will be given new bodies that will be perfect and free from pain, decay, or death (1 Corinthians 15:42-50). In contrast to these believers who awaken to experience everlasting life with Christ, nonbelievers will face an eternity of shame and everlasting contempt (Daniel 12:2).

Everybody will be judged (Matthew 25:32, 2 Corinthians 5:10, Hebrews 9:27). This judgment will be absolutely fair and impartial, because Jesus Christ is the ultimate Judge (John 5:22,27; Acts 10:42; 2 Corinthians 5:10; 2 Timothy 4:1). The judgment also appears to be permanent and irrevocable. There is no indication in the Bible that the verdict can be appealed or changed.

The outcome of the judgment will be different for nonbelievers than it will be for believers. Nonbelievers are those who have rejected Jesus Christ and refused His offer of salvation. Because of this refusal they are condemned already (John 3:18). At the judgment time they will be condemned to a place of endless punishment, anguish, and everlasting separation from God.[16] C. S. Lewis wrote that throughout life, unbelievers have sought to live independently of God and, in effect, have said, "Go away and leave me alone." Hell is God finally and reluctantly giving sinners what they insisted upon in life.

In contrast, believers will have a different type of judgment. They don't need to fear everlasting condemnation; they have been pardoned because of the sacrifice of Christ (Romans 8:1,31-39). But believers will be judged for their work on earth. All that we have done or even thought will be made visible and publicly appraised, as gold is tested in fire (1 Corinthians 3:8-15). There will be a rejection and destruction of all that was done independently of Christ's will, and there will be approval and reward for all that was done in His strength and in keeping with the will of God (1 Corinthians 3:8,12-15; 2 Corinthians 5:9-10; Colossians 3:24-25; John 15:5).

This judgment has nothing to do with salvation. Our destiny as believers has already been settled. As a gift from God, all believers will enter eternity with Christ. And all of us will go with a divine appraisal for the lives that we have lived on earth. For some, there will be special approval because they have served Christ faithfully on earth, giving Him praise and doing good in their lives (Hebrews 13:15-16).

In the end there will be a new creation. Sincere and dedicated Bible scholars disagree on the details concerning the end-time events. Some maintain that there will be a thousand-year reign of Christ on earth prior to the time when the new heaven and new earth are ushered in (Isaiah 11:6-9, Revelation 20:4-6). Others believe that Jesus will come at any time, that judgment will follow immediately, and that the new heaven and earth will follow shortly thereafter.[17] Due to the space limitations of this book, I have chosen to bypass the details of this significant and fascinating discussion, even though we all will be involved personally in these coming events.

Most Bible students will agree that at some time in the future, all of creation will be tested as gold is tested in fire and God will create a new heaven and a new earth (2 Peter 3:10-13). The Lord Himself will be there, and all of us who are present will be permanently transformed people, living together harmoniously in community. The image of God in us that was marred at the time of the Fall will be fully restored, and we will be able to relate without hindrance to God, to others, and to all of His creation. This is summarized at the bottom of figure 12.2, where the diagram that we have used through this book is completed.

Figure 12.2
THE CREATION, FALL, AND RESTORATION,
SANCTIFICATION, AND GLORIFICATION OF HUMAN BEINGS

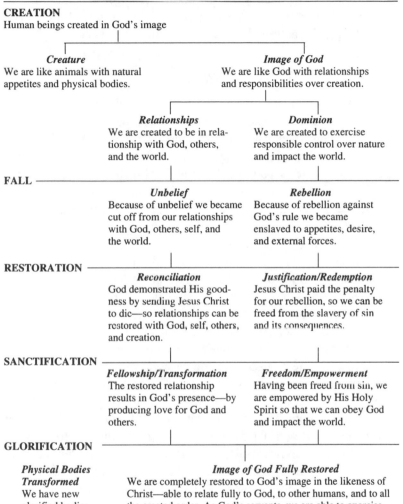

CREATION
Human beings created in God's image

Creature
We are like animals with natural appetites and physical bodies.

Image of God
We are like God with relationships and responsibilities over creation.

Relationships
We are created to be in relationship with God, others, and the world.

Dominion
We are created to exercise responsible control over nature and impact the world.

FALL

Unbelief
Because of unbelief we became cut off from our relationships with God, others, self, and the world.

Rebellion
Because of rebellion against God's rule we became enslaved to appetites, desire, and external forces.

RESTORATION

Reconciliation
God demonstrated His goodness by sending Jesus Christ to die—so relationships can be restored with God, self, others, and creation.

Justification/Redemption
Jesus Christ paid the penalty for our rebellion, so we can be freed from the slavery of sin and its consequences.

SANCTIFICATION

Fellowship/Transformation
The restored relationship results in God's presence—by producing love for God and others.

Freedom/Empowerment
Having been freed from sin, we are empowered by His Holy Spirit so that we can obey God and impact the world.

GLORIFICATION

Physical Bodies Transformed
We have new glorified bodies.

Image of God Fully Restored
We are completely restored to God's image in the likeness of Christ—able to relate fully to God, to other humans, and to all the created order. As God's servants, we are able to exercise responsible control over creation.

All of this pictures a new age that is far different from that envisioned by advocates of the new-age movement. The final outcome of history is a new age and a new creation, including a community of believers. This new creation worships God and brings glory to Him by reflecting His nature. This, indeed, will be a new age.

SO WHAT?

But what does all of this have to do with counseling?

Warren Heard is a seminary professor, a pastor, a professional counselor, and a scholar with advanced degrees in both psychology and New Testament studies. For a while we taught on the same faculty and sometimes still get together for lunch, where the conversations almost always are stimulating. Consider, for example, that time when he started talking about "eschatologically oriented psychology."

To understand Heard's position so that we can see its relevance for counseling, we have to pull ourselves through a brief theological discussion of two words: the *indicative* and the *imperative*. The epistles often begin by indicating things that are true (the indicative), but we also read about what we are to do (that's the imperative) as a result of these truths. In Scripture, how we are instructed to act always rests on and arises out of what we know to be true. Stated more formally, "the imperative rests upon the indicative and not vice versa. The imperative follows the indicative by way of conclusion, often with 'thus' or 'therefore'" (e.g., Romans 6:12-14; 12:1; 2 Corinthians 5:11,20; Colossians 3:5).[18] Colossians 3:1 is an example. Since you have been raised with Christ, Paul wrote, then you should set your hearts on things above. In Romans, the writer gave eleven chapters of indicatives, stating who we are in Christ and where we are going. Then he devoted four chapters to the imperatives of what we should do as a result.

Now we can apply this to counseling. As Christian counselors, we believe that the most beneficial and mentally healthy behavior is consistent with the biblical imperatives. As a result we encourage people to avoid envy, to maintain sexual purity, or to control their anger. These imperatives often make little sense to our counselees or to our nonChristian colleagues, unless they understand the biblical basics (the indicatives) on which the recommended behavior is built.

As an example, let us look again at the verses in Philippians where we are told to forget the past and focus instead on the future (3:13-14). Heard suggests that Paul was not suggesting that his readers forget everything in the past. In fact, Paul often mentioned things that are worth remembering. It seems more likely that Paul was advocating a selective forgetting. The apostle, himself, could have been paralyzed by guilt and despair if he had dwelt on thoughts of his past persecution of the Church, and he could have swelled with pride if he had focused on his accomplishments. Instead, he put most of his attention on what he knew for sure about God's actions now and in the future.

Heard gives the illustration of a young woman in her thirties who had been abused repeatedly by her stepfather when she was a child. Consider how this case history develops.

> This woman has recently become a Christian and has heard a number of sermons about forgiveness. She knows that she is being challenged to forgive, but her recollections maintain their power and immediacy as her mind relives the past events. Each time she thinks about these terrible incidents she is gripped afresh by the intense emotions attached to the memories. To control her cognitions and simply not to think about these events risks repressing the emotions, which then may well work themselves out in unhealthy ways. Thus it is important deliberately to access this material cognitively and emotionally. However, going over this highly emotive material again and again in psychotherapy to gain insight and process some of the residual emotion can only help so much. Instead, this client needs to be guided through these painful events from a new perspective: the perspective of the future. She must project herself into the future, appropriate her identity and position in Christ, see herself as one who is whole, and then, *from the perspective of the future*, be guided back through those old memories.
>
> It must also be emphasized that the achieving of this eschatological perspective is a *process* and takes place over a period of time. To be able to view events, past and present, from the standpoint of the future is not a product of repeated assertions, either by the therapist or by the client; it is a work of the Spirit, as the Spirit renews the client's mind.

Psychotherapy (which includes listening, support, prayer,
insight, admonition, Scripture, meditation, encouragement,
reading, reflection, advice, confrontation, confession, questioning, interpretation, evaluation, explanation, informing,
teaching, empathy, verbalizing feelings, unconditional love,
authenticity, trust, wholesome relational experiences, etc.)
is a powerful instrument that the Spirit is able to utilize.
The therapeutic process can best facilitate the Spirit's work
by having an eschatological orientation. Once this eschatological orientation is achieved, the client is able to pass
through those past painful events (as well as present ones),
not as one whose identity is that of an abused child, as one
who conceives of herself as damaged goods, but as one
who is healed and who is in Christ (the indicative). From an
eschatological perspective this woman is not captive to her
emotions and only able to return abuse for abuse in a retalia-
tory way, but she can now forgive (the imperative) because
she is able to envision her stepfather as God does and see
herself as whole in Christ.[19]

This case implies a worldview that combines an emphasis on
this present world with an awareness of the world to come. As long
as we live in the period of overlap between the Kingdom of God and
the kingdom of this earth, we must deal with both "this-worldly"
and "other-worldly" issues. We must focus, for example, on abuse,
pain, hunger, violence, injustice, interpersonal tension, and the other
stresses of this world. But we also keep aware of the long range biblical perspective that history is moving toward a conclusion, when
Christ will return and when believers will experience the fullness of
God's Kingdom.[20] We live and counsel in the present but also in the
light of eternity.

Not long ago, I read an interview with Charles Barkley, who
had been voted as the most valuable player in the National Basketball
Association. Barkley can be abrasive with the media, but sometimes
his honesty is disarming. When his team lost a championship game,
the famous athlete was besieged with shouting reporters who were
berating the team for the failure.

"Get real, you guys," Barkley responded. "It's not life or death.
The world's not going to stop if we lose. This is my job, not my
life."

Charles Barkley, and millions like him, may not think much about eternity, but this superstar basketball player was able to see the present from a broader perspective. That is the challenge for Christian counselors: to enable the people we help to see their problems and to live their lives in the light of what is certain about the future.

This gives our counseling a solid foundation and provides our counselees with a firm basis on which to built their lives. All of that is far more satisfying and useful than the speculations of the fortune tellers and those who give their "readings" to admiring followers but who have no personal walk with God and no clear understanding of God's plans for His coming new age.

❖

CHAPTER THIRTEEN

Spirituality and Counseling

THE COFFEE SHOP in a western hotel was our prearranged meeting place when I got together with two young psychologists who were interested in writing a book about Christian counseling. We had talked on the phone, but this was to be our first face-to-face get-acquainted meeting.

After we chatted about our families, backgrounds, and careers, I asked my new-found colleagues to tell me about their church involvements.

"I don't go to church," one of the counselors stated. "I'm a recovering Catholic." His colleague, who had been raised in a Protestant church, was also frustrated by a "dysfunctional" religious background, but instead of leaving the church, he had joined a congregation that rejected "rigid narrow-mindedness" and gave people freedom to believe pretty much what they wanted.

Both of these counselors were involved in the modern men's movement. They claimed to find "cleansing and true spirituality" in their monthly meetings by getting in touch with nature, beating drums, and sweating with other men. My recovering Catholic friend spoke with great approval about the writings of renegade priest

232 Spirituality and Counseling

Matthew Fox, whose books mix Christian theology with pagan concepts of spirituality and salvation through "mother earth."

Clearly the two men in that restaurant define spirituality in non-traditional ways. But each has a strong interest in what it means to be spiritual and both teach at respected universities where interest in spirituality is high, even among counselors.

This is a new trend. For decades, professional counselors have been willing to deal with almost any issue that a counselee raised, no matter how bizarre, but religion has been dismissed as being irrelevant or pathological. According to one report, 90 percent of Americans claim to believe in God, 82 percent believe in an afterlife that includes both Heaven and hell, 55 percent believe in the existence of Satan, and 58 percent went to religious services when they were growing up—services that presumably made some difference in their lives.[1] But textbooks in psychology, psychiatry, and counseling have ignored the study of religion and religious behavior, overlooked the impact of religion in people's lives, sought to explain religion away, or dismissed it as evidence of pathology.[2]

Why has this begun to change? What has made spirituality a popular topic and why have some university professors, professional organizations, and journals become more willing to treat religious issues with greater seriousness? When *Family Therapy Networker* magazine devoted an entire issue to "Spirituality and the Limits of Psychotherapy," the editor expressed what many secular counselors must feel. In spite of "all its fascination, therapy has no answers to the ultimate mysteries that surround our lives," editor Richard Simon wrote. "However intricately a clinical theory can help us analyze a client's dilemma, it cannot tell us why any of the various dramas in anyone's life is worth caring about, or what meaning our lives have. . . .We can do therapy, come up with clever interventions, but we're going to die anyway, just like everybody else."[3]

This realization has not sparked an interest in Christianity. Instead, it has brought counselors into a type of spirituality that involves "tapping into the unlimited power within us." Christian concepts of looking outward to Christ, seeking guidance in Scripture, worshiping with other believers in church services, or believing in the Son of God who came to a manger are all rejected as being narrow, insensitive, "arrogant and uncompassionate in a world of pluralism, a world in which there are many worthwhile religious ways."[4]

The new spirituality is a movement away from the rigorous,

rational, objective, logical, factual thinking of the past. In contrast, the new spirituality is subjective, mystical, feeling-oriented, intuitive, and devoted to urging people to look into themselves to find God, or to "get in contact with the higher self within." As we have seen in an earlier chapter, many spirituality seekers would add that we all are gods or in the process of becoming gods, and some would suggest that the ultimate goal of spirituality is to experience unity with one another and with the universe.

Psychiatrist M. Scott Peck, for example, divides spirituality into four levels. Lower levels view God as we have viewed Him in this book, as an eternal, transcendent Being. The top level is the most mature spirituality, which according to Peck, is "a mystical communical stage of spiritual development," a stage "of unity, of an underlying connectedness between things: between men and women, between us and the other creatures and even inanimate matter as well, fitting together according to an ordinarily invisible fabric underlying the cosmos."[5]

This may sound like pantheistic gobbledygook, but it isn't far removed from the thinking of many of our nonChristian and new-age–oriented colleagues. Their concepts of spirituality have been described as a modern resurgence of the ancient religion of mother earth, where all of nature is seen to be alive and filled with divine energy. From this perspective, true spirituality seeks to find the energy and unrealized potential within ourselves and within nature. It is a spirituality that is slipping unnoticed into many churches and into mainstream psychotherapy.

CHRISTIAN SPIRITUALITY

When he was asked about the growing ministry of Jesus, John the Baptist made a brief statement that gives the essence of spirituality for the follower of Christ: "He must become greater; I must become less" (John 3:30). Although the term *spirituality* has become increasingly vague, Rowland Croucher has captured the essence of spirituality from a Christian perspective. "Christian spirituality is about the movements of God's Spirit in one's life, in the community of faith, and in the cosmos," Croucher wrote. "It is concerned with how all realities relate, enlivened, enlightened, and empowered by the Spirit of Jesus. . . . *Spiritual formation is the dynamic process whereby the Word of God is applied by the Spirit of God to the heart and mind of the child of God so that she or he becomes more like the Son of God.*"[6]

Christians cannot conceive of true spirituality without the guidance of the Holy Spirit of God and the truth of the Word of God. Christian spirituality does not ignore human potential, interpersonal relationships, meditation, or even personal success or concern for the environment. But neither does Christian spirituality ignore the realities of sin, the significance of self-denial and self-control, or the centrality of obedience to God the Father and the formative influence of Jesus Christ, who is both our redeemer and our model.

Christian spirituality is a process of becoming increasingly Christlike—a process that goes beyond mere self-reflection to find hope, forgiveness, redemption, and ultimate meaning in the living Christ. Christian spiritual growth involves introspection and self-examination but goes much further to include reading and obeying the Scriptures, attendance at worship services, self-sacrificing service, personal discipline, and a firm commitment to Christ. Is it surprising that millions turn away, like the rich young ruler? Modern new-age views of spirituality are easier, less demanding, and much more vague.

The Christian counselor is in the process of growing in Christian spirituality and in helping others grow. This growth in spirituality involves developing a Christ-centered worldview and orientation toward God, nature, society, and oneself.[7] There are two facets to this growth process—becoming more like Christ, and allowing Christian concepts to permeate every area of our lives.

CHRISTIAN SPIRITUALITY: BECOMING MORE CHRISTLIKE

Every counselor knows about word association tests in which people hear a word and are invited to respond with the first thought that comes to mind. When we hear "salt," most of us respond with "pepper" (or maybe with "light" if we are familiar with Matthew 5:13-14). But how do you think most people would respond to the word *holy*? The Bible speaks often about our holy God and about holiness, but today the term arouses pictures of dour, joyless, irrelevant, unattractive, "holier-than-thou" religion.

Holiness, however, is at the essence of Christian spirituality. The Israelites were instructed to be holy, because God is holy (Leviticus 11:45). Jesus expressed a similar idea when He instructed His followers to "be perfect, therefore, as your heavenly Father is perfect" (Matthew 5:47). Paul wrote that all of us should present our bodies as "holy and pleasing to God" as a "spiritual act of worship" (Romans 12:1).

These, of course, are ideals that cannot be attained fully in this life, but the serious biblical call to a devout and holy life is at the core of Christian spirituality. Tucked on one of my bookshelves is a tiny volume with a title that summarizes the challenge for Christians: *The Call to Holiness: Spirituality in a Secular Age.*[8] Many counselors in the secular world may share our interest in spirituality, but for the Christian living in a secular age, spirituality means that we are called to be like Christ, to be holy, to imitate Him (1 Corinthians 11:1, 1 Thessalonians 1:6), and to be increasingly conformed to His likeness (Romans 8:29).

This is a noble thought when we read it on paper or hear it in a sermon, but the call to holiness is difficult to apply in day-to-day living. Some of our counselees, like some of us, try repeatedly to be "good Christians," but the failure rate is high and the resulting frustrations are common. Others may try a "let go and let God" approach that involves continual submission and a process of waiting for God to bring about the longed-for transformation. This too can lead to failure and disappointment. In contrast the Bible presents what might be called a "divine cooperative program" in which we take responsibility for becoming more Christlike *and* we trust continually that God will work within us to bring change.

This biblical approach to spirituality does not involve some twelve step program or the application of spiritual growth techniques. Certainly recovery programs and the use of techniques are helpful in many lives and with many types of problems. But the urge to put spirituality into a growth-inducing formula can distract us from Christ Himself. Adherence to spirituality programs can involve us in human-oriented ways to build power and control[9] or can force people into a rigid regimen that might fit some but not others.

Theologian James I. Packer notes that spirituality and growth in holiness are relational. God is a person and we are people who relate. The goal is the same for all of us—to be like Christ—but each spiritual journey is likely to be unique, guided by the Holy Spirit, and often helped along by other human beings.

Because human individuals differ from each other, no two marriages are ever identical, and in the same way no two lives of fellowship with God are ever quite the same. Every Christian must ultimately find his or her own way in the relationship, with such help as can be gained from friends, pastors, and those who since the seventeenth century have been called "spiritual directors" (nowadays more often described as "soul-friends").[10]

Packer adds that throughout history numerous traditions or paths to holiness have been developed. These include Catholic, Lutheran, Wesleyan, Reformed, mystically-oriented, charismatic, socially alert, individualistic and other approaches to spirituality. Each of these has enthusiastic devotees who see their own approach as being complete and self-sufficient, "with the added innuendo that none of the formulae really work save the one the speaker is currently peddling."[11] As a result, teachers of spirituality regularly omit helpful guidelines that are rejected because they are anchored in another tradition.

How, then, do we become Christlike, so that we are better able to counsel in ways that the Lord Himself would approve? There are at least two answers. We must focus on what Christ has done on our behalf and we must model our lives on how He lived.

Focus on What Christ Has Done
During the summer Olympics, an American super-heavyweight wrestler was expected to do well in his division. Sports writers thought he had the potential to win a gold medal, or at least a silver, but in one difficult match he lost in overtime, while his wife and six-year-old daughter watched.

Later that night, television audiences saw a film clip of the little girl crying as her father retreated from the competition. As the viewers watched, a commentator observed that "at her age, daddies aren't supposed to lose."[12]

In our society, nobody is supposed to lose. We are raised with the idea that all of us can be or can do whatever we set our minds to—if we work hard enough. This is a message that often is conveyed in the words, attitudes, and lifestyles of counselors, teachers, pastors, business leaders, coaches, and parents. The result is a whole society of individuals who measure their worth in terms of how much they accomplish. Many of us go through life caught in a performance trap or driven by a "success syndrome."[13]

In his nineteenth-century analysis of American culture, the much quoted Alexis de Tocqueville wrote that in our society, every person is supposed to earn a place on the ladder of success. Each works night and day to be successful, each is afraid of falling back, each wants to find a place in the world through personal achievements, and each wants to reach the heights quickly. Some contemporary baby boomers and others may resist this philosophy of drivenness, but it still floods into our counseling rooms and it permeates many churches.

It also has a subtle power in the lives of people who want to grow spiritually. We assume that God did His part by creating us in His image. Jesus did His part by redeeming us. The Holy Spirit does His part by guiding and teaching us. Now it is our job to do what we can to obey the laws of Scripture and to grow spiritually. We sense that God is watching us, arms folded and brow furrowed, waiting to see whether we love Him enough or have sufficient commitment to pull it off.[14]

It is true that the Christian life can be a struggle (Ephesians 6:12), but spiritual growth is not a performance-driven, success-oriented push for some victorious superspirituality. Salvation came because of the mercy and grace of God, and spiritual growth comes in the same way. We don't need works, ecstatic experiences, self-flagellation, special Spirit baptisms, spiritual twelve step programs or anything else to bring true spirituality. Christ's work on the cross is necessary and sufficient for both the new birth and Christian maturity.[15] Both depend on what Christ has done and is doing in the lives of people who have faith in Him. In the Bible, salvation refers to a growth process that begins with the new birth but continues throughout life as Christ molds us and makes us more like Him. We can resist the growth process, of course, or we can get distracted by our own efforts to perform and to reach spiritual success. But real growth comes only when we consistently and humbly submit to Christ, admit our weaknesses and sinfulness, and recognize the emptiness of efforts to reach spiritual maturity on our own.

Jesus once used the example of a branch on a vine. Cut off from the vine and on its own, the branch cannot thrive or produce fruit. But when the branch is part of the vine, the life-giving resources flow from the larger plant to give strength, growth, and productivity to the smaller branches (John 15:1-8). In a similar way, true Christian spirituality comes as a result of our being yielded to Christ, getting to know Him better, and acknowledging that we are loved and complete in Him.

During his times of great personal struggles and doubt, Martin Luther frequently repeated the words "I am baptized!" He was reminding himself that despite the struggles he was in union with Christ. Baptism symbolizes this (Romans 6:3-4). Although Christians use different types of baptism, perhaps baptism by immersion most clearly conveys the symbolism. Going down into the water and being raised out is a reminder that because of the death and resurrection of Christ, we die to the old person and are raised to become new persons in Christ, forgiven, accepted, loved, and in the process of growing in Christlikeness (2 Corinthians 5:17).

Model Our Lives on How Jesus Lived

In one of her counseling sessions, Leanne Payne worked with a Christian woman whose problems included self-hatred and spiritual confusion.[16] The counselee had come from a broken home where the father had divorced his wife and abandoned the family, leaving his daughter starved for love and guilty because of her attempts to find acceptance in sexual permissiveness.

For some time the woman had been keeping a journal, but like many of us who keep journals, this counselee tended to write mostly about her miseries and struggles. Writing in a journal can be healthy and useful, but Payne suggests that journaling too often becomes little more than a record of all our unhealthy attitudes, negative experiences, and introspective musings. Journals frequently reflect a "practice of the presence of self" in isolation from the presence of God and His words. Certainly this has been true of the entries in my journals over the years.

Payne's counselee was given a different assignment: to get a new notebook and to go through the gospels, personalizing every promise and every command that Christ gave to His disciples. The counselor knew that this exercise would focus attention away from the "I can'ts," and on to a new awareness of what Christ has done and continues to do in our lives. The new journal also gave this woman a new appreciation for how Christ wants obedience, and her journaling revealed a fresh recognition that He gives us the power to model our lives after His.

Paul instructed the Corinthian Christians to imitate Christ (1 Corinthians 11:1), and John gave a similar message by writing that believers "must walk as Jesus did" (1 John 2:6). These are not calls to herculean self-effort and neither do they imply that growth occurs in people who are isolated from others. Individuals are transformed into Christlikeness (2 Corinthians 3:18) through a slow process that often involves other human beings. Within the community of believers, we encourage, teach, strengthen, and sometimes rebuke or correct one another in a spirit of love. The Bible gives no approval to oppressive church leadership or legalistic rule-keeping. Instead we work together as a new community of redeemed, still imperfect, growing people who bear one another's burdens and help one another move toward maturity.

Most counselors are familiar with concepts of modeling and mentoring in which a more experienced and/or mature, usually older, person seeks to guide and encourage one who is less experienced and growing. Paul mentored Timothy and was a mentor-model to the Corinthians (1 Corinthians 11:1, 1 Timothy 1:3, 2 Timothy 2:2). Today, modeling and mentoring take place in both the counseling room and in the church where we learn from one another but have the same goal, to be like Christ. To help us understand what He is like, we can read about His life in the Bible and ponder (sometimes even with our counselees) the various biblical models that portray Jesus as a servant and shepherd among others.

What can we learn about spirituality by following Christ?

We learn that *Jesus lived in obedience to the Father*. Jesus stated His mission concisely. "I have come down from heaven not to do my will but to do the will of him who sent me" (John 6:38). Throughout the Bible we are commanded to obey God and to live in holiness, instead of following after our own lusts and desires (1 Peter 1:14-15). Like Jesus obeyed the Father's commands, we are to obey God as well. That is how we show him our love (John 15:10-11).

Everybody knows that this is difficult as long as we live here on earth and experience the continued temptations of Satan and his forces. The Bible is realistic enough to state that none of us is sinless and that we all are likely to fall at times. But we have Jesus Christ, who speaks to the Father in our defense (1 John 1:10–2:1), and we can step out through life believing that as we seek to do God's will, He will enable us.

By looking at the life of Christ, we see that *Jesus lived in dependence on the Holy Spirit*. The Spirit of God was present when Jesus was born, baptized, tempted, ministering, praying, crucified, commissioning His followers, and ascending into Heaven (Matthew 1:18, 3:16, 4:1; Luke 4:14, 10:21; John 20:22; Acts 1:1-2). Near the end of his life, he promised that the Holy Spirit would come to believers as their counselor, teacher, and guide (John 14:26, 15:26, 16:13).

When I was teaching an introductory counseling course, I often talked with the students about the importance of counselor empathy, warmth, genuineness, and sincere concern for people. Then I would suggest that the best counselors are people whose counseling and lives are characterized by love, joy, peace, patience, kindness, goodness, faithfulness, gentleness, and self-control. These, as you probably realize, are what the Bible calls the fruit of the Spirit, characteristics that develop in our lives through the activity of the Holy Spirit (Galatians 5:22-23). People with these growing attributes are best able to gently work with counselees and others who are caught in sin and other self-destructive behaviors (Galatians 6:1).

Jesus lived a disciplined life. If we read carefully through the Gospels, we see Jesus taking time for worship, prayer, communication with the Father, rest, ministry, and interaction with His critics. His life was disciplined, but there is no evidence that He was uptight, rule-dominated, or rigid. Instead He demonstrated what subsequent generations of spiritual giants have discovered: spiritual maturity and a sense of genuine freedom only come through embracing the spiritual disciplines.

Donald Whitney has used the example of guitarists Chet Atkins and Christopher Parkening to illustrate how freedom comes through mastery of a discipline. When they perform in public, these musicians give the impression that they were born with the instruments attached to their bodies. They have such an intimacy and freedom with the guitar that their playing looks effortless. But anyone who has tried to play knows that the musical freedom of such masters comes only after decades of disciplined practice.

The same is true of the athletic superstars, skilled debaters, master carpenters, insightful leaders, eloquent speakers, and highly skilled counselors whose familiarity with their crafts comes after years of consistent and often rigorous practice. These people are achievers who experience true freedom in their actions because of their submission to discipline. "Nothing was ever achieved without discipline; and many an athlete and many a man has been ruined because he abandoned discipline and let himself grow slack," wrote

William Barclay. "No one ever reached any eminence, and no one having reached it ever maintained it, without discipline."[17]

Christian Spiritual Formation

Sometimes I am surprised by the basic truths that I have missed in my journey through life. As a child in Sunday school I heard about prayer and Bible study, but over the years somehow I failed to grasp the importance of spiritual disciplines and the nature of spiritual formation. Without giving these issues much thought, I concluded that spiritual growth is a matter that concerns an individual and God, with a lot of the responsibility falling on us. If anybody had asked, I would have agreed with the divine cooperative program that was mentioned earlier. I knew that God works to bring change from within, and I was aware of my need to take responsibility for becoming more Christlike. But I began to see this with greater clarity when Richard Foster published his widely acclaimed book *Celebration of Discipline* and when other writers followed with similar thought-triggering volumes.[18]

These writers promised no magical formula for spiritual formation. They did not give lists of rules and neither did they prescribe a growth program that would be the same for everybody. But they agreed that nobody ever came to Christian spiritual maturity except through discipline.

Donald Whitney writes that God uses three primary means for changing us and conforming us to Christlikeness.[19] The first of these is *people*. Friends, mentors, pastors, prayer partners, neighbors, family members, writers, teachers, spiritual directors, critics, even nonbelievers—all can be used by God to make a difference in our lives. For some counselees, you or I may be the human instrument God uses, even without our being aware that this is happening.

Second, God uses *circumstances*. At the beginning of 2 Corinthians, Paul describes some of the hardships, pressures, and discouragements that he felt, but he is quick to point out that these were growth experiences. In the midst of his troubles, the apostle learned to praise God and to depend on Him. He saw how God brought deliverance and hope. And having been comforted by God, Paul could see that "we can comfort those in any trouble with the comfort we ourselves have received" (2 Corinthians 1:3-11).

These growth-inducing circumstances could be thought of as "spontaneous" events that God uses to reshape our worldviews, remold our personalities, and strengthen our beliefs.[20] Some of these events are positive, like a good marriage, a job promotion, or an awareness of good health that can cause us to reflect on God's goodness and mercy. Other circumstances are disruptive, leading to distress, confusion, and questioning. Months or even years may pass before the person begins to glimpse the purpose of God in allowing the crisis to occur or is able to reevaluate the situation and begin to heal and grow as a result.

Third, spiritual growth comes through the deliberate practice of *spiritual disciplines*. Writers give different lists of the disciplines and group them in different ways, but all include prayer, worship, Bible study, meditation on Scripture, fasting, serving, silence, giving, and evangelizing. These are spiritual exercises that keep us spiritually fit and growing, similar to the periodic physical workouts that keep us in good physical shape. The disciplines take time, determination, and effort, but they are not effective in themselves. The disciplines put us in a place where God is best able to change willing human beings, from the inside out. This is the deliberate cooperation with God where believers who have put their faith in Christ continue to "work out" that salvation through human efforts and experience God working in them to bring change and maturation (Philippians 2:12-13).

CHRISTIAN SPIRITUALITY: BELIEFS PERMEATING LIFE

Heaven is likely to be a place where a lot of us will be surprised. We might be surprised at some of the people who are there and at some who are missing. We might be surprised to discover that some of our gravest theological issues are of little concern to God, and probably we all will be surprised to find that some of our dearly held beliefs were wrong. I wonder, however, if the greatest surprises will come when we see how God evaluated people on earth.

When Jim Berry's wife died, he and I had a talk about their years together and Jim reflected on his future. Unlike the professors, students, and professional colleagues with whom I have interacted during much of my adult life, Jim never got beyond fourth grade. He is the first to admit that his grammar isn't always correct, he knows that his endless jokes and stories are as "corny" as they come ("but they're clean!"), and nobody would say that he has a lot of tact. But Jim is a motivator, a blatant extrovert, and in demand as a speaker who can entertain audiences with tales and truisms that leave people laughing and thinking.

When my wife, Julie, and I drove away from the funeral home after Jim's wife died, I can remember my comment: "Great will be that man's reward in Heaven." His entire life is a continual reflection of his beliefs. I don't know of anyone who is more dedicated to Christ, more willing to learn, more committed to evangelism. I have met some of the people Jim has led to Christ, ordinary women and men like Jim, neighbors and business associates whose lives have been changed for eternity by a man who even today has no hesitation in sharing his faith with any who will listen—and often with people who don't much want to listen. Even though he likes to read, I doubt that Jim Berry has plowed through many (or any) theology books, but his life reflects something that even theologians sometimes miss. True spirituality involves following the example of Jesus. His relationship with the Father was reflected in everything He did.

Sometimes we think of life as a dualism that divides everything into two realms, the spiritual and the ordinary. The spiritual part of life is assumed to include thoughts about God, spiritual discipline, religious observances, theological jargon, and mystical experiences. In contrast, the ordinary part of life includes our day-to-day activities, building our careers, taking care of our bodies, paying the bills, and having sex.

Jim Berry would never divide his life like this, and neither does the Bible. Earlier we described spirituality as a Christ-centered worldview and orientation toward God, nature, society, and oneself. This view of spirituality implies that Christian spirituality is concerned with theology, sociology, politics, economics, education, business, entertainment, the environment, child-rearing, marriage building, personal problem solving, and every other part of our existence. No area of life is excluded. At times Jesus withdrew from the crowds for time alone with the Father, but much of His life was spent involved with the ordinary experiences shared by human beings who live in the real world. Larry Richards captured the essence of this when he defined spirituality as "living a human life in this world in union with God."[21]

For most of us that doesn't mean having visions and ecstatic religious experiences. Unusual experiences are not to be ignored or dismissed as being irrelevant, but neither are they to be sought or lauded as evidence of superspirituality. Jesus warned the disciples

244 Spirituality and Counseling

against a fascination with the unusual and instructed them, instead, to rejoice that their names were written in Heaven (Luke 10:17-20). Sometimes miracles, unusual experiences, signs, and wonders are counterfeits that look like they come from God but really come from the Devil (2 Thessalonians 2:9). Discernment is important so that we distinguish between the unusual experiences that are genuinely from God and those that are not. The real essence of spirituality is living a Christ-pleasing life in the midst of our daily activities, far removed from thoughts of ecstasy and excitement.

C. S. Lewis learned that he could see God and undergo spiritual growth in the midst of pain and grief. As he faced death, David Watson experienced spiritual growth in the midst of suffering. Brother Lawrence knew that he could live out his spirituality in the noise and clutter of the kitchen "while several persons are at the same time calling for different things," just as easily as he could possess God in the tranquility of being on his knees at worship in the cathedral. "Lord of all pots and pans and things," he wrote. "Make me a saint by getting meals and washing up the plates!"[22]

Could something similar be said of counselors today who work, not with pots and pans, but with DSM-III-R's, insurance forms, crushed egos, addictions, and counselees in conflict? "Lord of all struggles and healing, make me a saint by listening empathically and being Your instrument for helping those who struggle in their daily lives." True spirituality includes doing our counseling and living our lives in union with God.

SO WHAT?

Gary Moon has told a parable of three sons who left the farm, where generations of their ancestors had labored for many years, and went to the university and into the city where they experienced success and satisfaction. The first brother to leave the farm was named Psychology; the other brothers, Pastoral Counseling and Christian Counseling, came later.

In this parable, the farm was described as the place where workers based their labors on insights gleaned from historical figures with names like Tertullian, Augustine, Luther, Calfin, Richard Baxter, and Jeremy Taylor. The "farming practices" included soul care activities like meditation, prayer, confession, dependence on Scripture, fasting, simplicity, and worship. The goal of work on the farm was the transformation of human character into the character of Christ.

The city, in contrast, was the place where the insights of Freud, Jung, Rogers, Sullivan, Berne, and others held supreme focus; the old farming masters were not even recognized. In place of the long-tested methods on the farm, the new insights and ways of operating in the city were called psychotherapeutic theories and methods.

Parts of Gary Moon's parable are worth reading carefully:

> Psychology distanced itself from both the practices of soul care and its other parent, philosophy, when it turned toward the "hard sciences" as role models in the late nineteen hundreds. Much was gained, but much was also lost.
>
> Psychology prospered in the city. It won a place in the academy, usually just down the hall and to the left from the physics departments. Hundreds of new divisions, schools, and departments were spawned. Scores of new academic journals were launched. National organizations, some with considerable political clout, were initiated. Human behavior was squeezed under a microscope and studied from the outside in. Life on the farm was a dim memory. . . . It would appear that the three sons from the farm quickly adapted to a more urban lifestyle.
>
> It is sadly ironic that Americans have recently been turning toward religious and spiritual interests in unprecedented numbers during a time when contemporary "soul care providers" have been turning away from spiritual practices. Fortunately, for those with spiritual appetites, life has continued on the "farm."
>
> . . . The purpose of this [parable] . . . is not to browbeat psychology, pastoral counseling, or professional Christian counseling. Each of these disciplines has made unique and profound contributions to human healing. I have deep gratitude for all of the accomplishments which have been made by these "brothers" during their sojourn in the city. However, perhaps it is good for us as Christian counselors to be reminded that in many ways we have left home—our historic roots as soul care provides. And, for those willing to make the trip, our home is a wonderful place to return. Perhaps "home" is where we will find the answers for many of our most perplexing questions.[23]

This parable is a good summary of what the pages of this book have attempted to convey. Like Dr. Moon, I do not advocate dumping the truck load of knowledge that has come from the city, knowledge about psychopathology, diagnosis, treatment strategies, scientific data, counseling methods. But we need to bring the truck load back home where we can sift carefully through the methods of psychotherapy, reembrace the rich heritage of soul care, and ground our feet firmly among the biblical roots that some Christian counselors forgot when they settled in the therapeutic city.

In research conducted by Moon and his colleagues, surveys were received from twenty-seven graduate schools that offer training for Christian counselors. The respondents were almost universal in their agreement that spiritual disciplines—like meditation, intercessory prayer, worship, confession, forgiveness, simplicity, and fasting—are both scripturally based and able to benefit people in therapeutic ways. But it is rare for students to get any training in the use of these disciplines, and there is little concern about developing, modeling, or teaching the spiritual disciplines so they can be applied by the students in their own lives.[24] At a time when our city colleagues have an interest in the soul care methods of the farm, even Christian counselors appear to be well entrenched in the city—perhaps too entrenched.

How Do We Then Live, and Counsel?
Unlike earlier parts of the book, this chapter has focused less on the basics of biblical doctrine and more on ourselves—on how we should seek to live and on goals for our counselees. Psychology, pastoral counseling, and Christian counseling, the three brothers in the parable, often seek to help counselees become well adjusted and able to cope effectively with the problems of life. These goals are achieved mostly by human efforts that include expressing emotion, gaining insight, learning new interpersonal skills, developing potential, resolving conflict, solving problems, maximizing life satisfaction, or medicating physical bodies so that emotional equilibrium is restored. Christian counselors might start with prayer and a determination to keep their words and counsel consistent with biblical morality, but in practice the actual counseling becomes an unthinking accommodation to the methods and assumptions of secular psychology.

In contrast, Christians are called to a radical realignment of our lives so that we live in accordance with the teachings of Scripture and the claims of Christ. We know that suffering and pain are inevitable, that fulfillment doesn't always come, and that we are called to be holy. This means that we seek to become more like Jesus and set apart for God's purposes, even when this goal is mocked, criticized, or even despised by our colleagues. Growth is important in the Christian life, but for the followers of Christ, we are called as well to be salt and light in the world, doing what we can to preserve the society from decay and illuminating the path to Christ. I agree with Jones and Butman who argue persuasively that "it is essential for Christian pastors, academicians, clinicians and researchers to take Christian world views and . . . beliefs seriously."[25]

I faced this when I left graduate school and started work as a counselor and teacher. Then, as now, I admired those Christian counselors who were working in secular counseling centers and academic institutions, maintaining their Christian perspectives, and striving for continued excellence in their therapeutic and teaching work. None of my training had been in a religious setting, and I had no desire to teach and work in the Christian college that encouraged me to accept their offer of a job.

But I sensed that this was where I should go, so with my wife of one month, I loaded our little car and moved to a part of the country where we knew nobody and were hundreds of miles from the nearest relatives. For several years I worked in that college and later moved on to other teaching positions. As I taught and built relationships with counseling colleagues, I became increasingly convinced that our Christian worldviews are crucial for growing in our own lives and for bringing genuine help to others.

You may work in a different setting, but the challenge is the same: to mature in your own spirituality, in communion with other believers, and to help others become men, women, and young people who know Christ and are growing in Christian maturity. Can anything in life be of greater importance?

❖

CHAPTER FOURTEEN

Keeping Perspective
in Christian Counseling

IT WAS CLEAR that the little girl was dying.

As he held the weakening body in his strong arms, the father could not hold back the tears.

"Magdalene," he whispered. "My dear little daughter, would you like to stay here with your father; or would you willingly go to your Father yonder?"

She opened her eyes and looked into the grief-stricken face of the one who knelt by her bedside. "Darling father," she replied, "as God wills."

Martin Luther continued to hold the girl in his arms as she quietly slipped away in death and into the presence of her heavenly Father.

When his daughter was laid in her coffin in September of 1542, Luther was able to look through his tears at her lifeless body and still find hope. "Darling Lena, you will rise and shine like a star, yea like the sun," the father declared. "I am happy in spirit, but the flesh is sorrowful and will not be content, the parting grieves me beyond measure.

"I have sent a saint to heaven."[1]

Sometimes the experiences of life jolt us into a clearer perspec-

250 Keeping Perspective in Christian Counseling

tive on what ultimately is important. The birth of a child, the terminal illness of a friend, the sudden destruction from a storm, the shock of a near-miss accident, the disruption of a heart attack, the death of a daughter or son—each can grab our attention away from the routine activities of life and force us to reconsider what we really believe and what really matters.

Reflecting on the death of Luther's daughter, New Testament scholar Don Carson wrote that, at times,

> We begin to wonder if some pain and sorrow in this life is not used in God's providential hand to make us homesick for heaven, to detach us from this world, to prepare us for heaven, to draw our attention to himself and away from the world of merely physical things. In short, we begin to look at all of life's experiences, good and ill, from the vantage of the End.[2]

Most of us are caught in the events surrounding our daily activities, our careers, or our families, and we don't think much about ultimate things, at least until we encounter a crisis. One of our tasks as counselors is to help people through these crises, but to do so we must draw on a storehouse of beliefs, values, and eternal truths that few counselors hear about during their training. Often we have no alternative but to pull from the limited Sunday school theology that we mentioned earlier, and as a result, we come up short in our efforts to give genuine help at the crisis points of life. In the pages of this book, I have tried to show how a deeper understanding of our faith can enable us to counsel more effectively.

Even with this awareness, however, we still will continue to have diversity in Christian counseling. Our worldviews, personalities, past experiences, work settings, training, and theoretical orientations all influence how we counsel. Each of us is a unique human being, we encounter differences in our counselees, we live in a time of history where change is rampant, and almost daily we face the impact of an information explosion that we cannot ignore if we want to counsel in relevant and genuinely helpful ways.

Many of our counselees and colleagues are adrift in a sea of uncertainty, looking for an anchor that will hold them to something they can know for sure. Despite the new-age gurus of spirituality and the ever-emerging new therapies, there is need for a rock of stability, a shelter in the storm, on which we can build our lives, our counseling, and the lives of our counselees. With a biblically based worldview, similar to what these pages have proposed, we can build our counseling on a solid foundation. From this we can seek to help people in accordance with all of our different personalities and with sensitivity to their diverse problems and crises.

When I had partially completed my work on this book, I met one day with a lady in her thirties whose life had been filled with tragedy, including the abuse that came from her pastor-husband. When we talked, she still was adjusting to life as a single parent and divorcee, in a family and church environment where people were not supposed to get divorced.

"Tell me about the counseling you had during the time of your divorce," I said in an interview.

She talked about counselors who had been helpful but went on to describe one who was not. Apparently the man was sincere and wanted to help, but he sat with a big open Bible on his lap and repeatedly read verses that instructed the lady how to live. She knew most of the verses, and she wanted to live a life pleasing to Christ, but in her time of crisis she needed a fellow human being who would understand, who would listen, who would gently remind her of the confidence that she could have in her compassionate Lord. The counselor gave the impression that he cared less about the counselee than about his agenda of pushing a correct biblical theology.

Jesus had correct theology, but His life was also marked by sensitivity, care, and understanding. As His followers, we too must be sensitive and compassionate, faithful to the Father, and always living our lives with the end and eternity in view. Our task is not to force some theological agenda on to the people who seek our help but to be informed, knowledgeable followers of Jesus Christ who are available to be guided by the Holy Spirit and used as His instruments in changing lives.

The Apostle Paul, who was used by God to change many lives, sent a letter to Timothy with instructions about his future ministry. Christians need to cleanse themselves from evil influences, the letter stated. They need to flee youthful evils and pursue righteousness, faith, love, and peace. Then each believer "will be an instrument for noble purposes, made holy and useful to the Master and prepared to do any good work" (2 Timothy 2:21-22).

That is the calling and a challenge for any people-helper who has a growing understanding of the biblical basis of Christian counseling.

Questions for Further Study

Chapter One—What Makes Counseling Christian?
1. What is a worldview and what is its purpose?
2. How does a person's worldview influence the way he or she views a problem and counsels?
3. List the elements that make up a worldview. Give an example of how a person's worldview can influence behavior in each of these areas.
4. Summarize your worldview. How does it influence your counseling?
5. Briefly discuss how you would determine the validity of a worldview.
6. What is distinctive about "Christian counseling"?

Chapter Two—The Bible and Counseling: Revelation
1. How do we learn about other people? How do we learn about God?
2. What is general revelation? List three types of general revelation. How does the concept of general revelation relate to psychology?
3. What is special revelation?
4. How is special revelation different from general revelation? Why is special revelation necessary?

5. Respond to these statements:
   - ❖ The Bible is our recipe book for counseling.
   - ❖ The Bible does not answer every question.
   - ❖ The Bible deals with all of the problems that people bring to counseling.
6. What are some of the results of looking to personal experience as the only source of authority in life? Name some other sources of authority.
7. If someone asked you why the Bible should be an authority, how would you respond?
8. What are some reasons for concluding that the Bible is God's Word?
9. In what ways is the Bible helpful to the counselor?

Chapter Three—Interpreting the Bible
1. Define the word *hermeneutics*. What is the purpose of hermeneutics?
2. What are the four gaps we must deal with in interpreting the Bible?
3. Briefly discuss the difference between "meaning" and "significance." How does confusing these two processes influence the interpretation of the Bible?
4. What are the three stages of biblical interpretation?
5. When applying the Bible to life situations what steps do Howard and William Hendricks follow? How does this relate to counseling?
6. What are the principles to keep in mind when you deal with a question that the Bible does not address directly? Think of a problem that might fit this category. How would you deal with this biblically?
7. How should/could you use the Bible in your counseling?

Chapter Four—God and Counseling
1. What are some common beliefs about God?
2. How does the idea of a personal God differ from the new-age concept of God? What difference does this make for counseling?
3. Why do you think the Bible does not spend a lot of time proving that God exists?
4. Why is it important to have a correct understanding of God's

nature? How does a faulty understanding of God's nature affect counselors and counselees?

5. What is the difference between "knowing God" and "knowing about God"?

6. List some of the ways that God has used in the Bible to tell us about Himself.

7. Choose two of God's attributes (table 4.1) and briefly discuss how you have experienced God's involvement in your life based on these character descriptions.

8. Discuss the results of taking one of the characteristics of God out of proportion to the rest (e.g., His love, transcendence, holiness). Can you think of counselees who have done this to their disadvantage?

9. Think of your counselees. How has their misunderstanding of God's nature created problems? Give specific examples. How could a clearer view of God be helpful to these people?

10. In what two ways is God active in our world?

11. What is your definition of worship? Based on your knowledge of God, how should He be worshiped? In what specific ways does this relate to counseling?

Chapter Five—Human Nature and Counseling

1. What does it mean to be a creature?

2. How should understanding God as the Creator make a difference in people's lives?

3. Briefly discuss how a person's view of human nature influences his or her counseling.

4. In what two ways is the image of God expressed in human beings?

5. How should understanding human beings influence the way we treat others?

6. How should our understanding of human beings as people "made to exercise dominion" influence the way we treat others?

7. According to the Christian worldview, what is the purpose of life?

8. How should the fact that human beings are created in God's image affect our self-understanding?

9. Do you think human nature is tripartite or bipartite? How does your view influence your counseling?

10. What does an integrated view of human nature mean? How does this influence counseling?

Chapter Six—Sin and Counseling

1. How does the Bible define sin?
2. Explain how one's view of sin influences his or her approach to life and style of counseling?
3. Contrast the Christian view of sin with other viewpoints.
4. Distinguish between sin as an act, sin as an attitude, sin as a force, and sin as a state.
5. Where did evil originate? How does this relate to your counseling?
6. How does unbelief work itself out in peoples' lives? Why is a lack of trust a problem in developing relationships?
7. What is the result of rebellion in our lives?
8. Briefly discuss the four areas of separation that are caused by sin. How do these areas of separation influence human behavior?
9. Under what circumstances should a counselor discuss sin with a counselee?
10. Can counseling really be Christian if sin is never mentioned? Explain your answer.

Chapter Seven—Christ and Counseling

1. Why should a counselor know who Jesus Christ is, what He has done, and what He does today?
2. What is unique about Jesus Christ?
3. What is the meaning of incarnation? What does the Incarnation say about our humanity?
4. Was the death of Jesus Christ really necessary? What does the death of Jesus Christ tell us about God? What does His death tell us about ourselves? How should we respond? How does this relate to counseling?
5. Briefly discuss the benefits of the resurrection.
6. Explain what it means to be reconciled to God. What are the benefits of reconciliation with God?
7. How might the parable of the prodigal son be useful in counseling?
8. What is justification? How does justification apply to the human condition?

9. How does redemption affect the human situation?
10. Discuss the ethical implications of telling people about Christ as a part of their counseling.
11. What counseling issues are affected by the work of Christ?

Chapter Eight—Guilt and Forgiveness in Counseling

1. What do you think about the statement that "considerations of guilt may be the place where religion and psychology often meet"?
2. Define *objective* and *subjective* guilt.
3. Why is theological guilt so serious? How does this differ from legal, social, and psychological guilt?
4. What is the relationship between guilt and the conscience? Why is it important for a person to pay attention to his or her conscience? Respond to the statement that some people are "caught by their own consciences and inclined to punish themselves by various forms of psychic and social misery."
5. Arc guilt feelings ever healthy? Is so, when? If not, why not? How do appropriate and inappropriate guilt feelings differ? Can you find examples of each from your counseling?
6. What are some of the healthy components of true forgiveness? Can you think of situations where a person failed to experience forgiveness because some of these components were lacking?
7. In what ways is the distinction helpful between parental and judicial forgiveness?
8. What are some of the benefits of confessing a sin to another person?
9. What are some of the benefits of practicing restitution?
10. Should Christians always forgive another person who has wronged them even if the person is not sorry for what he or she has done? Give biblical examples to support your answer. Can you think of instances in your life or in the life of a counselee when the failure to forgive has been negative?

Chapter Nine—The Holy Spirit and Counseling

1. When someone mentions the doctrine of the Holy Spirit what is your reaction? What leads you to react as you do?
2. What is the significance of the fact that the Holy Spirit is personal?

3. How does the Holy Spirit bring change in the lives of unbelievers and in believers? What is the relevance of this for counseling?
4. The Holy Spirit transforms us so that we are restored to relational wholeness and are able to impact the world. How does this transformation relate to counselees? How does it relate to counselors like you?
5. Think of some life situations where the presence of the Holy Spirit brings comfort. Think of some life situations where the presence of the Spirit produces accountability.
6. Why is the developing of community such an important part of the work of the Holy Spirit?
7. What is the primary purpose for the gifts of the Holy Spirit?
8. Give your reaction to the issue of "miraculous counseling." What about signs and wonders?
9. What is the role of the Holy Spirit in your counseling?

Chapter Ten—Supernatural Agents and Counseling
1. How does a person's worldview influence his or her beliefs about supernatural beings such as angels and demons?
2. C. S. Lewis described two extremes when it comes to belief about supernatural beings. What are those extremes, and how do these two extremes relate to counseling?
3. What ideas or experiences have shaped your beliefs about supernatural beings?
4. Why is it important for a counselor to understand the nature and the role of angels?
5. As a Christian counselor, what would be your response to a person who claimed to be receiving messages from angels? What if the person claimed the messages were coming from demons?
6. Why do Christians believe in Satan and demons?
7. What are some ways that demonic forces seek to disrupt people's lives?
8. Can you think of areas in your life and in your counselees where there are temptation and other demonic influences?
9. How can a person resist temptation?
10. Why is it dangerous for human beings to develop habitual patterns of sin?
11. What is your view of "demon possession"? Give scriptural

support for your conclusions. What is the place of deliverance in counseling?

Chapter Eleven—The Church and Counseling

1. What is the nature of the church?
2. Why is the church an important part of the Christian life? Why is it of importance for counselors?
3. Unity and diversity are both true of God's nature. How does the church reflect both of these truths about God's nature?
4. An understanding of the church as "the people of God" can create a sense of belonging. What are some positive results of experiencing a sense of belonging? What are the results of a lack of belonging?
5. Is the church primarily an institution or a living organism? What difference does this make?
6. List three reasons for the existence of the church. Of the three reasons listed, how do these reasons contribute to the well-being of individuals?
7. Why is worship important? How does it effect us as individuals?
8. What are some of the lessons a person can learn through being a part of a Christian community?
9. Define edification. How is the church like other groups that meet together to keep people accountable? In what ways are church-related groups unique?
10. How are people affected by being part of a group that impacts society?
11. How can we help people begin to focus on helping others? How does helping others help the person who helps?

Chapter Twleve—The New Age in Counseling

1. Why do you think human beings arc so interested in knowing about the future?
2. What specific problems result from anxicty concerning the future?
3. What does the phrase "Kingdom of God" mean? Is the "Kingdom of God" future or present reality? What is the relevance of this for counseling?
4. How can focusing on the future help reshape a person's perspective on life? Think of examples.

5. How does our culture avoid the reality of death? As a Christian counselor how can we speak about the issue of death?
6. How does the "age to come" influence a person today? Do counselors put too much emphasis on a person's past? How do we balance this past perspective with the Bible's emphasis on the future?
7. What does the Bible teach about the future judgment? Distinguish between the believers' judgment and the unbelievers' judgment. Does this have relevance for counseling?
8. Comment on the quotation from Heard (page 227).
9. How should the promise of a new creation affect our treatment of nature?

Chapter Thirteen—Spirituality and Counseling
1. Why is spirituality such a popular topic?
2. How do you define Christian spirituality? What makes Christian spirituality distinctive from other forms of spirituality?
3. What is the relationship between human effort and God's power in spiritual growth?
4. Is it possible to develop a plan for spiritual growth that fits every person? If not, why not?
5. Why is it important to focus on the work of Christ for spiritual development?
6. What are some ways that Christians can model their lives after Jesus Christ?
7. How can counselors implement spiritual disciplines in their counseling?
8. How do we teach spiritual disciplines without communicating that we earn God's favor by practicing certain techniques?
9. Think of some ways that God's presence can become more real in everyday experiences. Explain.
10. Do you think that people's problems are the result of spiritual issues?
11. What is the relationship between a counselee's spirituality and his or her ability to counsel others?
12. Give your response to Gary Moon's parable (page 245).

Appendix

Bibles

The King James Version (KJV). Translated in 1611 and often referred to as "The Authorized Version." The KJV uses very expressive language and is a good translation.

The Living Bible (TLB). A paraphrase that is good for daily Bible reading and reading to children.

The New American Standard Bible (NASB). This version is very accurate and therefore rather choppy at points. This is an excellent study Bible.

The New International Version (NIV). This version is an attempt to maintain accuracy while providing readability.

Bible Dictionaries

Tenney, Merrill (ed.). *The Zondervan Pictorial Bible Dictionary (Revised)*. This volume, the result of about sixty-five contributors, contains excellent evangelical scholarship (Zondervan, 1987).

Vine, W. E. *Vine's Expository Dictionary of Old and New Testament Words*. This work is extremely profitable for word studies (Academic Books, 1993).

Bible Handbooks

Eerdman's Handbook of the Bible. Edited by David Alexander. An excellent work on biblical backgrounds (Eerdmans, 1973).

The Handbook of Life in Bible Times. J. A. Thompson. Includes maps and illustrations (InterVarsity Press, 1986).

Concordances

Strong, James. *The New Strong's Exhaustive Concordance of the Bible*. This older concordance is good for using with older versions of the Bible (Thomas Nelson, 1990).

Young, Robert. *Young's Analytical Concordance to the Bible*. A classic concordance of the Bible (Eerdmans, 1970).

Notes

Chapter One—What Makes Counseling Christian?

1. Roland H. Bainton, *Here I Stand: A Life of Martin Luther* (New York: Abingdon, 1950), page 363.
2. James W. Sire, *The Universe Next Door: A Basic Worldview Catalog* (Downers Grove, IL: InterVarsity, 1976), page 17.
3. This in itself may reflect the worldview of pragmatism, the idea that if something works, it must be true.
4. C. S. Lewis, "Christian Apologetics," in W. Hooper ed., C. S. Lewis, *God in the Dock: Essays on Theology and Ethics* (Grand Rapids, MI: Eerdmans, 1970), page 93 (originally published by C. S. Lewis in 1945).
5. Ronald H. Nash, *Faith and Reason: Searching for a Rational Faith* (Grand Rapids, MI: Zondervan, 1988). The following paragraphs are adapted from pages 30-33 of Nash's book.
6. Nash, page 33.
7. Once again, I am grateful to Nash for his helpful insights. See *Faith and Reason*, chapter 4.
8. Don Matzat, "A Better Way: Christ Is My Worth," in Michael Scott Horton ed., *Power Religion: The Selling Out of the Evangelical Church* (Chicago: Moody, 1992), page 253.
9. Gary R. Collins, *Case Studies in Christian Counseling* (Dallas, TX: Word, 1991), page 4.
10. At the seminary I attended, I taught my first ever counseling course. My class was in the evening, in the basement of the men's dormitory. I tried not to be paranoid but at times I felt like I was being sneaked into the curriculum, in a corner of the campus, where nobody would find me and I wouldn't be free to do much harm.

Chapter Two—The Bible and Counseling: Revelation

1. John Warwick Montgomery, *Where Is History Going?* (Grand Rapids, MI: Zondervan, 1969).

2. C. S. Lewis, *Mere Christianity* (New York: Macmillan, 1952), page 19.
3. Millard J. Erickson, *Christian Theology* (Grand Rapids, MI: Baker, 1985), page 155.
4. Dave Hunt, *Beyond Seduction* (Eugene, OR: Harvest House, 1987), page 130.
5. William Kirk Kilpatrick, *The Emperor's New Clothes: The Naked Truth About Psychology* (Westchester, IL: Crossway, 1985), page 4.
6. I attempted to answer some of the criticisms in Gary R. Collins, *Can You Trust Psychology?* (Downers Grove, IL: InterVarsity, 1988).
7. Martin Robinson, *A World Apart* (Turnbridge Wells, England: Monarch, 1992), page 99.
8. Lawrence J. Crabb, Jr., *Understanding People* (Grand Rapids, MI: Zondervan, 1987), page 66.
9. Crabb, pages 44-45.
10. See, for example, John Warwick Montgomery ed., *God's Inerrant Word: An International Symposium on the Trustworthiness of Scripture* (Minneapolis, MN: Bethany Fellowship, 1973); John R. Stott, *The Authority of the Bible* (Downers Grove, IL: InterVarsity, 1974); and Earl D. Radmacher, *Can We Trust the Bible?* (Wheaton, IL: Tyndale, 1979).
11. Charles Colson with Ellen Santilli Vaughn, *The Body: Being Light in Darkness* (Dallas, TX: Word, 1992), page 335.
12. Colson, page 336 footnote.
13. James Patterson and Peter Kim, *The Day America Told the Truth* (New York: Prentice-Hall, 1991), page 25.
14. George W. Cornell, "'Situation Ethics' Still Finding Favor," *Arlington Heights (Ill.) Daily Herald*, 23 May 1992, sec. 5, page 4.
15. Much of the material in this section is adapted from Kenneth Boa and Larry Moody, *I'm Glad You Asked* (Wheaton, IL: Victor Books, 1982), pages 76-94.
16. Josh McDowell, *Evidence That Demands a Verdict: Historical Evidences for the Christian Faith* (San Bernardino, CA: Campus Crusade for Christ, 1972), chapters 9 and 11.
17. Lee Strobel, *Inside the Mind of Unchurched Harry & Mary* (Grand Rapids, MI: Zondervan, 1993).
18. See, for example, F. F. Bruce, *The New Testament Documents: Are They Reliable?* (Grand Rapids, MI: Eerdmans, 1974); Frederic Kenyon, *The Bible and Archaeology* (New York: Harper, 1940); Frederic Kenyon, *Our Bible and the Ancient Manuscripts* (New York: Harper, 1958); Josh McDowell, *Evidence that Demands a Verdict* (San Bernardino, CA: Campus Crusade for Christ, 1972); Bruce Metzger, *The Text of the New Testament* (New York: Oxford University Press, 1964); John W. Montgomery, *Christianity and History* (Downers Grove, IL: InterVarsity, 1964); and William Ramsay, *St. Paul the Traveller and the Roman Citizen* (New York: G. P. Putnam's Son, 1896).
19. This conclusion of Glueck is cited in a section on archaeology by R. K. Harrison, *Introduction to the Old Testament* (Grand Rapids, MI: Eerdmans, 1969), page 94.

20. Cited by Clark H. Pinnock, *Set Forth Your Case: An Examination of Christianity's Credentials* (Chicago: Moody, 1967), page 102.

Chapter Three—Interpreting the Bible

1. Henry A. Virkler, *Hermeneutics: Principles and Processes of Biblical Interpretation* (Grand Rapids, MI: Baker, 1981), page 15.
2. Bernard Ramm, *Protestant Biblical Interpretation: A Textbook of Hermeneutics for Conservative Protestants* (Boston, MA: Wilde, 1956), pages 167, 175.
3. Some of the material in this section is adapted from Howard G. Hendricks and William D. Hendricks, *Living By the Book* (Chicago: Moody, 1991).
4. Adapted from Hendricks and Hendricks.
5. Adapted from Hendricks and Hendricks, pages 292-308.
6. Adapted from Hendricks and Hendricks, pages 304-308.
7. The statistics in this paragraph are taken from an article by Nancy Gibbs, "'Til Death Do Us Part," *Time*, 18 January 1992, pages 38-45.
8. Lawrence J. Crabb, Jr., *Understanding People: Deep Longings for Relationship* (Grand Rapids, MI: Zondervan, 1987), page 63.
9. Richard K. Lore and Lori A. Schultz, "Control of Human Aggression: A Comparative Perspective," *American Psychologist* 48, January 1993, pages 16-25.

Chapter Four—God and Counseling

1. James Patterson and Peter Kim, *The Day America Told the Truth: What People Really Believe About Everything that Really Matters* (New York: Prentice Hall, 1991), page 199.
2. George Barna, *What Americans Believe* (Ventura, CA: Regal Books, 1991), page 200.
3. Patterson and Kim, page 201.
4. Os Guinness, "America's Last Men and Their Magnificent Talking Cure," in Os Guinness and John Seel ed., *No God But God: Breaking with the Idols of Our Age* (Chicago: Moody, 1992), page 119.
5. For a summary of these arguments see Norman Geisler, *Christian Apologetics* (Grand Rapids, MI: Baker, 1976), chapter 13; Ronald H. Nash, *Faith and Reason: Searching for a Rational Faith* (Grand Rapids, MI: Zondervan, 1988), chapters 9–12.
6. Stuart Hample and Eric Marshall, *Children's Letters to God: New Collection* (New York: Workman, 1991).
7. J. I. Packer, *Knowing God* (Downers Grove, IL: InterVarsity, 1973), page 29.
8. Jack Hayford, *The Heart of Praise: Daily Ways to Worship the Father with Psalms* (Ventura, CA: Regal Books, 1992), page 52.
9. A. W. Tozer, *The Knowledge of the Holy: The Attributes of God: Their Meaning in the Christian Life* (New York: Harper & Row, 1961), pages 7-11.
10. Packer, page 32.

11. Tozer, page 16.
12. Tozer, page 20.
13. Floyd H. Barackman, *Practical Christian Theology* (Grand Rapids, MI: Kregel, 1981), page 50.
14. John Townsend, *Hiding from Love* (Colorado Springs, CO: NavPress, 1991), pages 62-69.
15. John A. T. Robinson, *Honest to God* (Philadelphia: Westminster, 1963), pages 14 and 13, 40.
16. Robinson, pages 118-119.
17. © 1988 Edward Grant, Inc. Used by permission. CCLI #540301.
18. Frieda Fordham, *An Introduction to Jung's Psychology* (Baltimore, MD: Penguin Books, 1966), page 123.
19. For Jung's view of the quaternity, see C. G. Jung, "The Problem of Quaternity," in *Psychology and Religion: West and East,* vol. 11 of *Collected Works of C. G. Jung* (Princeton, NJ: Princeton University Press, 1969), pages 164-180. See also, C. G. Jung, *Psychology and Religion* (New Haven, CT: Yale University Press, 1972), pages 73-74.
20. James Montgomery Boice, *The Sovereign God* (Downers Grove, IL: InterVarsity, 1978), page 147.
21. Millard J. Erickson, *Christian Theology* (Grand Rapids, MI: Baker, 1985), pages 338-342.
22. Erickson, page 368.
23. Stephen Arterburn and Jack Felton, *Toxic Faith: Understanding and Overcoming Religious Addiction* (Nashville, TN: Thomas Nelson, 1991).
24. For discussions of the role of modern heresy, see Hank Hanegraff, *Christianity in Crisis* (Eugene, OR: Harvest House, 1993); Hendrik H. Hanegraff and Erwin M. de Castro, "What's Wrong with the Faith Movement? Part Two: The Teachings of Kenneth Copeland," *Christian Research Journal* 15, no. 2, spring 1993, pages 16-23, 44-45.

Chapter Five—Human Nature and Counseling

1. Carl A. Raschke, *Painted Black* (New York: HarperCollins, 1990).
2. Malcolm Muggeridge, *Something Beautiful for God: Mother Teresa of Calcutta* (Garden City, NY: Doubleday-Image Books, 1977), pages 52-53.
3. Jay E. Adams, *More Than Redemption: A Theology of Christian Counseling* (Grand Rapids, MI: Baker, 1979), page 94.
4. George Carey, *I Believe in Man* (Grand Rapids, MI: Eerdmans, 1977), page 26.
5. Stanton L. Jones and Richard E. Butman, *Modern Psychotherapies: A Christian Appraisal* (Downers Grove, IL: InterVarsity, 1991), page 49.
6. James W. Sire, *The Universe Next Door: A Basic World View Catalog* (Downers Grove, IL: InterVarsity, 1976), page 31. Italics are in the original, but I have taken the liberty of listing the six characteristics one below the other, rather than leaving them together in a one-sentence paragraph.
7. R. C. Sproul, *Essential Truths of the Christian Faith* (Wheaton, IL: Tyndale House, 1992), page 132.

8. Jones and Butman, page 48.
9. In a concise summary of existential therapy, Gerald Corey suggested that existential concepts and insights never gained widespread acceptance in the United States because North American psychology has been dominated by the empirical approach. See chapter 4, "Existential Therapy," in Gerald Corey, *Theory and Practice of Counseling and Psychotherapy*, 3rd ed. (Monterey, CA: Brooks/Cole, 1986), pages 72-97.
10. Corey, page 79.
11. Wayne Grudem, *Systematic Theology*, chapter 21, unpublished manuscript, pages 3-4.
12. John R. W. Stott, *The Cross of Christ* (Downers Grove, IL: InterVarsity, 1986), page 281.
13. See, for example, Paul C. Reisser, Teri K. Reisser, and John Weldon, *The Holistic Healers: A Christian Perspective on New-Age Health Care* (Downers Grove, IL: InterVarsity, 1983); Elliot Miller, *A Crash Course on the New Age Movement* (Grand Rapids, MI: Baker, 1989), chapters 3 and 4.
14. H. McDonald, *The Christian View of Man* (Westchester, IL: Crossway,1982).
15. Sproul, pages 133-134.

Chapter Six—Sin and Counseling

1. O. Hobart Mowrer, *The Crisis in Psychiatry and Religion* (Princeton, NJ: Van Nostrand, 1961), page 60.
2. Jay E. Adams, *Competent to Counsel* (Grand Rapids, MI: Baker, 1970). See also, Jay E. Adams, *The Christian Counselor's Manual: The Sequal and Companion Volume to "Competent to Counsel"* (Nutley, NJ: Presbyterian and Reformed Publishing, 1973).
3. The quotation is from page 40 of Mowrer, see, especially, chapters 3 and 4.
4. Karl Menninger, *Whatever Became of Sin?* (New York: Hawthorn, 1973), page 188.
5. In one study of what Americans really believe, researchers found that most people define for themselves what is sinful and what is not. James Patterson and Peter Kim, *The Day America Told the Truth* (New York: Prentice-Hall, 1991), page 203.
6. Robert H. Schuller, *Self-Esteem: The New Reformation* (Waco, TX: Word, 1982), page 14.
7. Millard J. Erickson, *Christian Theology* (Grand Rapids, MI: Baker, 1985), page 562.
8. Cited by A. McGrati, *Self Esteem* (Wheaton, IL: Crossway, 1992), page 72.
9. Adapted from J. Rodman Williams, *Renewal Theology: God, the World and Redemption* (Grand Rapids, MI: Zondervan Academic Books, 1988), pages 221-222.
10. This conclusion is based on a research review by the American Psychological Association's Commission on Violence and Youth, cited by Peter L. Benson and Eugene C. Roehlkepartain, "Youth Violence in Middle America," *Search Institute Source* (Search Institute, 122 W. Franklin Ave. Suite 525, Minneapolis, MN 55404), September 1992.
11. M. Scott Peck, *People of the Lie: The Hope for Healing Human Evil* (New

York: Simon & Schuster, 1983).

12. Floyd H. Barackman, *Practical Christian Theology* (Grand Rapids, MI: Kregel, 1992), pages 297-300. Readers might notice that Barackman lists four influences of original sin, but I list only three of these in the text. Barackman's conclusions about the "sin-principle" are summarized in my earlier discussion of sin as a force.

13. One other "timeout" issue might be the status of infants and other young children who die before they are old enough to willfully sin or to accept God's free gift of salvation. Are these little ones lost and condemned to eternal death? Most theologians would answer "no" and argue that young children are, indeed, saved. I have chosen not to discuss this issue in this book but to suggest, instead, that interested readers look at Erickson's treatment of this issue in *Christian Theology*, pages 637-639; Barackman, "The Salvation of Infants," *Practical Christian Theology*, pages 367-368.

14. Robert C. Roberts, *Taking the Word to Heart: Self and Other in an Age of Therapies* (Grand Rapids, MI: Eerdmans, 1993), pages 158-159.

15. Larry Crabb, *Who We Are and How We Relate* (Colorado Springs, CO: NavPress, 1992), pages 74-76.

16. William Morris, *News from Nowhere* (London: Routledge & Kegan Paul, 1890 [1970]).

17. With the exception of the last sentence, this paragraph draws heavily on the writing of James W. Sire, *The Universe Next Door: A Basic World View Catalog* (Downers Grove, IL: InterVarsity, 1976), pages 35-36.

18. The summary sentence that ends the paragraph in the text is adapted from Erickson, pages 615-618. *Whatever Became of Sin?* is by Menninger.

19. Paul Aurandt, *Paul Harvey's The Rest of the Story* (New York: Bantam, 1977).

Chapter Seven—Christ and Counseling

1. George Barna, *What Americans Believe* (Ventura, CA: Regal Books, 1991), page 191.

2. C. S. Lewis, *The Screwtape Letters* (Glasgow, Scotland: Collins-Fontana Books, 1942), page 118.

3. J. Rodman Williams, *Renewal Theology: God, the Word and Redemption* (Grand Rapids, MI: Zondervan Academic Books, 1988), page 323.

4. John R. W. Stott, *The Cross of Christ* (Downers Grove, IL: InterVarsity, 1986), page 159.

5. Paul L. Maier, *First Easter: The True and Unfamiliar Story* (New York: Harper and Row, 1973), page 78.

6. Critics still deny the reality of the resurrection, but evidence is very strong. See, for example, Josh McDowell, *Evidence that Demands a Verdict: Historical Evidences for the Christian Faith* (San Bernardino, CA: Campus Crusade for Christ, 1972), chapter 10; J. P. Moreland, *Scaling the Secular City* (Grand Rapids, MI: Baker, 1987); Merrill C. Tenney, *The Reality of the Resurrection* (New York: Harper and Row, 1963); and Maier, *First Easter* (New York: Harper and Row, 1973).

7. Stott, page 190.

Chapter Eight—Guilt and Forgiveness in Counseling

1. David Belgum, *Guilt: Where Religion and Psychology Meet* (Minneapolis, MN: Augsburg, 1963).
2. Belgum, page 52.
3. This section is adapted from my earlier book *Christian Counseling: A Comprehensive Guide*, rev. ed. (Dallas, TX: Word, 1988), pages 135-136.
4. LeRoy Aden and David G. Benner ed., *Counseling and the Human Predicament: A Study of Sin, Guilt, and Forgiveness* (Grand Rapids, MI: Baker, 1989), page 105.
5. L. I. Granberg and G. E. Farley, "Conscience," in Merrill C. Tenney ed., *The Zondervan Pictorial Encyclopedia of the Bible*, vol. 1 (Grand Rapids, MI: Zondervan, 1975), page 942.
6. Bonnidell Clouse, "Conscience," in J. D. Douglas ed., *New Twentieth Century Encyclopedia of Religious Knowledge* (Grand Rapids, MI: Baker, 1991), page 232.
7. Granberg and Farley, page 944.
8. The following paragraphs are adapted from Jay E. Adams, *More Than Redemption* (Grand Rapids, MI: Baker, 1979), pages 210-219.
9. At this point, we should note that Christians differ on the issue of whether or not a believer can lose his or her salvation and be "kicked out of the family." Some believers would say that a person could become hardened to the conviction of the Holy Spirit as a result of continued rebellion and disobedience. Because of this they could lose their salvation.
10. Adams, page 215.
11. S. Bruce Narramore, *No Condemnation* (Grand Rapids, MI: Zondervan, 1984), page 155.
12. Lyman T. Lundeen, "Forgiveness and Human Relationships," in Aden and Benner, page 188.
13. Richard S. Nixon, *In the Arena: A Memoir of Victory, Defeat and Renewal* (New York: Simon & Schuster, 1990), page 18.
14. Michael E. McCullough and Everett L. Worthington, Jr., *Two Group Interventions for Promoting Forgiveness,* unpublished manuscript (1993).
15. Allen C. Guelzo, "Fear of Forgiving," *Christianity Today* 37, 8 February 1993, pages 42-45.
16. Guelzo, page 45.
17. For the view that forgiveness should be unconditional, whether or not the guilty party expresses sorrow or repentance, see Lewis Smedes, *Forgive and Forget: Healing the Hurts We Don't Deserve* (San Francisco, CA: Harper & Row, 1984); Charles Stanley, *Forgiveness* (Nashville, TN: Thomas Nelson, 1987), pages 122-133; and Educational Psychology Study Group, "Must a Christian *Require* Repentance Before Forgiving?" *Journal of Psychology and Christianity* 9, fall 1990, pages 16-19.
   An alternative view maintains that there is no need to forgive unless the offender repents. See Jay Adams, *More Than Redemption* (Grand Rapids, MI: Baker, 1979), pages 229-232; John R. W. Stott, *The Cross of Christ* (Downers Grove, IL: InterVarsity, 1986), page 296; and Floyd H. Barackman, *Practical*

Christian Theology (Grand Rapids, MI: Kregel, 1992), pages 537-538.
18. Guelzo, page 45.
19. Pattison, page 172.

Chapter Nine—The Holy Spirit and Counseling

1. The story of Ralph Hamburger and the others who have been dedicated to evangelism and the growth of believers in Eastern Europe is told by Walter E. James with Christy Hawes Zatkin, in *Tumbling Walls: A True Story of Ordinary People Bringing Reconciliation in Extraordinary Ways to an Alienated World* (La Jolla, CA: The Diaspora Foundation, 1990). The book is self-published and not easily available in bookstores, but you can get a copy from The Diaspora Foundation, Inc., 7504 Olivetas Avenue #C37, La Jolla, CA 92037.
2. "Counselor" is the word used in the *New International Version* of the Bible—the version that is quoted most frequently in this book.
3. Millard J. Erickson, *Christian Theology* (Grand Rapids, MI: Baker, 1985), page 846.
4. Erickson, page 847.
5. Throughout this chapter and this book, you will notice that I refer to God as "He." I seek to avoid sexist language in my writing, speaking, and thinking, but I do not believe that using the masculine pronoun to describe God is sexist. The original biblical texts never describe God using the feminine pronoun "she," and I do not think we have reason to do this either—despite the urgings of some feminists. The Scriptures are not implying that God is masculine; the pronoun "He" is used by biblical writers in the broad sense to include a divine being who is neither male nor female.

   Biblical scholars have noted that the word translated "spirit" is neuter (neither male nor female), but that the Holy Spirit is described with a masculine pronoun in John 15:26; 16:7,13-14; and Ephesians 1:14. Erickson suggests that the biblical writers have deliberately chosen to use the masculine pronoun to convey to us that the Holy Spirit is a Person and not a thing.
6. Modern translations of the Bible and most Christians today prefer to use *Holy Spirit* rather than *Holy Ghost* to refer to the third Person of the Trinity. In this book, I rarely refer to the Holy Ghost, but we should note that this is the preferred term in many older theological publications.
7. The *New American Standard Bible* translation of John 16:7 describes Christ's departure and the coming of the Holy Spirit as an advantage: "But I tell you the truth, it is to your advantage that I go away; for if I do not go away, the Helper shall not come to you; but it I go, I will send Him to you."
8. Writers of theology books often give different lists to summarize the Holy Spirit's activities. If you look closely, however, you will discover that these lists often contain the same material, even though it is presented in different ways. What I list as five works of the Holy Spirit, for example, some other writers might put into a list of three, four, six, or some other number of categories.

9. No pun intended!

10. Gilbert Bilezikian, *Christianity 101: Your Guide to Eight Basic Christian Beliefs* (Grand Rapids, MI: Zondervan, 1993), page 106.

11. Bilezikian, page 106.

12. Brother Lawrence, *The Practice of the Presence of God* (Old Tappan, NJ: Revell, 1958).

13. M. Scott Peck, *The Different Drum: Community Making and Peace* (New York: Simon & Schuster, 1987), pages 299-300. See also M. Scott Peck, *A World Waiting to be Born: Civility Rediscovered* (New York: Bantam Books, 1993).

14. See "The Holy Spirit and Counseling Ministries: An Interview with Dr. Siang-Yang Tan," *The Christian Journal of Psychology and Counseling* 7 (3), July 1992, pages 8-11.

15. See, for example, Stanley M. Horton, "The Gifts of the Spirit," in Marvin G. Gilbert and Raymond T. Brock ed., *The Holy Spirit and Counseling: Theology and Theory* (Peabody, MA: Hendrickson Publishers, 1985), pages 39-54.

16. Several very good books critique such new-age claims. One of the best is written by Vishal Mangalwadi, *When the New Age Gets Old: Looking for a Greater Spirituality* (Downers Grove, IL: InterVarsity, 1992).

17. J. I. Packer, *Rediscovering Holiness* (Ann Arbor, MI: Servant, 1992), page 214.

18. Demons and the demonic are discussed in the next chapter.

19. Packer, pages 218-219, 205.

20. Packer, page 212.

21. Floyd H. Barackman, *Practical Christian Theology* (Grand Rapids, MI: Kregel, 1992), page 216.

22. Barackman, page 216.

Chapter Ten—Supernatural Agents and Counseling

1. George H. Gallup, Jr., and Frank Newport, "Belief in Paranormal Phenomena Among Adult Americans," *Skeptical Inquirer* 15, winter 1991, pages 137-146.

2. William M. Alnor, *UFOs in the New Age: Extraterrestrial Messages and the Truth of Scripture* (Grand Rapids, MI: Baker, 1992), page 71.

3. Carl G. Jung, *Flying Saucers: A Modern Myth of Things Seen in the Sky* (London: Ark Paperbacks, 1959).

4. Budd Hopkins, David M. Jacobs, and Ron Westrum, *Unusual Personal Experiences: An Analysis of the Data from Three National Surveys* (Las Vegas, NV: Bigelow Holding Corporation, 1992). See also Lloyd Stires, "3.7 Million Americans Kidnapped by Aliens?" *Skeptical Inquirer* 17, winter 1993, pages 142-144.

5. David Icke, *The Truth Vibrations* (London: The Aquarian Press, 1991), page 117.

6. Cited by Timothy Jones, "Rumors of Angels," *Christianity Today* 37, 5 April 1993, pages 18-22.

7. In this section I rely heavily on the analysis of Vishal Mangalwadi, *When*

the New Age Gets Old: Looking for a Greater Spirituality (Downers Grove, IL: InterVarsity, 1992), pages 15-16, 70.

8. Mangalwadi, page 16.
9. Mangalwadi, chapter 5, "Tantric Sex: A Celebration of Life?" pages 108-126.
10. C. S. Lewis, *The Screwtape Letters* (London: Fontana, 1942), page 9.
11. Mangalwadi, page 97.
12. William J. Doherty, "Family Therapy Goes Postmodern: Deconstructing Clinical Objectivity," *Family Therapy Networker* 15, September/October 1991, pages 36-42.
13. R. Kearsley, "Angels," in Sinclair B. Ferguson, David F. Wright, and J. I. Packer ed., *New Dictionary of Theology* (Downers Grove, IL: InterVarsity, 1988), pages 20-21.
14. Jones, 20-22.
15. Corrie ten Boom, *A Prisoner and Yet* (Fort Washington, PA: Christian Literature Crusade, 1954).
16. Andrew J. Bandstra, "A Job Description for Angels," *Christianity Today* 37, 5 April 1993, page 21.
17. J. Rodman Williams, *Renewal Theology: God, the World and Redemption* (Grand Rapids, MI: Zondervan, 1988), pages 194-195.
18. Mangalwadi, pages 101, 106.
19. Neil T. Anderson, *The Bondage Breaker* (Eugene, OR: Harvest House, 1990), page 130.
20. For a list of the activities and facts about fallen angels, with Scripture references, see Cecil B. Murphey, *The Dictionary of Biblical Literacy* (Nashville, TN: Thomas Nelson, 1989), pages 490-491.
21. M. Scott Peck, *People of the Lie: The Hope for Healing Human Error* (New York: Simon & Schuster, 1983), pages 182-183.
22. Millard J. Erickson, *Christian Theology* (Grand Rapids, MI: Baker, 1985), page 451.
23. In the following discussion, I have been guided by the writing of Clinton E. Arnold, *Powers of Darkness: Principalities and Powers in Paul's Letters* (Downers Grove, IL: InterVarsity, 1992), pages 123-127.
24. Wayne Grudem, *Systematic Theology*, unpublished manuscript, chapters 16, 20. Writers who agree with this interpretation include Neil T. Anderson, *The Bondage Breaker* (Eugene, OR: Harvest House, 1990); Fred C. Dickason, *Demon Possession and the Christian* (Westchester, IL: Crossway, 1989), pages 37-40; Ed Murphy, *The Handbook of Spiritual Warfare* (Nashville, TN: Thomas Nelson, 1992), pages 51-52; and Timothy M. Warner, *Spiritual Warfare* (Wheaton, IL: Crossway, 1991), pages 79-80.
25. Murphy, pages 51-52.
26. Murphy, page 134.
27. Murphy, pages 437-448.
28. Murphy, page 437.
29. Roger Bufford, *Counseling and the Demonic* (Dallas, TX: Word, 1988), pages 151-155.
30. Erickson, page 451.

Chapter Eleven—The Church and Counseling

1. Scholars disagree about the role that Boisen played in the pastoral counseling movement. In *Professional Education for Ministry: History of Clinical Pastoral Education* (Nashville, TN: Abingdon, 1970), Edward E. Thornton wrote that "Boisen's place in the organizational development of clinical pastoral education is peripheral," but Thornton quoted another writer who concluded that "the modern clinical pastoral training movement is due almost entirely to the genius of one man: the Reverend Anton T. Boisen," pages 56 and 55.

2. A detailed discussion of these four pastoral functions is given in an out-of-print book by William A. Clebsch and Charles R. Jaekle, *Pastoral Care in Historical Perspective* (Englewood Cliffs, NJ: Prentice-Hall, 1964), pages 32-66.

3. From Michael Douchette's foreword to Stephen Arterburn and Jack Felton, *Toxic Faith: Understanding and Overcoming Religious Addiction* (Nashville, TN: Oliver-Nelson, 1991), pages ix, x.

4. Gilbert Bilezikian, *Christianity 101: Your Guide to Eight Basic Christian Beliefs* (Grand Rapids, MI: Zondervan, 1993), page 177.

5. Some biblical scholars would add that Galatians 3:28 goes further and teaches that ethnic, social, and sexual differences don't exist among the people in God's new community. Concerning Jews and Gentiles, for example, Bilezikian wrote, "Their commitment has shifted from their Jewishness or Gentileness to the unity they have in Christ. They still remain Jew and Gentile, but such distinctions are immaterial to their equal participation in the life of the church." See Gilbert Bilezikian, *Beyond Sex Roles: What the Bible Says About a Woman's Place in Church and Family* (Grand Rapids, MI: Baker, 1989), page 127.

6. Bilezikian, *Christianity 101*, page 194.

7. Charles Colson with Ellen Santilli Vaughn, *The Body: Being Light in Darkness* (Dallas, TX: Word, 1992), page 73.

8. Millard Erickson, *Does It Matter What I Believe?* (Grand Rapids, MI: Baker, 1992), page 140.

9. Cited by Greg Oden, *The New Reformation: Returning the Ministry to the People of God* (Grand Rapids, MI: Zondervan, 1990), pages 42-43.

10. In 1 Corinthians 3:16, we read, "Don't you know that you yourselves are God's temple and that God's Spirit lives in you?" Does this apply to individuals or to the church? The footnote to this verse in *The NIV Study Bible* clarifies: In this verse, "Paul does not mean here that each of his readers is a temple of the Holy Spirit. He says 'You yourselves (plural) are God's temple (singular).' In 6:19 he speaks of each Christian as a temple of the Holy Spirit."

11. Bilezikian, *Christianity 101*, page 203.

12. These thoughts are adapted from a sermon by John Shaeffer, Grace Community Church, Palatine, Illinois, 16 May 1993.

13. Howard E. Snyder, *Liberating the Church: The Ecology of Church and Kingdom* (Downers Grove, IL: InterVarsity, 1983), page 79.

14. David Watson, *Fear No Evil: One Man Deals with Terminal Illness*

(Wheaton, IL: Harold Shaw, 1985), pages 60 and 59.

15. Richard N. Ostling, "The Church Search," *Time*, 5 April 1993, pages 44-49.
16. Snyder, page 80.
17. David Watson, *Called and Committed: World-Changing Discipleship* (Wheaton, IL: Harold Shaw, 1982), pages 34, 37, emphasis added.
18. This paragraph is adapted from Watson *Called and Committed*, 36-37. For ease of reading I have chosen to put Scripture references here rather than in the text. Here is the text with references: It is generous and from the heart (1 Peter 1:22), marked by the sacrificial giving of time, money, energy, and gifts to people in need. It a forgiving love (Colossians 3:12-14), sensitive to the needs of others (Romans 14:15); an upbuilding love that avoids backbiting or putting people down (Ephesians 4:15, 2 Timothy 2:22-26); a unifying love that works to heal divisions and restore relationships (Ephesians 4:3, Philippians 2:2, Colossians 2:2); and a positive love that believes the best about others and doesn't focus on the negatives (1 Corinthians 13:4-7).
19. Millard J. Erickson, *Christian Theology* (Grand Rapids, MI: Baker, 1985), page 1053.
20. Colson, page 123.

Chapter Twelve—The New Age in Counseling

1. Reports of the growth of psychic readings and use of divination cards often appear in the media. In these introductory paragraphs I have drawn from William Mullen, "Futures Market: Fortunetellers See Boom in Their Present," *Chicago Tribune*, 28 February 1993; Steve Rabey, "Divine Decks: More People Seeking Life Answers in 'Divination System' Cards," *Colorado Springs Gazette Telegraph*, 27 March 1993.
2. Quoted by Elliot Miller, *A Crash Course on the New Age Movement* (Grand Rapids, MI: Baker, 1989), page 27.
3. Douglas R. Groothuis, *Unmasking the New Age* (Downers Grove, IL: InterVarsity, 1986), pages 26-27.
4. Stanley J. Grenz, *The Millennial Maze: Sorting Out Evangelical Options* (Downers Grove, IL: InterVarsity, 1992), pages 198-199.
5. This is the opinion of William A. Dyrness, *Let the Earth Rejoice: A Biblical Theology of Holistic Mission* (Westchester, IL: Crossway, 1983), page 126.
6. Gilbert Bilezikian, *Christianity 101: Your Guide to Eight Christian Beliefs* (Grand Rapids, MI: Zondervan, 1993), page 229. A non-sympathetic critique of the excesses in prophetic conferences is presented by Paul Boyer, *When Time Shall Be No More: Prophecy Belief in Modern American Culture* (Cambridge, MA: Harvard University Press, 1992).
7. Adapted from Eldon Ladd, *A Theology of New Testament* (Grand Rapids, MI: Eerdmans, 1974), pages 68-69.
8. "Sociological Perspectives on Christian Counseling: An Interview with Dr. Anthony Campolo," *The Christian Journal of Psychology and Counseling* 7, no. 2, April 1992, page 8. (This journal ceased publication in 1992.) For a highly technical discussion of this topic, see Warren J. Heard, Jr., "Eschatologically Oriented Psychology: A New Paradigm for the Integration of

Psychology and Christianity," in D. A. Carson and John D. Woodbridge ed., *God and Culture* (Grand Rapids, MI: Eerdmans, 1993), pages 106-133. This issue is also discussed further in the last section of this chapter.

9. Ernest Becker, *The Denial of Death* (New York: The Free Press, 1973), page ix.

10. For a brief discussion of these issues, see John P. Newport, *Life's Ultimate Questions: A Contemporary Philosophy of Religion* (Dallas, TX: Word, 1989), pages 285-290.

11. Millard Erickson, *Does It Matter What I Believe?* (Grand Rapids, MI: Baker, 1992), page 154. For a further discussion of death and why we fear dying, see Gary R. Habermas and J. P. Moreland, *Immortality: The Other Side of Death* (Nashville, TN: Thomas Nelson, 1992), page 200.

12. Millard Erickson, *Christian Theology* (Grand Rapids, MI: Baker, 1985), page 1169.

13. Summarized from an article by William F. Nicholson in *USA Today*.

14. This illustration is from Bruce Shelley, *Theology for Ordinary People* (Downers Grove, IL: InterVarsity, 1993), page 200. The story was found originally in a book by A. M. Hunter, *Taking the Christian View* (Atlanta, GA: John Knox Press, 1974), page 83.

15. Erickson, *Does It Matter*, 155.

16. Erickson, *Does It Matter*, 158. Erickson notes that hell sometimes is described as a place of darkness (Matthew 22:13, 25:30), but elsewhere described as a place of fire (Mark 9:43-49). Since fire and darkness cannot exist together, these may be images that are used to point to the greater truth that hell will be agonizing and lonely as people live through eternity cut off from God.

17. For brief and clear discussions of the different options, see Millard J. Erickson, *Contemporary Options in Eschatology: A Study of the Millennium* (Grand Rapids, MI: Baker, 1977), or Grenz.

18. Heard, page 126

19. Heard, pages 128-129.

20. Newport, page 95.

Chapter Thirteen—Spirituality and Counseling

1. James Patterson and Peter Kim, *The Day America Told the Truth* (New York: Prentice-Hall, 1991), pages 200-202.

2. The following paragraphs are adapted from the lead article that I wrote for a short-lived mental-health newsletter "Spiritual and Mental Health," *Christian Mental Health For the Professional Therapist* 1, fall 1991, pages 1-4.

3. Richard Simon, "From the Editor: Psychotherapy and Spirituality," *Family Therapy Networker* 14, no. 5 (1991), page 2.

4. Donald G. Bloesch, "Lost in the Mystical Myths," *Christianity Today* 35, no. 9 (1991), pages 22-24.

5. M. Scott Peck, *The Different Drum: Community Making and Peace* (New York: Simon & Schuster, 1987), page 192.

6. Rowland Croucher, "Spiritual Formation," *Grid*, a publication of World Vision of Australia, winter 1991, pages 1-2.

7. Alan Sager, *Gospel-Centered Spirituality: An Introduction to Our Spiritual Journey* (Minneapolis: Augsburg, 1990), page 25.
8. Martin Parsons, *The Call to Holiness: Spirituality in a Secular Age* (Grand Rapids, MI: Eerdmans, 1974). For a classic treatment of this subject, see William Law, *A Serious Call to a Devout and Holy Life* (Grand Rapids, MI: Eerdmans, 1728/1966). For a more modern discussion see James I. Packer, *Rediscovering Holiness* (Ann Arbor, MI: Servant, 1992).
9. James Houston, *In Search of Happiness* (Oxford: Lion, 1990), pages 116-117, 131.
10. Packer, page 97.
11. Packer, page 97.
12. Chap Clark, *The Performance Illusion* (Colorado Springs, CO: NavPress, 1993), page 41.
13. For further discussion of these issues, see Clark; David A. Seamands, *Freedom from the Performance Trap* (Wheaton, IL: Victor Books, 1988); Kent and Barbara Hughes, *Liberating Ministry from the Success Syndrome* (Wheaton, IL: Tyndale, 1988).
14. Adapted from a cover statement on the book by Clark.
15. Ronald Macaulay and Jerram Barrs, *Being Human: The Nature of Spiritual Experience* (Downers Grove, IL: InterVarsity, 1978), page 69.
16. Leanne Payne, *Restoring the Christian Soul Through Healing Prayer* (Wheaton, IL: Crossway, 1991), page 158.
17. Cited by Donald S. Whitney, *Spiritual Disciplines for the Christian Life* (Colorado Springs, CO: NavPress, 1991), pages 20-21. For other excellent discussions of spiritual disciplines, see Richard Foster, *Celebration of Discipline* (San Francisco, CA: Harper and Row, 1988); Dallas Willard, *The Spirit of the Disciplines* (San Francisco, CA: Harper and Row, 1988).
18. The first edition of Foster's book appeared in 1978. The best known and respected follow-up books, at least in Protestant evangelical circles, are the books by Willard and by Whitney.
19. Whitney, pages 15-16.
20. Julie Gorman, "Christian Formation," *Christian Education Journal* 10, no. 2, pages 65-73. Gorman suggests two major "formats" of Christian character formation. Spontaneous formation involves growth that follows circumstances in our lives; deliberate formation comes as the result of spiritual discipline.
21. Lawrence O. Richards, *A Practical Theology of Spirituality* (Grand Rapids, MI: Zondervan, 1987), page 53.
22. Brother Lawrence, *The Practice of the Presence of God* (Old Tappan, NJ: Spire Books/Revell, 1958), page 8.
23. Gary Moon, "Christian Counseling: You Can Go Home Again," *The Christian Journal of Psychology and Counseling* 7, no. 2, April 1992, pages 12-16.
24. Gary W. Moon, Judy W. Bailey, John C. Kwasny, and Dale E. Willis, "Training in the Use of Christian Disciplines as Counseling Techniques Within Religiously Oriented Graduate Training Programs," *Journal of Psychology and Christianity* 10, no. 2, summer 1992, pages 155-165.

25. Stanton L. Jones and Richard E. Butman, *Modern Psychotherapies: A Comprehensive Christian Appraisal* (Downers Grove, IL: InterVarsity, 1991), page 57.

Chapter Fourteen
1. Cited in E. G. Rupp and B. Drewery ed., *Martin Luther* (London: Edward Arnold, 1971), page 162.
2. D. A. Carson, *How Long, O Lord? Reflections on Suffering and Evil* (Grand Rapids, MI: Baker, 1990), page 130.

Index

Author

Gary R. Collins, Ph.D., is a licensed clinical psychologist and author of about fifty books, including *Christian Counseling: A Comprehensive Guide* and *Family Shock*. He is president of the American Association of Christian Counselors and editor of *Christian Counseling Today* magazine. He taught at Trinity Evangelical Divinity School for 20 years, serves part time as Distinguished Professor of Counseling at Western Seminary, and speaks at Christian counseling conferences around the world.